Get the eBook FREE!

(PDF, ePub, Kindle, and liveBook all included)

We believe that once you buy a book from us, you should be able to read it in any format we have available. To get electronic versions of this book at no additional cost to you, purchase and then register this book at the Manning website.

Go to https://www.manning.com/freebook and follow the instructions to complete your pBook registration.

That's it!
Thanks from Manning!

Conversational AI

Conversational AI

CHATBOTS THAT WORK

ANDREW R. FREED

MANNING

SHELTER ISLAND

For online information and ordering of this and other Manning books, please visit
www.manning.com. The publisher offers discounts on this book when ordered in quantity.
For more information, please contact

    Special Sales Department
    Manning Publications Co.
    20 Baldwin Road
    PO Box 761
    Shelter Island, NY 11964
    Email: orders@manning.com

Manning Publications Co.
20 Baldwin Road
PO Box 761
Shelter Island, NY 11964

Development editor:	Tricia Louvar
Technical development editor:	Frances Buontempo
Review editor:	Mihaela Batinić
Production editor:	Rachel Gibbs
Copy editor:	Keir Simpson
Proofreader:	Melody Dolab
Technical proofreader:	Bhagvan Kommadi
Typesetter:	Gordan Salinovic
Cover designer:	Marija Tudor

ISBN 9781617298837

Printed in the United States of America

To my family. I love you all!

brief contents

contents

preface

I've been a software developer and architect for 18 years, with half of that time spent building artificial intelligence solutions. I've built several conversational AI solutions and various other AI assistants. In those 18 years, I've read and learned from more books, blogs, and podcasts than I can count. I'm excited to give back by producing original content of my own. I like to say that I've been standing on the shoulders of giants for long enough now; I'd like to be a giant for someone else. I look forward to hearing about the wonderful solutions that readers of this book are going to build.

In this book, I will walk you through all aspects of building, designing, training, testing, and improving an AI assistant, with a primary focus on conversational AI. This book includes several hard lessons I've learned along the way and shared with you so that you don't have to make the same mistakes.

When I first learned about conversational AIs, I assumed that they were just a handful of dialogue rules sprinkled on top of a machine learning algorithm. I've come to appreciate that there is so much more to building an AI assistant than that.

AI assistants are a powerful new technology that allow users to do what they want, when they want to, the way they want to. You use AI assistants every day, from the assistant on a smartphone, to a chatbot or automated voice system, to email systems that sort your incoming mail.

The global COVID-19 pandemic accelerated a trend towards self-service automation through conversational AI assistants. Now more than ever, companies are looking for ways to increase self-service capability. A common path is to automate routine customer inquiries and free up support staff for higher-value activities.

The book is written from the perspective of the company Fictitious Inc. and tells how they have built their first conversational AI to serve their customer service needs. The book is not tied to a specific AI platform. The demo in chapter 2 is built on IBM's Watson Assistant, but includes conceptual translations on how to build this AI assistant in any other platform. The other chapters use generic Python code or pseudocode that can be adapted to your platform of choice. After reading this book, you will have a solid foundation in AI assistants.

AI assistants have come a long way since I've started building them. The technology gets better every day. Even so, the basic technology can only take you so far. This book shows you how to make AI technology work for you.

acknowledgments

You may have heard that writing a book is a lot of work. I've come to understand what an understatement that is. While this book only has one name on the cover, it took a lot of people to make this book a reality.

Thank you to my wife, Elise, and my sons, Greg and Jeff. I spent so much time away from you this year. Thank you for supporting me throughout this project. Special thank you to Mom and Dad for a lifetime of encouragement.

Thank you to Michael Stephens for believing I could write a book. Thank you to my editor, Tricia Louvar, for teaching me how to write a book and for keeping the project on track. Thank you to my technical editor, Fran Buontempo, for your insightful remarks on every chapter and your fresh perspective, which taught me so much. Thank you to Bert Bates for teaching me how to teach through a book. Thank you to Jennifer Houle for taking my drawings and making them look amazing. Thank you to Keir Simpson for polishing the entire manuscript.

To all the reviewers: Aaron Barton, Bhagvan Kommadi, Bill LeBorgne, Daniel Carl, Fernando Antonio da Silva Bernardino, Håvard Wall, Irfan Ullah, James Black, John Stephen Villarosa, Jr., Jon Riddle, Jose Luis Perez, Joseph Perenia, Lokesh Kumar, Lonnie Smetana. Marc-Anthony Taylor, Maxim Volgin, Richard Vaughan, Salil Athalye, Shivakumar Swaminathan, Simeon Leyzerzon, Sowmya Vajjala, Steve Grey-Wilson, Steven Herrera Corrales, Thomas Joseph Heiman, and Zoheb Ainapore, your suggestions helped make this a better book.

Thank you to my colleagues at IBM for reviewing my early drafts: Anuj Jain, Cheryl Howard, Leo Mazzoli, Marco Noel, Murali Vridhachalam, Preeth Muthusamy,

Rebecca James, Rich Nieto, Saloni Potdar, Sheetal Reddy. Special thanks to Cari Jacobs for her exceptionally thorough reviews. You all made this book better!

Thank you to my mentors who encouraged me and showed me the way: Stacey Joines, Rob Murgai, Dick Darden, Naeem Altaf, and Kyle Brown. The smallest of encouraging nudges can go a long way.

Thanks to my colleagues who build conversational AI assistants with me, and thanks to my customers for the opportunity to build. I've learned something from working with each of you. Those lessons are distributed throughout this book.

about this book

Conversational AI is written to give you an understanding of all the AI assistant fundamentals, with a focus on conversational AIs. It starts with a description of why AI assistants are important and then includes demonstrations of AI assistant technology. From there the book continues on to designing, training, testing, and improving an AI assistant.

Who should read this book

Conversational AI is written for developers and business analysts who are interested in building AI assistants. Software development experience is useful for building these assistants but is not required. Many AI platforms are moving toward low-code or no-code development. Even if you are not writing code, this book teaches you the fundamentals you need to ensure that the assistant you build is successful. There are many disparate resources for each aspect of AI assistant development; this book ties a cohesive thread through each of them.

How this book is organized: A roadmap

This book has five sections and 12 chapters, plus a glossary.

Part 1 explains what AI assistants are and why you would use them, and walks through several examples:

- Chapter 1 describes several types of AI assistants, where you have interacted with them, and a brief breakdown of how they work. It also outlines common use cases and platforms offering AI assistant technology.

- Chapter 2 introduces the key building blocks of intents, entities, and dialogue responses. It uses these building blocks to construct a conversational AI assistant for Fictitious Inc. The assistant answers routine customer service questions for this generic retailer.

Part 2 explains how to design an AI assistant that will achieve your goals and satisfy your users:

- Chapter 3 teaches how to select the problems your AI assistant should solve and how to solve them. Not every process is suitable for automating via an assistant.
- Chapter 4 describes how to design dialogue for your conversational AI. It includes dialogue practices that work well in both voice and text channels, as well as pointing out practices that work in one channel but not the other.
- Chapter 5 outlines measurement metrics that tell you how much an AI assistant is meeting your business needs. These metrics ensure that the assistant is successful for both you and your users.

Part 3 explains the development cycle for AI assistants:

- Chapter 6 covers how to find data to train your assistant. It also takes a data-driven approach to evaluating the volume, variety, and veracity of your training data, and how that affects your assistant.
- Chapter 7 teaches the data scientist aspect of testing your assistant: verifying how accurate it is. It introduces several accuracy metrics and shows how to interpret these metrics so that you know what improvements are needed.
- Chapter 8 describes the functional aspects of testing your assistant: verifying that each of the dialogue flows perform as designed. This chapter additionally covers how to automate your tests and test your assistant with many concurrent users.

Part 4 explains the life cycle of AI assistants after the initial build phase. An assistant should be continuously monitored and improved:

- Chapter 9 outlines a methodology for tracking your AI assistant software assets and managing multiple separate environments. It also demonstrates strategies for updating these assistants with both new features and bug fixes.
- Chapter 10 walks through how to analyze and improve an AI assistant, and how to prioritize these based on a success metric. It shows several ways of finding problem spots and how to fix them.

Part 5 explains useful AI assistant concepts that apply to special assistant scenarios:

- Chapter 11 shows you how to build your own classifier. While most people do not build classifiers from scratch, this chapter demonstrates how they work mathematically. This underpinning helps the reader understand why AI assistants are trained and tested the way they are.

- Chapter 12 describes how to train and test speech recognition for voice assistants. This includes how to gather speech data and three different methodologies for training a custom speech recognition model.

The glossary contains more than 100 terms used in this book and their definitions.

The first four parts are written in the same order in which AI assistants are created: foundation, design, train/test, and maintenance. Developers new to AI assistants should read these parts in order. Experienced developers can read the chapters in any order based on their own needs. The fifth part is optional, based on what type of assistant you are creating.

About the code

Source code for this book is available at http://mng.bz/1AZQ.

Chapter 2 was written against the IBM Watson Assistant v1 Dialog API. Chapter 11 was written against Python 3.7.4 and jupyter-notebook 6.0.1. Other chapters include pseudocode, contained in the book itself.

This book contains many examples of source code, both in numbered listings and in line with normal text. In both cases, source code is formatted in a `fixed-width font like this` to separate it from ordinary text. Sometimes code is also **in bold** to highlight code that has changed from previous steps in the chapter, such as when a new feature adds to an existing line of code.

In many cases, the original source code has been reformatted; we've added line breaks and reworked indentation to accommodate the available page space in the book. In rare cases, even this was not enough, and listings include line-continuation markers (➥). Additionally, comments in the source code have often been removed from the listings when the code is described in the text. Code annotations accompany many of the listings, highlighting important concepts.

The code for the examples in this book is also available for download from the Manning website at https://www.manning.com/downloads/2254.

liveBook discussion forum

Purchase of *Conversational AI* includes free access to a private web forum run by Manning Publications where you can make comments about the book, ask technical questions, and receive help from the author and from other users. To access the forum, go to https://livebook.manning.com/#!/book/conversational-ai/discussion. You can also learn more about Manning's forums and the rules of conduct at https://livebook.manning.com/#!/discussion.

Manning's commitment to our readers is to provide a venue where a meaningful dialogue between individual readers and between readers and the author can take place. It is not a commitment to any specific amount of participation on the part of the author, whose contribution to the forum remains voluntary (and unpaid). We suggest you try asking the author some challenging questions lest his interest stray! The forum and the archives of previous discussions will be accessible from the publisher's website as long as the book is in print.

Other online resources

My personal website and blog are at http://freedville.com. Now that I'm done writing this book, I promise to start blogging again!

My colleagues and I frequently blog about many different AI topics, including AI assistants. That blog is found at https://medium.com/ibm-data-ai.

about the author

 Andrew R. Freed is a Senior Technical Staff Member and Master Inventor at IBM. He studied computer science at Penn State University, has more than 100 software patents, and is a devoted husband and loving father.

Andrew has 18 years of experience as a software developer and architect. He has been building artificial intelligence solutions since 2012. He has broad experience building conversational AI assistants, including complex solutions for both text- and voice-based assistants.

about the cover illustration

The figure on the cover of *Conversational AI* is captioned "Femme Touralinze," or a woman from the Tyumen region in Siberia, Russia. The illustration is taken from a collection of dress costumes from various countries by Jacques Grasset de Saint-Sauveur (1757-1810), titled *Costumes civils actuels de tous les peuples connus,* originally published in France in 1784. Each illustration is finely drawn and colored by hand. The rich variety of Grasset de Saint-Sauveur's collection reminds us vividly of how culturally apart the world's towns and regions were just 200 years ago. Isolated from each other, people spoke different dialects and languages. In the streets or in the countryside, it was easy to identify where they lived and what their trade or station in life was just by their dress.

The way we dress has changed since then and the diversity by region, so rich at the time, has faded away. It is now hard to tell apart the inhabitants of different continents, let alone different towns, regions, or countries. Perhaps we have traded cultural diversity for a more varied personal life—certainly for a more varied and fast-paced technological life.

At a time when it is hard to tell one computer book from another, Manning celebrates the inventiveness and initiative of the computer business with book covers based on the rich diversity of regional life of two centuries ago, brought back to life by Grasset de Saint-Sauveur's pictures.

Part 1

Foundations

Have you ever used a chatbot? Do you turn the lights on and off by speaking to your phone? Does your email client sort your mail and filter out spam automatically? If so, you've interacted with an AI assistant. These are just a few examples of the ways that AI assistant technology is used.

Conversational AI and other AI assistants are transforming the way businesses interact with their customers. These assistants bring self-service power to users, helping them get what they want, when they want it, the way they want it. Businesses around the world are saving millions of dollars by using AI and making their customers happier at the same time.

In chapter 1, you'll learn about three types of AI assistants and when they are appropriate to use. You'll also learn about the most common AI assistant use cases and platforms. In chapter 2, you'll see how a conversational AI is assembled from three core building blocks: intents, entities, and dialogue responses.

When you complete this part, you'll be ready to start designing your AI assistant solution.

Introduction to conversational AI

AI assistants are an exciting new technology that is being used in an increasing number of places and use cases. The odds are good that you have interacted with an AI assistant. From the assistants on our phones ("Hey Siri") to automated customer service agents to email filtering systems, AI assistant technology is widespread and growing in use.

In this book, you will learn how and why AI assistants work. You will learn when AI assistant technology is appropriate and how to apply the technology effectively. You will also learn how to develop, train, test, and improve your AI assistant. Finally, you will learn about advanced topics, including enabling a voice channel for your AI assistant and deeply analyzing your assistant's performance.

> **Who is this book for? Who is this book not for?**
>
> This book is written for someone who is interested in developing AI assistants. We will start with broad coverage of multiple assistant types and how they are used; then we will take a deep dive into all aspects of creating a conversational AI assistant, including design, development, training, testing, and measurement.
>
> If you have already developed several assistants, you'll probably want to skip to specific chapters later in the book. If you are not a developer, you can read the first couple of chapters and then skim or skip the rest.

1.1 *Introduction to AI assistants and their platforms*

Why are AI assistants popular? Let's examine one industry that frequently uses AI assistants: customer service. A new call or case at a customer service center averages between 8 and 45 minutes, depending on the product or service type. Customer service call centers spend up to $4,000 for every agent they hire, and even more money in training costs, while experiencing employee turnover of 30–45%. This situation leads to an estimated annual loss of $62 billion in sales annually in the United States alone (http://mng.bz/G6rR). AI assistants can help with these problems and more.

You've probably had several recent interactions with different kinds of AI assistants:

- Chat interfaces for customer service and guided buying
- Smartphones and connected homes that are controlled by voice ("Alexa, turn on the light!")
- Email software that automatically sorts your mail into folders such as Important and Spam

AI assistants are pervasive and used in a wide variety of ways. How many of the AI assistants in table 1.1 have you interacted with? The rest of this section dives into the mainstay platforms and AI assistant types in this ecosystem.

Table 1.1   Examples of AI assistants and their platforms

AI assistant type	Uses	Skills you'll need to build one	Technology focus	Example platforms
Conversational AI (sometimes called a *chatbot*)	Customer service Guided buying experience New employee training	Designing and coding process flows with one or many steps Using conversational state to determine the next step Writing dialogue Classifying utterances into intents Extracting entities from utterances to support the intent Writing code to call external application programming interfaces (APIs)	Conversation and dialogue flow	IBM Watson Assistant Microsoft Azure Bot Service Rasa

Table 1.1   Examples of AI assistants and their platforms

AI assistant type	Uses	Skills you'll need to build one	Technology focus	Example platforms
Command interpreter	Natural language or voice interface to devices	Classifying statements into commands Extracting supporting parameters from a command statement Writing code to call external APIs	Classification and calling APIs	Apple Siri Amazon Alexa
Event classifier	Sorting email into folders Routing messages (such as emails) to an appropriate handler	Classifying messages based on message content and metadata Extracting many entities that support or augment the classification	Classification and entity identification	Google Gmail Natural Language Understanding services

A wide variety of platforms can help you build AI assistants. Most of the platforms are usable in a variety of AI assistant scenarios. You should consider a few things when you choose a platform:

- *Ease of use*—Some platforms are intended for business users, and some are for software developers.
- *APIs and integration*—Does the platform expose APIs or have prebuilt integrations to third-party interfaces and tools? An AI assistant is usually integrated into a larger solution.
- *Run-time environment*—Some platforms run only in the cloud, some run only on-premise, and some run in both environments.
- *Open or closed source*—Many AI assistant platforms do not make their source code available.

Let's look at a couple of assistants in more detail.

1.1.1   Types of AI assistants

AI assistants come in many shapes and sizes. When you see the term *AI assistant*, you may think *chatbot*, but there are multiple applications of AI assistant technology. AI assistants can be used to have a full conversation with a user, use dialogue to execute a single command, or work behind the scenes without any dialogue. AI assistants fall into three categories:

- *Conversational AI*—These assistants are full systems that use full conversational dialogue to accomplish one or more tasks. (You may be used to calling these assistants *chatbots*.)
- *Command interpreters*—These assistants use enough dialogue to interpret and execute a single command. (You probably use a command interpreter on your phone.)
- *Event classifiers*—These assistants don't use dialogue; they read a message (such as an email) and perform an action based on the type of message.

When a user sends textual input to an AI assistant, that input is generally understood to contain an *intent* (what the user wants to achieve) and optionally some parameters that support that intent. We'll call these parameters *entities*.

Figure 1.1 shows a generalized AI assistant architecture.

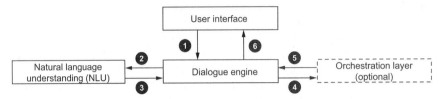

Figure 1.1   Generalized AI assistant architecture and control flow

This architecture includes four primary components:

- *Interface*—The way end users interact with the assistant. The interface can be a text or voice interface and is the only part of the AI assistant that is visible to users.
- *Dialogue engine*—Manages dialogue state and coordinates building the assistant's response to the user.
- *Natural language understanding (NLU)*—This component is invoked by the dialogue engine to extract meaning from a user's natural language input. The NLU generally extracts an intent as well as information that supports the intent.
- *Orchestrator*—(Optional) Coordinates calls to APIs to drive business processes and provide dynamic response data.

Let's examine how these components can work in a single turn of dialogue. When I set an alarm on my phone, a command interpreter is my AI assistant, and it executes a flow like that shown in figure 1.2.

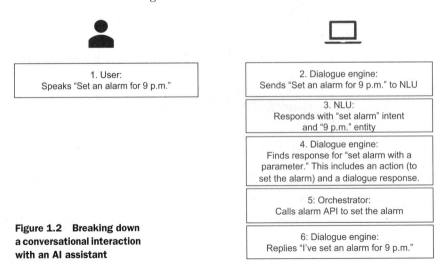

Figure 1.2   Breaking down a conversational interaction with an AI assistant

In figure 1.2, we see how the components interact in a conversation with a single turn:

1 The user starts the conversation by asking for something ("Set an alarm for 9 p.m.").

2 The user interface passes this text to the dialogue engine, which first asks the classifier to find the intent. The NLU identifies a "set alarm" intent.

3 The NLU also detects an entity; the phrase *9 p.m.* represents a time.

4 The dialogue engine looks up the appropriate response for the "set alarm" intent when a time parameter is present. The response has two parts: an action (performed by the orchestrator) and a text response.

5 The orchestrator calls an API exposed by an alarm service to set an alarm for 9 p.m.

6 The dialogue engine responds to the user via the user interface ("I've set an alarm for 9 p.m.").

> ## Terminology alert
>
> The terms in this section are meant to be generic across AI assistant providers. Depending on your provider, you may see slightly different terminology:
>
> - *Interface*—Many AI assistant providers do not include a user interface, exposing their capabilities only through APIs. Your provider might use integrations, connectors, or channels to supply a user interface.
> - *NLU*—Nearly every AI assistant includes an NLU component, sometimes referred to as Cognitive Language Understanding. The NLU component usually includes a classifier and an entity (or parameter) detector.
> - *Dialogue engine*—This component has the least-consistent terminology across AI assistant platforms. Each platform lets you associate responses to conversational conditions. Some platforms expose this component only as code; others offer a visual editor.
> - *Orchestration*—AI assistants sometimes let you code backend orchestration (webhooks) directly into the assistant. Generally, you can write an orchestrator that interfaces with an AI assistant through an API. Many platforms have built-in orchestration interfaces to third parties, which may be referred to as integrations or connectors. Sometimes, the platform uses the same terminology to refer to frontend and backend components.

CONVERSATIONAL AI

Conversational AI is the type of assistant that most frequently comes to mind when you hear the words "AI assistant." A conversational AI assistant has a conversational interface and services a variety of requests. Those requests may be satisfied with a simple question-and-answer format or may require an associated conversational flow.

Throughout 2020, many private and public entities built conversational AIs to handle questions related to the novel coronavirus. These assistants fielded most responses via a simple question-and-response format. Many of these assistants also included a symptom checker that walked a user through a diagnostic triage process. These assistants were critical in quickly disseminating the latest expert and official advice to constituent populations.

Conversational AIs can be trained to answer a wide variety of questions. The answers returned by the assistant can be static text or may contain information from external sources. In figure 1.3, we see a user being greeted by a conversational AI and asking a simple question ("What is the coronavirus?"). The AI returns with an answer: a description of the coronavirus. At this point, the user's request is considered to be complete: a question has been asked, and an answer has been provided.

1. **The assistant starts the conversation with a greeting.**

2. **The user asks a simple question.**

3. **The assistant returns a static answer. No follow-up is necessary to complete the request. The user may ask another question.**

Figure 1.3   A simple question-and-answer scenario with a static answer (from U.S. Centers for Disease Control; https://www.cdc.gov/coronavirus/2019-ncov/faq.html).

Figure 1.3 demonstrates a simple question-and-answer response. The question "What is the coronavirus?" has a simple response—in this case, a definition of the coronavirus. Everyone who asks that question gets the same answer, and the answer rarely changes. This question was answered by the interface, NLU, and dialogue engine. No API call had to be made, so no orchestrator was required.

Many coronavirus assistants also answer questions such as "How many COVID cases are there?" In this case, the answer changes daily. The number of cases cannot be hardcoded into the dialogue engine; you would have to update it every day! The answer is still a simple response ("There have been x cases"), but an orchestrator is required to query a case count API to return a complete answer.

Conversational AI in action

The U.S. Centers for Disease Control has its own conversational AI assistant to let people check their symptoms and see whether they should be tested for COVID-19. Try it at http://mng.bz/gxdx.

In figure 1.4, the user has asked a more complex question ("Do I have the coronavirus?"). This question is difficult to answer. Although we could return a static result, it would be paragraphs or pages in length and would require a lot of work on the user's part to interpret. To deliver a satisfactory answer, we need additional information from the user. The assistant asks a series of follow-up questions, in this case asking about fever and itchy eyes. After a series of back-and-forth messages, the assistant will make a final recommendation, such as beginning self-isolation or seeking immediate medical assistance.

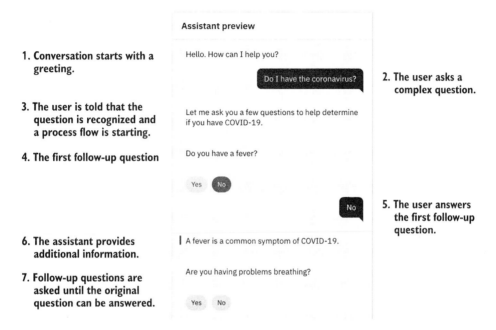

Figure 1.4　A new conversation in which the user asks a question that requires a process flow before providing the final answer

A conversational AI assistant is frequently expected to service multiple requests in a single conversational session, whether these requests follow a simple question-and-answer format or involve a detailed process flow. When you're designing a process flow, be sure to sketch it in a flow chart, as shown in figure 1.5.

WARNING　Do not take medical advice from this book.

A conversational AI requires the most up-front design work of the three AI assistant types due to the amount of work required to gather and write the responses. I describe those design aspects in chapter 3.

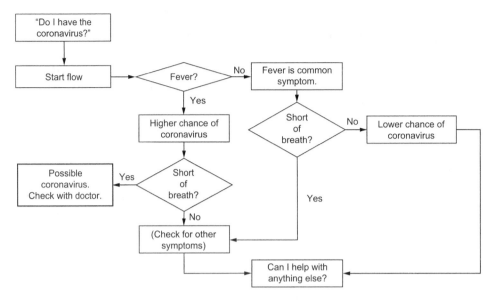

Figure 1.5 Exemplary process flow for a coronavirus assistant, inferred from the table at http://mng.bz/YAYK.

COMMAND INTERPRETER

A simpler use of AI assistant technology is the command interpreter pattern. This pattern is prevalent in smart devices such as phones, remote controls, and appliances. The command interpreter deals with a limited vocabulary, enough to invoke the commands it supports, and the interaction is finished as soon as the information needed to execute the task is collected. A smart television remote, for example, is tuned to recognize words such as *channel* and *volume* but won't recognize a command like "Set air temperature to 76 degrees." Table 1.2 shows example command interpreters and commands that are in their vocabulary.

Table 1.2 Example command interpreters and supported commands

Command interpreter type	Example commands
Smartphone	"Set an alarm for 9 p.m."
	"Call Mom."
	"Open Facebook."
Voice-powered television remote	"Increase volume."
	"Turn to channel 3."
Smart home controller	"Turn on the light."
	"Set air temperature to 76 degrees."

My favorite command on my phone is the "Set alarm" command, which has two parameter slots: the alarm time and the alarm reason. On my phone, the alarm time is a required parameter, and the alarm reason is optional. In figure 1.6, I've mapped out the simplest "set alarm" invocation: "Set an alarm." The interpreter knows that setting an alarm without an alarm time is impossible, so it prompts me for the alarm time.

The command interpreters with which you are most familiar with require activation via a physical button or a wake word. Several wake words you may be familiar with include "Hey Siri," "OK Google," and "Alexa." Devices that wake via a button don't start listening until you press that button. Devices that are always listening don't jump into action until you use a wake word.

Figures 1.6 and 1.7 demonstrate how several command interpreters parse your input into an actionable command. Try experimenting with your devices to see how many ways you can execute a command, either by changing the words ("create alarm" versus "set an alarm") or changing the order of the information given.

The command interpreter's job is to identify a command (such as "set alarm") and fill all the parameter slots (such as time of alarm) for that command. When the command interpreter is invoked, it will ask as many follow-up questions as needed to fill all the required slots—no more and no fewer. This process is similar to how conversational AIs work, except that command interpreters service only a single request:

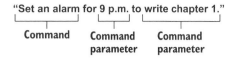

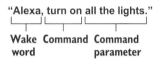

Figure 1.6   Exploring the parts of a command

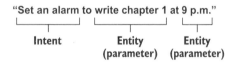

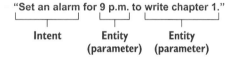

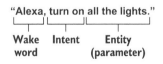

Figure 1.7   Alternative terminology for the command interpreter pattern

the entire conversation is finished when the required parameters are gathered and the initial command is executed. Figure 1.8 shows a command interpreter using slots to set an alarm.

Do AI assistants always have commands?

Terminology differs. Generally, in this book I will refer to *intents* and *entities*; nearly every AI assistant platform uses *intent*. Some platforms use *action* and *intent* interchangeably.

In the case of command interpreters, commands are intents, and parameters are entities.

1. The user invokes a command.

3. The user supplies the missing parameter.

2. The command is recognized but is missing a required parameter.

4. The command is executed, and the conversation is over.

Figure 1.8 A command can require follow-up questions from the command interpreter.

Command interpreters can also be coded to receive multiple parameters at the same time as long as there is a way to distinguish them. In figure 1.9, I provide all the alarm parameters in a single statement: "Set an alarm for 9 p.m. to write chapter 1." The phone gladly obliges. Figure 1.9 shows how the command interpreter reacts when all parameters are passed at the same time.

1. The user invokes a command with two parameters:
   - Alarm time
   - Alarm label

2. All required parameters are present. The command is executed, and the conversation is over.

Figure 1.9 When all required parameters are passed to the command interpreter, it completes the command and ends the conversation.

When you're developing a command interpreter, you need to be able to separate the parameters from the command. In the case of setting an alarm, this task is not too difficult. The command will be something like "Set an alarm"; the alarm time will be text that parses to a time; and any remaining text (minus filler words such as *for, to,* and *at*) will be the reason.

EVENT CLASSIFIER

The final category of AI assistant technology is the event classifier pattern, which frequently has no dialogue at all. You are probably most familiar with this pattern through your email client. This pattern is typically used in email routing and email assistants, but it has also been used for routing support tickets to appropriate queues. Like the command interpreter pattern, this pattern can also use parameter slots to ensure that enough information is provided.

The event classifier pattern has been part of most email platforms since the rise of spam in the late 1990s and early 2000s. Some providers make it almost invisible to you (your internet service provider likely filters out spam before you even have a chance to download it), and some providers let you peek behind the curtain. The Gmail client runs an event classifier to sort your mail into separate mailboxes.

Event classifiers use a mixture of rules and machine learning techniques to decide how mail should be routed. In Gmail's case, the classifier decides which inbox to choose. Gmail offers several ways for the user to personalize or train the classifier through a mix of rules and training options. I selected an email in my Promotions folder and was offered the following training options:

- Add *sender* to contacts
- Block sender
- Report spam
- Report phishing
- Filter messages like these

Figure 1.10 shows how classification logic can work inside an email client.

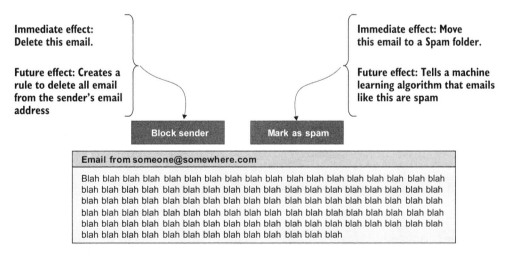

Figure 1.10 Actions in your email client can personalize the classification of your email.

The first two options are exposing rules: putting a sender in your contacts list means that their messages should always go to your primary inbox, and blocking a sender prevents their messages from appearing in your primary inbox. The last three options are likely providing training to a machine learning algorithm. Additionally, you can drag a message from one inbox to another. When I moved a message from my Promotions to my Primary folder, I was prompted as follows: "Conversation moved to Primary. Do this for future messages from sender?" Gmail is asking whether the rules and training for the event classifier should be updated.

Behind the scenes, additional rules are applied. Did the email originate from an IP address that is known to send spam? Did thousands of other Gmail users get the same message? Is the email filled with nonsensical words (such as v1agra)? Google is continually updating its training and rules based on the actions you and other users take.

Event classifiers can also be used in forms for bug reports and trouble-ticket submissions. A software product support team could use an online event classifier tied to a form that lets users request help. Users can be instructed to describe their problem in natural language, and the event classifier can decide how the problem should be handled.

Like the conversational AI and command interpreter patterns, the event classifier needs to find an overall intent in the message. This intent will be used to direct the message. Often, different teams support different issues, such as installation, crashes, and general questions. As with parameters in the command interpreter pattern, each issue type requires supporting details (such as product version and operating system), and the event classifier can request these parameters if they are not provided.

Figure 1.11 shows a form in which a user has entered a vague description. The description is enough to route the request to the installation team, but that team will need more details to solve the problem quickly. The user can proceed or can update the description.

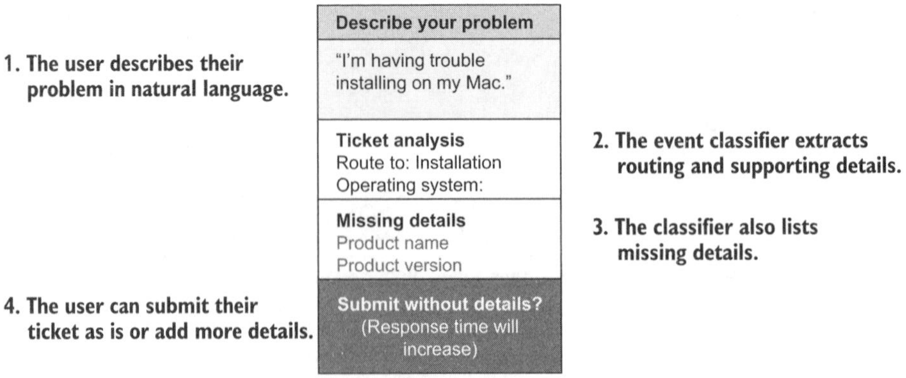

1. **The user describes their problem in natural language.**

Describe your problem

"I'm having trouble installing on my Mac."

Ticket analysis
Route to: Installation
Operating system:

2. **The event classifier extracts routing and supporting details.**

Missing details
Product name
Product version

3. **The classifier also lists missing details.**

4. **The user can submit their ticket as is or add more details.**

Submit without details?
(Response time will increase)

Figure 1.11 An event classifier helps classify support requests. Even better, it tells users what information will be needed to get a faster answer.

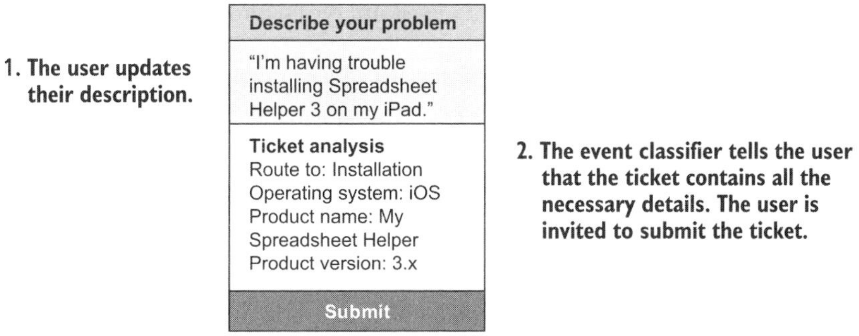

1. The user updates their description.

Describe your problem
"I'm having trouble installing Spreadsheet Helper 3 on my iPad."
Ticket analysis Route to: Installation Operating system: iOS Product name: My Spreadsheet Helper Product version: 3.x
Submit

2. The event classifier tells the user that the ticket contains all the necessary details. The user is invited to submit the ticket.

Figure 1.12 The user updates their problem description, and the event classifier finds all the required parameters.

In figure 1.12, the user takes the opportunity to improve the problem description, and the event classifier tells them that all the required information is present.

Why not use a form with drop-down menus?

You may be inclined to present a form to the user with all the required elements and options available from drop-down menus. Many support forms work that way. This approach has a few challenges, however:

- The number of drop-down menus can be intimidating to a user.
- Different request types might require different parameters, increasing the size and complexity of the form.
- The user may not know all the right options to select. (In figure 1.12, the event classifier inferred the iOS operating system from *iPad* in the description.)

A simple form with a single natural language field is approachable, and the event classifier can nudge the user to provide additional useful information.

Classifiers are powerful sorting technology. All AI assistants have a classifier at their heart, whether that classifier uses rules, machine learning, or both. (I will discuss this topic more in future chapters.)

1.1.2 A snapshot of AI assistant platforms

Several AI assistant platforms are available, most of them suitable for building multiple kinds of AI assistants.

MICROSOFT

Microsoft offers a full catalog of software services that you can use to build your own solution. Their solutions are friendly to developers. Microsoft offers separate Azure Cognitive Services: Language Understanding Intelligent Service (for natural language understanding) and Bot Framework (for dialogue and response). Microsoft's services are suitable for building all three AI assistant types and integrate into a variety of external interfaces.

Wolford deployed a guided self-service shopping assistant powered by Microsoft Azure Bot Service to consumers in 14 countries (https://customers.microsoft.com/en-US). The assistant answers common questions from shoppers and provides personalized "style me" recommendations from Wolford's product catalog.

AMAZON

Amazon also has a full catalog of software services. Amazon Lex is the primary service used for building AI assistants but integrates easily with Amazon's other cloud-based services as well as external interfaces. Amazon Lex uses the same foundation as Alexa.

Amazon's Alexa is available on more than 100 million devices worldwide and is configurable with more than 100,000 Alexa skills. These skills are usually command interpreters, but you can use Lex to build conversational AIs as well. Amazon offers several other services for building your own event classifiers.

GOOGLE

Google is another platform with a variety of software services in its catalog and many prebuilt integration points. Google's Dialogflow is the primary service used for conversational AI, and several other services are available for building your own event classifiers.

Gmail is a quintessential event classifier, with 1.5 billion users worldwide. Gmail sorts incoming mail into specific categories and detects spam. Nest is a configurable command interpreter used in many homes and businesses.

RASA

Rasa is the only open source platform in our list, giving you full control of the software you deploy. The other vendors in this list have you control the classifier by changing training data, but Rasa lets you change the entire classification process.

Rasa is deployed at Align (https://rasa.io/pushing-send/case-study-align) in a smart newsletter. Align uses Rasa's AI assistant as a concierge. The assistant increases engagements with Align's newsletter and decreases friction in processes such as webinar registration.

IBM

IBM offers a platform with easily integrated services. Watson Assistant is IBM's AI assistant platform, and it is suitable for building all three types of AI assistants.

Humana fields thousands of routine health insurance queries per day with a voice-enabled self-service conversational AI. Watson Assistant serves these callers at one-third of the cost of Humana's previous system while doubling the call containment rate (https://www.ibm.com/watson/stories/humana).

1.2 *Primary use cases for AI assistant technology*

The three primary use cases for AI assistant technology align with the technical categories described earlier in this chapter. These categories include self-service assistant, agent assist, and classification and routing. These use cases are distinguished by who interacts with the assistant and the way in which they interact.

1.2.1 *Self-service assistant*

The self-service assistant pattern is the most familiar pattern. In this pattern, a user interacts directly with the AI assistant. The AI assistant is generally, but not always, set up to handle inquiries that are otherwise answered by human agents.

This pattern is frequently used in

- *Customer service*—Resolving frequently asked questions without a wait or hold time
- *Conversational commerce*—Guiding a consumer through an exploration and purchasing experience
- *Employee productivity*—Helping employees find enterprise guidance quickly
- *Home/personal assistant*—Performing tasks through a conversational interface

When you use the assistant on your smartphone, you are interacting with an AI assistant. This style of AI assistant is increasingly common in automated customer support. You may interact with touchtone voice agents ("Press 1 for billing, press 2 to open an account") when you call your bank or favorite retailer; these agents are technically AI assistants. In this book, we will focus on assistants that use a conversational interface rather than a button- or keyword-driven interface. Figure 1.13 shows how self-service assistants are generally deployed.

The actor diagram in a self-service assistant is simple: a user interacts directly with an AI assistant, which does its best to handle any requests. Optionally, the assistant may detect that it is unable to satisfy the user's request and can escalate the conversation to a human agent. This pattern can work in web (text) and voice channels.

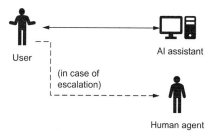

Figure 1.13 Model for how users interact with support agents

1.2.2 *Agent assist*

Agent assist is a twist on the self-service pattern. In this pattern, the user interacts directly with a human agent. That human agent can augment their intelligence by using an AI assistant. That AI assistant is like an expert adviser to the human agent.

The agent assist pattern has two significant variations. In the first variation (figure 1.14), input from the user is sent directly to the AI assistant, and the AI assistant sends output to the human agent.

The agent assist pattern reduces the burden on the human agent by seamlessly providing additional information. The human agent can decide whether to include information from this response to the user. The downside of this approach is that it may require more AI assistant training: the user is likely to include additional, irrelevant context when speaking to another human.

The other significant variation is for the human agent to use the AI assistant only when needed. This pattern is shown in figure 1.15. In this variation, the human agent forms a question, possibly well-structured, to the AI assistant and receives a response. The human agent can incorporate this information into their response to the user. This pattern requires active participation from the human agent, who has to type a question to the AI assistant, but requires less AI assistant design and implementation work.

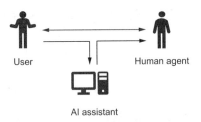

Figure 1.14 First model for interactions in an agent assist scenario. The user interacts only with the agent, but the assistant is listening to the conversation and advising the agent.

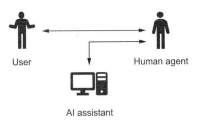

Figure 1.15 Alternative agent assist pattern. The assistant is invoked by the agent only when required.

Both scenarios are commonly used in training and supporting new customer service agents. Customer service departments frequently have high turnover, and the agent assist pattern is a great way to raise the average agent's ability. Agent assist can also work in web (text) and voice channels.

1.2.3 Classification and routing

The final use case uses an AI assistant to classify data that's already been received. This classification pattern is commonly run on emails but is suitable for many other input types, including submitted forms and social media posts and comments. A classifier can quickly sort through a large volume of incoming requests, and the resulting classification informs how the requests should be routed. Figure 1.16 shows an example of the classification and routing pattern.

A variation is to run the AI assistant before a form is submitted. The AI assistant can run on free text in a form and detect what critical information is provided. In a bug-report form, for example, the assistant can detect whether the user provided information on their operating system, product version, and general problem type.

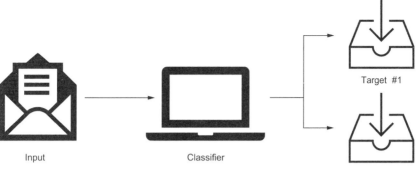

Figure 1.16 Example classifier and routing pattern

1.3 *Follow along with this book*

The techniques in this book apply to most AI assistant platforms. I will reference Watson Assistant (https://www.ibm.com/cloud/watson-assistant), an AI assistant platform that is suitable for implementing the solutions outlined in this book. You need not use Watson Assistant to implement your assistant, however. The book's examples are helpful guides in the spirit of all AI assistant platforms. Feel free to use Azure Bot Service, Lex, Dialogflow, Rasa, or any other platform you prefer.

Watson is designed to run wherever you need it, whether that's on a public cloud or on your premises. The interface is suitable for both technical and nontechnical users. You will be able to build your own AI assistant on Watson Assistant by using a Lite (free) account.

1.3.1 *What you need to create your assistant*

If you are following along in Watson Assistant, you will need the following:

- *IBM Cloud account*—You can register for a free IBM Cloud account at https://cloud.ibm.com.
- *Watson Assistant instance*—With your IBM Cloud ID, you can create a Watson Assistant instance at https://cloud.ibm.com/catalog. A Lite plan is available free of charge and is sufficient to run all the examples in this book.

> **Terminology alert**
>
> Many AI assistant platforms are hosted on vendor clouds and generally include the following concepts:
>
> - *Account*—You have to register with the provider, at minimum with an email address or account identifier.
> - *Try before you buy*—At the time of this writing, all major platforms provide some sort of free, light, or trial option. Be warned: some platforms require you to register a credit card with your account, even if you use only free services. If your provider requires a credit card when you sign up, be sure to read the fine print.

> **(continued)**
> - *Instance*—An *instance* is your personal "copy" of the AI assistant software. It may also be called a *service*, *service instance*, or *resource*, depending on your platform. You may see references to resource groups or service groups, which are intended to help enterprises keep many separate instances segregated. If you're presented an option for something like a resource group, you can safely accept the default.
>
> If you are not using a cloud-based platform, you may not see any of these terms.

If you are using a different AI assistant provider, look through its documentation for an option to use the software for free.

1.3.2 Useful spreadsheet software

Regardless of platform, you will find it handy to have spreadsheet software. You can use any software that is capable of reading a comma-separated-values (CSV) file. Spreadsheet software commonly works with this format.

AI assistants are commonly trained with two-column CSV files. Each row of the file is used to train the assistant, with the first column being an input and the second column being the expected output. We'll get deeper into the specifics in chapters 6 and 7.

1.3.3 Recommended programming language and code repository

The book includes a small number of code examples for testing AI assistants. To run these examples, you will need the following:

- *Python*—This programing language provides an environment in which to run Python scripts and Jupyter Notebooks. You can download Python at https://www.python.org/downloads. You can download Jupyter at https://jupyter.org/install.
- *Git*—A Git client is needed to download code samples from the internet. The code samples are available at the book's GitHub repository: https://github.com/andrewrfreed/ConversationalAI.

When the code assumes a particular AI assistant platform, I will describe what the code is doing and how to achieve the same results in other AI assistant platforms.

Summary

- AI assistants are suited to solving a variety of tasks, most commonly through a conversational interface and with varying amounts of dialogue. Some AI assistants have no dialogue (event classifiers). Some assistants use only enough dialogue to get the information needed to execute a single command. Conversational AI is used in both web and voice.

- AI assistants can be used by consumers for self-service tasks or to augment the intelligence of a human agent.
- Some commands and questions can be answered immediately by an AI assistant, and others require follow-up questions to gather additional detail.
- When you mark an email as spam, you are training an AI assistant.

Building your first
conversational AI

This chapter covers

- Identifying the intent and entity in a single user utterance
- Implementing a question-and-answer dialogue for a recognized intent
- Adding contextual information to answers when an entity is recognized
- Implementing a multiple-question process flow to satisfy a user request

In chapter 1, we learned about what AI assistants are and why people use them, and saw some examples of AI assistants that we encounter every day. In this chapter, you will learn how they work, and you will build an assistant from the ground up. We will work through a case study for a retail company looking to build its first conversational AI.

The first thing assistants need to do is recognize what a user's utterances mean. A conversation starts with a user stating an intent and any related entities. The intent will help the assistant understand what to do next, such as respond with an answer or start a new dialogue flow. First, we will see in detail how the assistant breaks a user utterance into intents and entities.

The simplest response is for the assistant to respond to each intent with a single answer response. We will configure an assistant to recognize a variety of intents and to give a unique response for each. We will further explore how to provide additional information in a response based on the entities detected in the user's utterance.

Some user intents require a multistep process flow that includes one or more follow-up questions. We will also explore methods for building these process flows in a conversational AI assistant. We will implement a two-strikes rule so that if the assistant consistently doesn't understand the user, the user will be given a different resolution option.

By the end of this chapter, you will be able to build your first conversational AI, implement simple question-and-answer responses, tailor a response based on contextual details in the user's utterance, and implement multistep process flows that guide a user through a series of steps, ending with resolution for the user. Armed with this knowledge, you will be ready to design the process flows for your next conversational AI.

2.1 Building a conversational AI for Fictitious Inc.

Fictitious Inc. is a growing retail chain looking to reduce the burden on its support representatives. The company wants to build a self-service conversational AI to handle their most frequent customer questions, which are primarily about store locations and hours, scheduling appointments, and job applications. In this chapter, we will start building the assistant.

Fictitious Inc.'s use case is a typical retail scenario. Customer service departments are often overloaded with routine inquiries that can easily be automated. Fictitious Inc. will offer a conversational AI to give users a fast way to get answers without needing to wait for a human. When the conversational AI cannot answer a question, the user will be redirected to the existing human-based customer service processes.

Fictitious Inc. prefers to use pretrained content to reduce its conversational AI development time, though this requirement is not a hard one. The company has made it clear that it will use any technology that works, giving you free range to pick the AI platform of your choice. The only requirement is that the platform include a "try before you buy" option. In this chapter, I will demonstrate the Fictitious Inc. scenario by using Watson Assistant.

First, Fictitious Inc. needs to get some AI software. For this demo, I registered an account on the IBM Cloud and created a personal (free) instance of Watson Assistant by importing it from the IBM Cloud Catalog. I'm asked to configure a service instance name (any name will do) and select a geographic region (the one closest to your users is best).

If you are using a different cloud-based platform, you will encounter a similar workflow. You generally need to sign up (possibly with a credit card) and can find a free/limited/trial option. If you are not using a cloud-based platform, you will need to download and install the AI software and any dependencies it requires; be sure to check the documentation.

After this AI software is configured for your use, you need to create a specific conversational AI that uses this software. Figure 2.1 demonstrates the relationship between the former and latter steps.

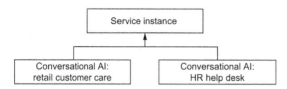

Figure 2.1   After configuring the service instance (or synonymous item) for your platform, you'll need to create a conversational AI for your specific use case. You can create separate conversational AIs by using the same service instance.

The next step is creating a conversational AI that's specific to your use case. The specific ways you'll do this will vary greatly, depending on your platform of choice.

Terminology alert

You want to create a conversational AI, but your platform may call it an assistant, a bot, an agent, or something else entirely. Sometimes, the assistant/bot/agent has everything you need; sometimes, you have to couple it with a skill, another service, or raw code.

The different naming schemes are sometimes cosmetic and sometimes indicative of different architectural patterns. Many platforms use a layered architecture that allows you to connect to a variety of frontend user interfaces and backend service integrations. For the Fictitious Inc. demo, we will not worry about integrating with any other systems.

There's one exception to this rule: if your AI platform separates the conversational service from the classifier or NLU service, you need to integrate the classifier and NLU to build your assistant. Check your platform's documentation when you get to the intent training section.

Because I am working with Watson Assistant, I have two more components to create. (Your platform will likely use different terminology. See figure 2.2 to figure out what your AI platform requires.) The smallest possible configuration in Watson Assistant's v2 API uses these two parts:

- *Assistant*—The interface integration layer (http://mng.bz/zGwX)
- *Skill*—The dialogue engine (http://mng.bz/0rXl)

When I created a new Watson Assistant instance, it came preloaded with an assistant called My first assistant. No other default configuration was provided, so I added a dialogue skill to implement Fictitious Inc.'s scenario. The Add Dialog Skill button creates a new, empty dialogue skill, as shown in figure 2.3.

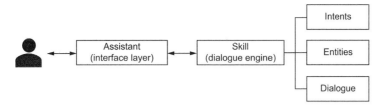

Figure 2.2   The Watson Assistant components used for Fictitious Inc. The terms *assistant* and *skill* may vary in your platform, but you can expect to find *intents*, *entities*, and *dialogue*.

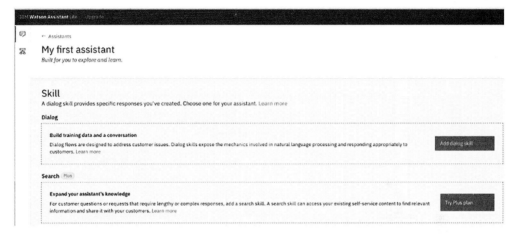

Figure 2.3   Adding a dialogue skill to the assistant. Your platform likely has choices that differ in name but are similar in function.

When creating a skill, you will be prompted to provide a name, description, and language. (Your platform will collect similar data.) Be sure to provide a useful name. The name and description are made available for your benefit. (I created the Fictitious Inc. skill with the name Customer Service skill, the description Answer most common customer service questions, and the English language.) After you click Create Dialog Skill, the skill is linked to the assistant.

If you are using another AI platform, you will have similar options. You may be prompted to pick a specific language that the assistant will converse in. Some of the AI platforms I surveyed allow you to create an assistant based on a sample provided by the platform. For following along in this chapter, I suggest creating a new, empty assistant.

With the basic conversational AI infrastructure (assistant and skill in Watson Assistant, a bot, assistant, or agent in other platforms) in place, it's time to start implementing Fictitious Inc.'s use case. We configure three specific components inside the AI assistant:

- *Intents*—Shows us all the training data made available to the assistant. This component will be empty until we provide some intents manually or import them from the content catalog.
- *Entities*—Identifies several Fictitious Inc. store locations.
- *Dialogue*—Holds the dialogue flows used in Fictitious Inc.'s assistant.

Our new AI assistant is almost empty. Let's start by adding some intents so that the assistant can understand what the user means.

2.2   What's the user's intent?

A conversation in an AI assistant generally starts with the following pattern (figure 2.4):

1 The user speaks/types something (the *utterance*).
2 The assistant determines what the utterance means or what the user is trying to accomplish (the *intent*).
3 The assistant formulates a response and sends it to the user. This response may be an answer or a request for additional information.

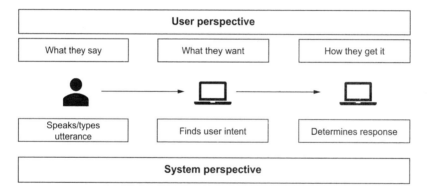

Figure 2.4   One turn of a conversation, from the user and system perspectives

Terminology alert

Every AI platform I surveyed at the time of this writing used the term *intent* the same way. Hooray for consistency! Some platforms are starting to hide the intent terminology (are they afraid that it scares users?), even though they use intents under the covers.

Fictitious Inc.'s users will use a nearly infinite number of utterances, which will map to a finite set of intents. For Fictitious Inc.'s assistant, we will need to create a set of intents and map dialogue responses to those intents.

2.2.1 What's an utterance?

The user interacts with assistants primarily through natural language. The user's input is an *utterance*, which is literally what the user says (to a telephone assistant) or types (in a web/chat assistant).

Terminology alert

Nearly every AI platform I surveyed used the term *utterance*, but a few platforms used *example* or *training phrase*. Search your platform's documentation for the section on training intents, and you'll quickly find how it refers to utterances.

Example utterances include

- "Where are you located?"
- "What time do you open?"
- "How can I reset my password?"
- "Tell me a joke."

Can users provide other types of input to an AI assistant besides text?

Yes. There are other ways for users to provide input. In a web channel, the user may also provide input by clicking a button. In a voice channel, the user may enter numeric values on their keyboard with dual-tone multi-frequency (DTMF) signals. Conversational AIs still generally treat this input as being textual.

2.2.2 What's a response?

The goal of a conversational AI is to respond appropriately to a user's utterance. A *response* is whatever the assistant returns to the user. A set of example utterances that Fictitious Inc.'s users might make, along with likely Fictitious Inc. responses, are shown in table 2.1.

Table 2.1 Example dialogue utterances and responses

Example user utterance	Example system response
"Where are you located?"	"We have two locations near you: 123 Maple Street and 456 Elm Drive."
"What time do you open?"	"Our hours are 9 a.m. to 8 p.m. on weekdays and 10 a.m. to 10 p.m. on weekends."
"How can I reset my password?"	"What's your user ID?"
"Tell me a joke"	"I'm not trained to handle that. I can help you with several other common IT requests, like password resets."

> **Terminology alert**
>
> Nearly every AI platform I surveyed used the term *response*. I also saw *dialogue response*, *action*, *message*, *prompt*, and *statement*.
>
> If you consider "If this, then that," the *that* is the response.

Table 2.1 shows what the user sees, but the assistant does a little work internally to determine that response. The assistant uses NLU to extract an intent from the user's utterance and uses it to drive the conversation further. Let's look at how an NLU module does that job.

> **Can conversational AIs respond with output other than text?**
>
> Yes. There are multiple ways to provide output in a conversational AI. Web assistants can use buttons, images, hyperlinks, and other rich media in their responses. Voice assistants can add music or other audio in a response.

2.2.3 *How does the assistant understand what the user means?*

The assistant uses an NLU engine that finds meaning in the user's utterance. The NLU component has two parts:

- *Intent classifier*—Finds meaning that applies to the entire utterance. The meaning is generally expressed as a (verb-based) intent and is extracted via machine learning.
- *Entity extractor*—Finds zero or more subsets of the utterance with a specific meaning, such as dates, locations, and other objects. The entities are usually noun-based and may be extracted by machine learning, hardcoded rules, or both.

The NLU component in your platform may offer separate training options for the classifier and the entity extractor. Table 2.2 summarizes the uses of intents and entities, both of which are extracted by an NLU component.

Table 2.2 Key differentiation between intents and entities

Intent	Entity
Verb-based	Noun-based
Considers the whole utterance	Extracted from a word or segment in the utterance
Usually uses machine learning	Uses rules and/or machine learning

2.2.4 Why machine learning?

A classifier uses machine learning because learning to understand text by example is a more scalable approach than implementing rules. Utterances come in natural language, which has nearly infinite variations. It is difficult to code enough rules to handle all possible variations in text, but a machine learning classifier can scale quickly. Table 2.3 shows several possible ways that a user may state that they need their password reset. Set A is handled easily with rules, but Set B is more easily handled with a machine learning classifier.

Table 2.3 Example utterances of a user whose intent is to reset their password

Set A	Set B
• "Reset my password"	• "I forgot my password"
• "Please help me reset my account password"	• "Reset my login information"
• "My password needs to be reset"	• "I can't sign into the intranet"
	• "I'm locked out of my email account"

A first and naive approach to intent detection would be to use keywords to apply structure to unstructured text. Set A is easily handled with a rule: any utterance containing *reset* and *password* should be treated as a password-reset request. Set B shows why a *rules-based* approach grows unwieldy quickly. There are nearly infinite ways to express most intents in natural language, and it is too hard to write rules to cover them all.

The classifier uses machine learning techniques at its heart. We'll see how the classifier learns to identify a user's request in chapter 11; for now, we can assume we have one trained and ready to use. The classifier attempts to derive intent from every input phrase and passes this intent to the dialogue engine. Then the dialogue engine can use structured rules to determine the next dialogue step.

2.2.5 What's an intent?

An *intent* is a normalization of what the user means by their utterance or what they want to do. An intent is generally centered on a key verb. Note that this verb may not be explicitly included in the utterance.

> **NOTE** By convention, I will reference intents with their name preceded by a pound (#) sign, such as #reset_password. This convention is used by most of the popular assistant platforms.

Table 2.4 shows sample utterances by Fictitious Inc.'s users along with the identified intents and the verbs at the center of those intents.

An intent represents a logical group of similar utterances that have the same user meaning (user intent). As in section 2.2.4, both "I need to reset my password" and "I'm locked out of my account" indicate locking or resetting problems. A classifier is

Table 2.4   Sample utterances with associated intents and implied verbs

Utterance	Intent	Implied verb(s) of the Intent
"Where are you located?"	`#store_location`	Locate
"What time do you open?"	`#store_hours`	Operate/Open/Close
"How can I reset my password?"	`#reset_password`	Reset/Unlock
"Tell me a joke"	`#chitchat`	N/A

more powerful than a simple keyword matcher and uses contextual clues in the natural language to derive the user's intent.

> **NOTE**   Classifiers are trained with a series of examples and their corresponding intents.

It is possible that a user utterance will not map to any of the intents the classifier is trained on. In this case, the classifier will respond with some indication that the utterance is poorly understood, either by not returning an intent or by returning an error condition. In Watson Assistant's development interface, this scenario is flagged as `#Irrelevant`, and no intents are returned in the API. Your AI platform of choice will do something similar when a user utterance is not well understood.

A classifier needs careful training for optimal performance. This training will be covered more thoroughly in chapter 6. For now, consider that intents are trained with a variety of example utterances with similar meanings and that intents should be clearly differentiated from one another. In the end, the classifier will evaluate the user utterance for an intent and send that intent back to the dialogue engine.

2.2.6   *What's an entity?*

An *entity* is a noun-based term or phrase. An intent applies to the entire user utterance, but an entity applies to part of the utterance, often a single noun or noun phrase. By convention, AI platforms reference entities with an at (@) sign preceding their name. Table 2.5 shows some example entities that Fictitious Inc. can use in its assistant.

Table 2.5   Example entities for Fictitious Inc.

Entity type	Entity value (canonical form)	Entity synonyms (surface forms)
`@store`	Elm	Elm Dr, Elm Drive
`@store`	Maple	Maple St, Maple Street
`@contact_method`	phone	mobile, SMS, smartphone
`@contact_method`	email	webmail

The simplest entity pattern is to use a data structure called a *dictionary*—an enumerated list of all possible words and phrases that you want to treat the same way.

> ## Terminology alert
>
> Most AI platforms use the term *entity*. Occasionally, I have seen *parameter* and *slot type*. Entities are typically defined in one of three ways:
>
> - A predefined, static list (sometimes called a *dictionary* or *lookup table*)
> - Regular expression patterns
> - Training by example
>
> Conversational AIs often come with built-in system entities to detect things such as dates and countries.

If all the entity variations are known ahead of time, the dictionary-based approach works well. Fictitious Inc.'s assistant will use dictionary-based entities for its customer service use case.

> ## What's a dictionary?
>
> The traditional use of a dictionary is as a book or other repository containing a list of words and information about those words, such as definition, pronunciation, part of speech, and other features (such as synonyms). In this context, a synonym for a given word is meant to be a similar but different word.
>
> In the context of AI assistants, a *dictionary* is a list of known words, with each word having an associated type. Synonyms in this kind of dictionary are interchangeable.
>
> In table 2.5, @store is a type, so Elm, Elm Drive, and Elm Dr can be treated interchangeably. Many AI assistants have spelling correction or a fuzzy-matching feature, which allows misspellings like Eml Drvie to be treated as though they too are in the dictionary.

2.2.7 Combining intents and entities

Conversational AI platforms use entities to provide additional contextual information beyond the intent that can be used to provide a response. When utterances share an intent but differ only in their nouns, entities are the best way to determine a response. Table 2.6 compares two assistants, one that does not use entities and another that does. The assistant without entities will be much harder to train.

Table 2.6 Comparing two conversational AIs

Utterance	Without entities	With entities
"Where are your stores?"	`#store_location_all`	`#store_location`
"Where is your Elm store?"	`#store_location_elm`	`#store_location, @store:Elm`
"Where is your Maple store?"	`#store_location_maple`	`#store_location, @store:Maple`

You might try to treat "Where is your Elm store?" and "Where is your Maple store?" as different intents, but machine learning has difficulty distinguishing multiple intents that use nearly identical utterances. We will explore that reasoning in chapter 7. For now, we can assume that using entities will help us build a more accurate conversational AI.

> **NOTE**   Use entities when multiple questions have the same intent but need different responses.

2.2.8   Adding intents to the Fictitious Inc. assistant

Fictitious Inc.'s new assistant is almost empty. Critically, it does not include any intents; therefore, it will not understand any user responses. If you are using Watson Assistant, you can import intents from the Watson Assistant Content Catalog, which provides some initial training data for the general customer service intents Fictitious Inc. is interested in.

Not using Watson Assistant? No problem!

If your platform does not have sample intents for a retail scenario, you can create your own training data. In this chapter, we will use the following intents, and you can create a few example utterances for each as noted in this sidebar. Add a few utterances of your own to increase the training quality:

- #Customer_Care_Store_Location—"Where are you?" and "How do I find your store?"
- #Customer_Care_Store_Hours—"What times are you open?" and "When do you close tonight?"
- #Customer_Care_Employment_Inquiry—"I need a job application" and "Can I work for you?"
- #Customer_Care_Appointments—"I need to schedule an appointment" and "When can I see a manager?"

After clicking the Content Catalog menu item, I selected the Customer Care category and clicked Add to skill. The assistant was populated with 18 customer service intents, each of which has 20 examples—a robust set of starter training data for Fictitious Inc.'s assistant. Now the assistant will be able to recognize store-location questions such as "Where is your store?" via the #Customer_Care_Store_Location intent.

As soon as the Customer Care content is loaded into the assistant, you need to train the NLU component. Your platform may train automatically (Watson Assistant is one such platform), or you may need to invoke a training action explicitly (check your platform's documentation). Regardless of platform, the training process should take only a few minutes.

Conversational AI platforms generally include a testing interface. In Watson Assistant, the interface is called Try It Out. I've also seen the test interface referred to as a *simulator* or *developer console*. Some platforms do not provide a graphical testing interface but expose APIs that you can use for testing. The testing interface usually includes information that helps you debug your assistant but that you won't expose to users (such as the name and confidence of any intents found). When your assistant is trained, you can explore how well it recognizes intents by using your platform's testing interface.

Test your assistant with questions that were not included in your training data. (Use your imagination!) I asked my assistant, for example, "What time do you open?" and "Where is the nearest store?" As shown in figure 2.5, the assistant recognized the intent behind these statements (`#Customer_Care_Store_Hours` and `#Customer_Care_Store_Location`, respectively) but responded to the user as though it didn't understand.

TIP　See how your assistant responds to phrases you did not explicitly train on.

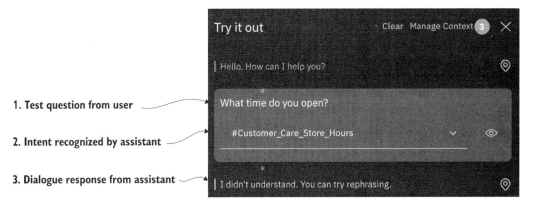

Figure 2.5　A testing interface shows some information that you won't expose to users (such as the name of the intent). Here, you can see that the new assistant recognizes my intent. You can infer that the "I didn't understand" response means that no dialogue condition was associated with that intent.

The assistant understands several intents but doesn't know how to respond to any of them. Figure 2.6 summarizes what our assistant can (and can't) do.

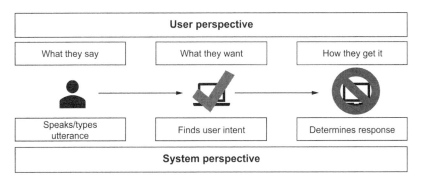

Figure 2.6　When you add intent training data but do not configure dialogue responses, you are here.

We've made nice progress, but we're only halfway there. Let's teach the assistant how to respond to the user in a meaningful way.

> ### Why are intents and responses separated?
>
> In many AI platforms, finding the intent is only one part of generating a response. Training an intent classifier and building dialogue rules to generate responses are two separate skills.
>
> Nonetheless, there is a growing trend among conversational AI providers to combine these steps. You may be using a platform that abstracts away intents. The training interface may ask you to provide only *this* (utterance) and *that* (response) in an "If this, then that" pattern.

2.3   Responding to the user

As a brand-new assistant needs to be loaded with intents, the assistant needs to be populated with dialogue rules. It's not sufficient to recognize the user intent; you also need to respond appropriately to that intent. AI assistants use conditional logic to determine which response to give the user. The simplest conditional logic is "If the user's intent is this, respond with that."

> ### Terminology alert
>
> Dear reader, dialogue logic causes the most variation among AI vendors! All vendors use some form of conditional logic, but the specifics of this logic vary.
>
> One major difference is the interface paradigm. Some vendors use a graphical interface, and others require you to write code by using their libraries to implement dialogue logic.
>
> Most conversational AIs have an event loop at their core. Most interactions with the assistant follow an "If this, then that" pattern until a conversation ends. AI platforms have similar conditional logic primitives even if they use different names for them.
>
> In this section, I will use lots of screenshots because a picture is worth a thousand words. I am confident that you can map each of the examples in this section to your AI platform of choice.

Your conversational AI platform provides some method to implement dialogue logic, either through a graphical editor or through pure code. A common way to reason about dialogue logic is to think of the dialogue as being a decision tree. (This example recalls call centers, which train employees on scripted call trees.) In this methodology, every decision point in the dialogue could be called a *dialogue node*. You'll be creating several dialogue nodes as you implement all the conversational paths supported by your assistant.

Before creating new dialogue response nodes for Fictitious Inc., let's explore the default dialogue nodes. (AI platforms generally include a few dialogue nodes or rules to help you get started in your assistant.) Figure 2.7 shows an example set of default dialogue nodes.

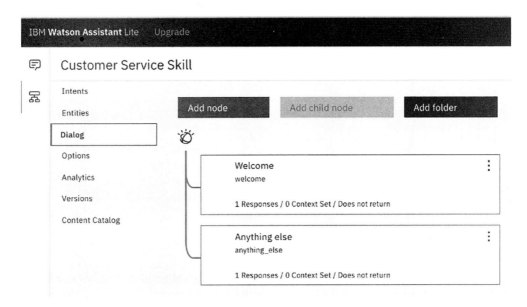

Figure 2.7 Dialogue nodes created automatically by Watson Assistant. Your AI platform of choice will come with some default conditions and/or dialogue nodes.

Each of the dialogue nodes in figure 2.7 includes a special condition that allows it to execute. The first condition is the Welcome node, which contributed the "Hello. How can I help you?" greeting. The second condition is the Anything Else node, which provided all the other dialogue responses, such as "I didn't understand. You can try rephrasing."

The two nodes and their conditions are described in table 2.7. Other platforms have similar conditions, intents, events, and/or dialogue nodes that handle these common situations.

Table 2.7 Precreated dialogue nodes and associated conditions in Watson Assistant

Dialogue node title	Node condition	Description
Welcome	`welcome`	This node represents your bot's greeting to users. The `welcome` condition is true only in a user's first interaction with the assistant. In most conversational AI instances, the assistant "speaks" first as a response to a user who opens a chat window.
Anything Else	`anything_else`	This node represents a fallback or catch-all condition. The `anything_else` condition is always true; thus, it can be used to catch utterances that the bot does not understand.

Way back in figure 2.5, we saw an assistant that recognized intents but responded with "I didn't understand. You can try rephrasing." Now we know why. An assistant must be configured both to recognize intents and to respond to conditions. If the assistant is not configured for both tasks, it will fall back to some default behavior. Our new assistant has only a message that it uses to start a conversation (Welcome) and a message that it uses for every other response (Anything Else).

Terminology alert

Your AI platform comes with some built-in conditions, events, or triggers that you can use:

- `welcome` may be expressed as a conversation start event or a welcome intent. It means that a new conversation has started.
- `anything_else` may be referred to as the *fallback intent*, *default intent*, *default condition*, or *catch-all*.

These two conditions are so prevalent in conversational AI that your platform's tutorial is sure to include them.

Fictitious Inc. needs rules coded into the assistant telling it how to respond when more interesting conditions are met, such as when the `#Customer_Care_Store_Hours` intent is recognized in a user question. The assistant should respond to any `#Customer_Care_Store_Hours` question with some sort of answer about when stores are open.

2.3.1 Simple question-and-answer responses

The simplest possible dialogue response is to provide a single, static answer based on the recognized intent. Fictitious Inc. most commonly receives questions about store hours, store locations, and job applications. Sample responses for these conditions will be coded into Fictitious Inc.'s assistant, as shown in table 2.8.

Table 2.8   The responses we'll code into the Fictitious Inc. assistant when certain intents are recognized

When the assistant recognizes this intent . . .	. . . it gives the following response
`#Customer_Care_Store_Hours`	"All of our local stores are open from 9 a.m. to 9 p.m."
`#Customer_Care_Store_Location`	"We have two locations near you: 123 Maple Street and 456 Elm Drive."
`#Customer_Care_Employment_Inquiry`	"We accept job applications at FictitiousInc.com/jobs. Feel free to apply today!"

After we code these responses into the assistant, anyone who asks the assistant a related question will get a more useful response.

Figure 2.8 shows how to configure the first dialogue rule for Fictitious Inc. If the assistant recognizes the user input as `#Customer_Care_Store_Hours`, it will respond with "All of our local stores are open from 9 a.m. to 9 p.m." and then wait for the user to provide additional input.

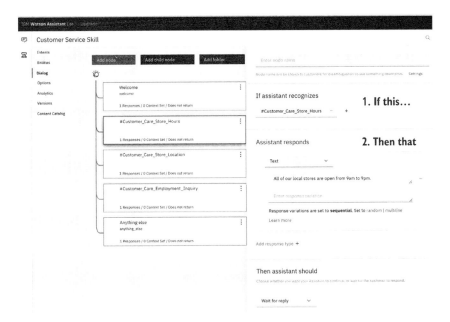

Figure 2.8   A simple dialogue rule takes the form "If this condition, then give this response."
Your conversational AI platform may have a different interface, but you will surely be able to
connect conditions to responses.

Figure 2.9 shows a test of the dialogue configured per table 2.8. Note that we have provided answers to only three of the intents. For the remaining Customer Care intents, even if the intent is recognized, the assistant will use the catch-all Anything Else dialogue node to respond. Each intent-specific response needs to be coded into the dialogue as shown in figure 2.8.

Figure 2.9   Testing after we associate intent conditions with dialogue responses. Now the interface
shows both the correct intent and the correct dialogue response—a successful test.

Now the assistant is more useful to users, at least when it comes to three question types (store hours, store locations, and employment inquiries). Fictitious Inc., however, has two retail locations, one on Maple Street and one on Elm Drive. If users ask about a specific store, they should get a store-specific response. The current implementation gives the same response for an intent no matter how detailed the user's question gets. The assistant needs to understand more-detailed context from the conversation.

2.3.2 *Contextualizing a response by using entities*

Giving a store-specific answer has two parts: detecting that a specific location was mentioned, and replying with a specific condition. The specific location will be detected by training the assistant to recognize entities; the entity will be used to give a specific response.

DETECTING AN ENTITY

Because the number of Fictitious Inc. stores is limited and well-defined, the simplest solution is to use a static dictionary-based entity. We open the Entities tab and create a new entity called @store_location with two possible values: Elm and Maple. We'll include a couple of variations with the Street/Drive qualifier as well, though variations are not strictly required. We will also enable fuzzy matching so that our entity dictionary will be robust in the case of user typos and misspellings (figure 2.10).

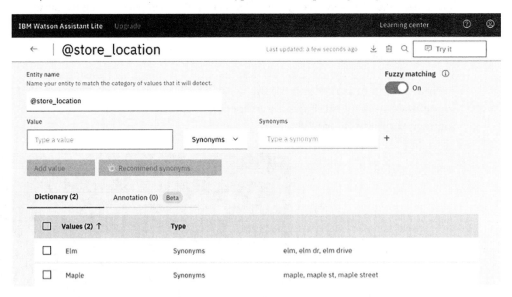

Figure 2.10   Example interface for defining entities. Fictitious Inc. uses a @store_location entity with values for its two stores: Elm and Maple.

> **Terminology alert**
>
> *Fuzzy matching* is a common term, used by all the AI platforms I surveyed. Use fuzzy matching so that your assistant is resilient against typos and misspellings.

USING AN ENTITY TO GIVE A SPECIFIC RESPONSE

Next, we have to update the dialogue conditions to check for a mention of one of our `@store_location` values in the user's utterance. We need to update the `#Customer_Care_Store_Location` node to check for a `@store_location` and to give a targeted response (if `@store_location` is present) or a generic response (if `@store_location` is not present). Follow these steps to update the dialogue (figure 2.11):

1 Find the `#Customer_Care_Store_Location` condition.
2 Within that conditional block, create child conditions for `@store_location:Elm`, `@store_location:Maple`, and another fallback or Anything Else node for use when `#Customer_Care_Store_Location` is detected but no `@store_location` is present.
3 Associate a dialogue response with each new condition.

1. First dialog node detects the intent.

2. Defer a response until the child nodes are evaluated for entities.

3. If the user asked about Elm, tell them about the Elm location.

4. If the user asked about Maple, tell them about the Maple location.

5. Otherwise, give the generic #Customer_Care_Store_Location response.

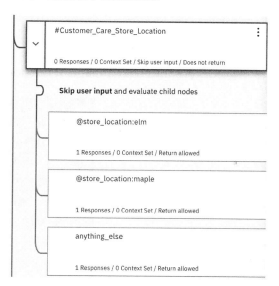

Figure 2.11 Dialogue rules for detecting a specific store location. Three answers will be given to a store-location question based on the specific store, or lack of a specific store, in the user's utterance. You can also put multiple conditions in each dialogue, joined by `and`.

This may look different in your AI platform

"Skip user input and evaluate child nodes" is my favorite way to implement this pattern. I like having one condition per dialogue node, which makes the nodes easier to read. The last three nodes in figure 2.11 effectively have two conditions by being children of the first node.

Alternatively, you could write three nodes with these conditions:

```
#Customer_Care_Store_Location and @store_location:Elm
#Customer_Care_Store_Location and @store_location:Maple
#Customer_Care_Store_Location
```

Your choice depends on what your platform supports and your preference.

In table 2.9, you can see that the assistant detects the three separate variations of the #Customer_Care_Store_Location intent based on the contextual clues.

Table 2.9   How the assistant interprets three `#Customer_Care_Store_Location` utterances when entities are used

User utterance	Assistant detects	Assistant responds
"Where is the Elm store?"	`#Customer_Care_Store_Location` `@store_location:Elm`	"That store is located at 456 Elm Drive."
"What's the address for the Mapel store?"	`#Customer_Care_Store_Location` `@store_location:Maple`	"That store is located at 123 Maple Street."
"Where are your local stores?"	`#Customer_Care_Store_Location`	"We have two locations near you: 123 Maple Street and 456 Elm Drive."

Figure 2.12 shows one variation of the store-location questions in Watson's interface.

1. User misspells "Maple."

2. Assistant understands the intended location "Maple."

Figure 2.12   The assistant has been trained to detect specific stores via entities and gives targeted responses. The assistant is even adaptive to misspellings (such as *Mapel*) thanks to fuzzy matching.

The ability to tailor a specific response based on one or more contextual clues is a powerful way to satisfy your users.

This may look different in your AI platform

Each of the AI platforms I surveyed provided some way to inspect entities by telling you the entity type (@store_location), value ("Maple"), and covered text ("Mapel") in the testing interface.

2.3.3 *An alternative way to provide contextual responses*

Fictitious Inc. provided contextual responses to #Customer_Care_Store_Location questions via four dialogue nodes. The pattern used requires $n + 2$ dialogue nodes, where n is the number of unique entity values. Fictitious Inc. will also provide contextual responses to the #Customer_Care_Store_Hours intent based on store-location variations. For this intent, however, the company uses a technique called *multiple conditioned responses* (http://mng.bz/9NGo), which allows you to put conditional response logic in a single dialogue node. To update this dialogue with multiple conditioned responses (figure 2.13), follow these steps:

1 Enable multiple conditioned responses on the dialogue node by using the settings (triple dot) icon.
2 Create conditioned responses for @store_location:Elm, @store_location: Maple, and an Anything Else node for use when no @store_location is present.

Coding conventions and style

Your platform may support multiple ways to implement complex conditions. Methods such as multiple conditioned responses have the advantage and disadvantage of being more compact. These responses use less screen real estate, allowing you to see more of your dialogue nodes on the screen at the same time.

Consistency is important in software development. Consistency makes software easier to read and understand. However you choose to implement complex conditions, try to do it consistently.

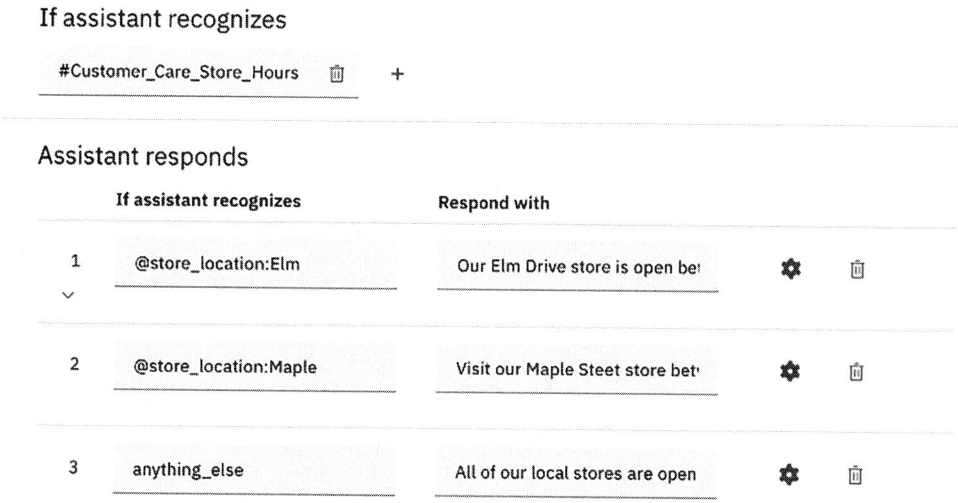

If assistant recognizes

#Customer_Care_Store_Hours 🗑 +

Assistant responds

	If assistant recognizes	Respond with		
1	@store_location:Elm	Our Elm Drive store is open beⁱ	⚙	🗑
2	@store_location:Maple	Visit our Maple Steet store betⁱ	⚙	🗑
3	anything_else	All of our local stores are open	⚙	🗑

Figure 2.13 Giving a targeted store-hours response based on which store (if any) the user asked about. A single dialogue node is configured with three possible responses. This response is more compact on the screen (compared with the exercise in figure 2.11) but can be harder to read.

We've seen two possible ways to improve the assistant's responses by using contextual information. Either method will satisfy your users and make them feel understood. When the user asks a specific form of a question ("Where's the *Elm* store?"), it's important to give a specific response ("The *Elm* store is at . . .").

Dictionaries seem to be static; would I use them to list my stores?

The preceding examples, which use dictionary-based entities, are intended to be simplistic. A national retail chain would prompt for zip code and use a store-locator service called from an orchestrator to select a store or get the zip code from the user's profile. The chain would not code hundreds or thousands of entities for each store. A dictionary-based entity works best for a relatively small and finite list of possibilities.

2.3.4   *Responding with a process flow*

Many self-service interactions require a process flow or other some way of collecting all the information necessary to complete a task. Fictitious Inc. will implement a simple process flow for setting up an appointment.

When Fictitious Inc. first configured the dialogue for its assistant, it created only static responses. The response to a `#Customer_Care_Employment_Inquiry` was a redirection to a website ("Apply on FictitiousInc.com/jobs now!"). Instead of doing a similar redirection for `#Customer_Care_Appointments`, however, the assistant should book an appointment. Booking an appointment has a process flow: an appointment consists of a date, time, and specific store location.

Fictitious Inc. can implement this process flow in one dialogue node by using a capability called *slots*. It will also use built-in entities (called *system entities*) to gather the date and time of the appointment.

Terminology alert

Each AI platform I surveyed had slots capability, though some gave it a different name, such as *parameters and actions*. Most AI platforms fill slots with *entities* and others with *slot resolution*.

Think of slots as being something that must be filled before a request can be worked on. Setting an alarm has one slot (the time of the alarm). Setting an appointment may have three slots (the date, time, and location of the appointment).

Conversational AI platforms usually come with system or default entities to cover basic scenarios such as detecting dates. (Building your own date detection is fiendishly difficult; be glad that your platform does the work for you!)

Check your platform's documentation to see how slots are implemented. Slots are a cool feature, and platform providers can't help but brag about it.

Figure 2.14 shows how the appointment flow might look in an AI platform that uses slots. Although the specific steps may vary in other platforms, the Watson Assistant steps are listed here:

1 Enable slots on the dialogue node, using the settings (triple dot) icon.
2 Enable system entities for sys-date and sys-time.
3 Create conditions for each of the slot variables: how to detect them, where to store them, and how to prompt for them.
4 Create a text response for use when no slot variables are present.
5 Create a response for use when all variables are filled in.

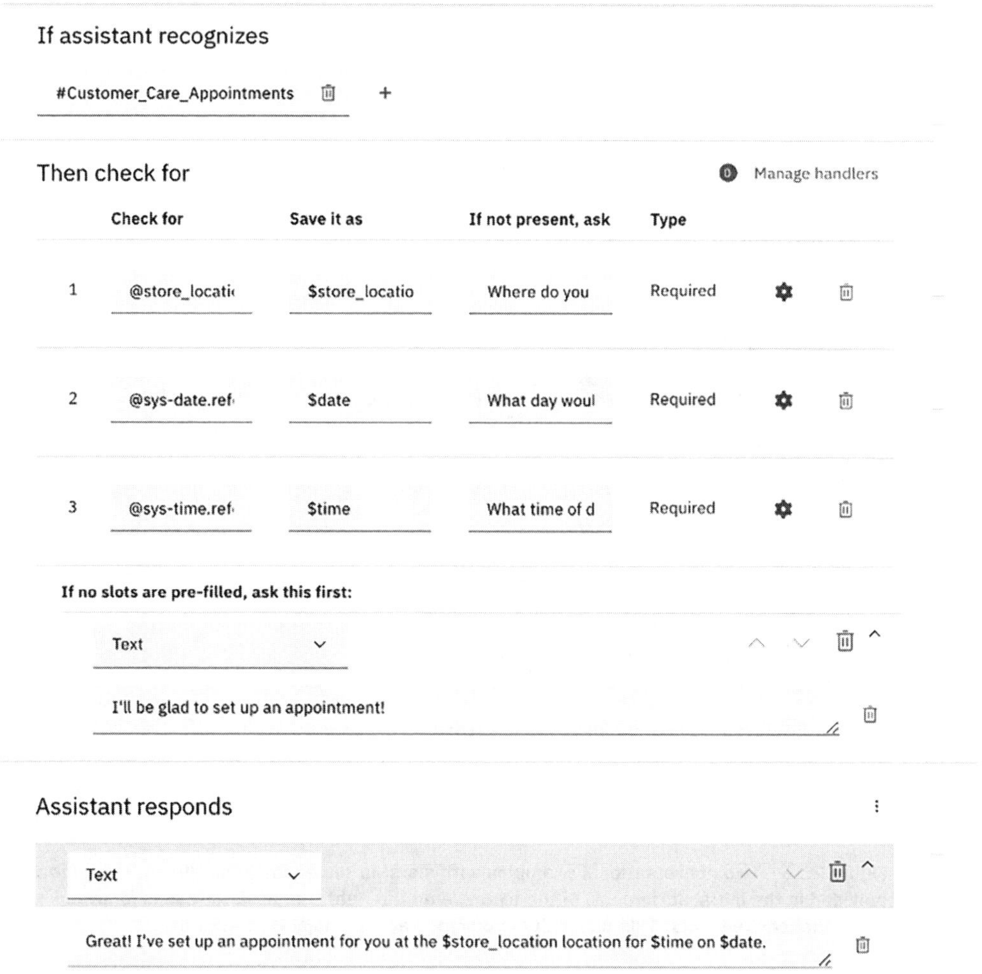

If assistant recognizes

#Customer_Care_Appointments 🗑 +

Then check for

0 Manage handlers

	Check for	Save it as	If not present, ask	Type		
1	@store_locatic	$store_locatio	Where do you	Required	⚙	🗑
2	@sys-date.ref	$date	What day woul	Required	⚙	🗑
3	@sys-time.ref	$time	What time of d	Required	⚙	🗑

If no slots are pre-filled, ask this first:

Text ⌄ ∧ ⌄ 🗑 ^

I'll be glad to set up an appointment! 🗑

Assistant responds

⋮

Text ⌄ ∧ ⌄ 🗑 ^

Great! I've set up an appointment for you at the $store_location location for $time on $date. 🗑

Figure 2.14 **Configuring dialogue to set up an appointment by using slots. The dialogue flow has slots for collecting the appointment location, date, and time. The user will be asked follow-up questions until all the slots are filled, because an appointment cannot be scheduled without all three pieces of information. Your platform may have a different interface but probably still has slots.**

Now that the dialogue engine is coded with these conditions, it can respond with a message that reflects all the appointment details, such as "Great! I've set up an appointment for you at the `$store_location` location for `$time` on `$date`." Your assistant will fill in the details dynamically, as shown in figure 2.14.

Technique alert

Your platform will let you use variables in your responses; check the syntax from your provider's documentation. Common patterns are $ plus a variable name (`$time`) or a variable name in braces (`{name}`). Search your platform's documentation for *variables* or *parameters*, and you should find what you need.

Figure 2.15 shows two examples of conversational flows that use slots. In the first example, the user supplies all three pieces of information in a single statement: "I'd like to set up an appointment at *Maple* for *9:15* on *Friday*." All information has been provided, so the system responds that the appointment has been set up. In the second example, the user's statement "I'd like to set up an appointment at *Maple* for *9:45*" does not include a date, so the system prompts the user with "What day would you like to come in?"

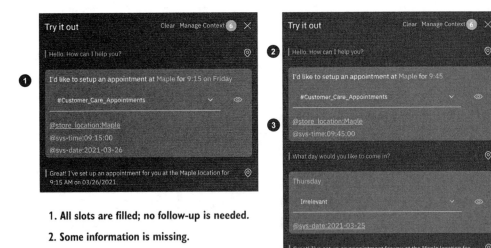

1. **All slots are filled; no follow-up is needed.**

2. **Some information is missing.**

3. **Follow-up question fills empty slot.**

Figure 2.15   Two conversational examples with slots. In the example on the left, all information is provided in the initial statement. In the example on the right, the assistant asks follow-up questions to fill all the required slots. This capability is common across major AI platforms.

The example ends with a message to the user: "Great! I've set up an appointment for you at the `$store_location` location for `$time` on `$date`." I used Spring Expression

Language (SpEL) expressions to reformat the date and time to a more user-friendly representation than the internal date format.

Platform variation

Watson Assistant uses SpEL (http://mng.bz/jBxp) for low-code manipulation within the conversational AI dialogue response. Your platform may require you to use no code, low code, or plain code in your responses. Check your platform documentation for details on customizing dialogue responses with system variables.

Listing 2.1 The SpEL logic used in the Watson Assistant date formatting example

```
{
  "context": {
    "date": "<? @sys-date.reformatDateTime(\"MM/dd/yyyy\") ?>"
  }
}
```

Listing 2.2 The SpEL logic used in the Watson Assistant time formatting example

```
{
  "context": {
    "time": "<? @sys-time.reformatDateTime(\"h:mm a\") ?>"
  }
}
```

This appointment flow ends with a dialogue response to the user, telling them about their appointment, but does not book the appointment. Booking an appointment would require an API call to an external booking system, coordinated by the orchestration layer. For the sake of brevity, this feature was not demonstrated.

Booking an appointment can be slightly more complex

We have walked through an example of appointment booking. A more robust example would include calling an appointment service API to check availability, book the appointment, and return a success or failure response. Your platform may enable this feature; search for *webhooks, orchestration, connectors, integration,* or anywhere you can write code.

Slots are useful for implementing a process flow that needs to collect multiple pieces of information before proceeding. Slots provide a syntax shortcut for gathering multiple input variables in a coordinated way. You can choose to implement process flows with or without slots. Anything you could implement in slots could also be implemented in regular dialogue nodes.

Further discussion of conventions and style

As in the entities example, you have multiple ways of implementing process flows. You may want to gather slot variables one by one and do an external validation. When you're authenticating with two pieces of information, such as user ID and date of birth, you may want to validate that the user ID exists in the system before prompting for date of birth, and you'll want to execute a resolution flow if the user ID is not correct.

2.4   *Other useful responses*

Fictitious Inc.'s assistant now has the following capabilities:

- Greeting the user
- Providing a static, noncontextual answer to employment inquiries
- Providing static, contextual answers to requests for store locations and store hours
- Executing a process flow to set up appointments
- Responding to any other utterances with "I didn't understand"

Before Fictitious Inc. accepts this demonstration, it needs two more capabilities:

- Determining when the assistant is unsure of the user's intent
- Handing the user to another channel when the assistant repeatedly misunderstands the user

Three strikes and you're out

Conversational AIs often use a baseball metaphor. When a batter swings and misses, that action is called a *strike*. If the batter accrues three strikes before hitting the ball, they're out.

Similarly, if a conversational AI assistant misunderstands the user, we can call that behavior a *strike*. If the assistant misunderstands the user three times, the assistant should hand the user off to get resolution elsewhere. Many conversational AI implementers use a two-strikes rule with similar logic.

Let's update the assistant with a two-strikes rule. We'll implement two pieces of logic in the dialogue nodes:

- Detecting low-confidence conditions from the classifier and routing them to the Anything Else node
- Counting how many times the Anything Else node is visited

2.4.1   *Detecting low confidence*

Most conversational AI classifiers not only predict an intent, but also tell you the confidence in that prediction. By default, they return an intent only if the best prediction has confidence exceeding some threshold (0.2 in Watson Assistant). Intent predictions with low-confidence values are frequently incorrect, and you may need to tune this threshold for your particular assistant.

In chapter 7, we will see how the confidence value is derived. For now, consider that the lower the confidence value is, the more likely the predicted intent is to be wrong. Figure 2.16 shows how you can inspect the confidence values in a testing interface.

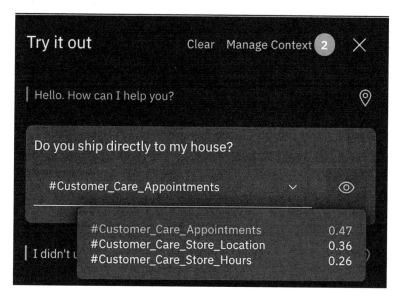

Figure 2.16 The most likely intents and associated confidence value for an input utterance. Note that low-confidence results are often wrong. The utterance "Do you ship directly to my house?" does not match any of the intents coded into this assistant.

The confidence values can be used in conditional logic in dialogue nodes.

Listing 2.3   Conditional logic for low-confidence intent selection in Watson Assistant

```
intents.size() > 0 && intents.get(0).confidence < 0.5
```

Terminology alert

Each platform I surveyed had a *confidence* term. Hooray again for common terminology!

The platforms differed in how they referred to the threshold and how you configure it. The threshold is also called *confidence cutoff*, *intent threshold*, or *classification threshold*, though it is still described as a threshold.

Most AI platforms have a single setting for this classification threshold to apply globally to your assistant. Some platforms let you use a higher threshold in specific dialogue logic.

2.4.2   *Counting misunderstandings*

When the dialogue reaches the catch-all Anything Else node, the implication is that the user was not understood, and their satisfaction with the assistant will decrease. Therefore, it's a good idea to count how many times this dialogue node has been visited. The second time the catch-all node is visited, we should respond by offering the user an alternative channel before they get frustrated.

Most conversational AI platforms come with a way to store arbitrary information in variables during a conversation. These variables are often called *context variables*. We'll use a context variable to count how many times the catch-all node is visited.

> **NOTE**   Some platforms automatically count the number of visits to the catch-all node. Be sure to check the documentation to see whether your platform has this feature, which will save you some time.

Thus, the two-strikes rule is implemented by storing the number of visits to the catch-all Anything Else node in a context variable. After two strikes (two visits to this node), the assistant should send the user to another channel, such as a customer service phone line, a website, or another human-backed process.

Fictitious Inc. wants to be conservative with its first assistant, wanting it to respond to a user's intent only if that intent is detected with high confidence. Thus, the assistant should treat low-confidence predictions as being misunderstandings. Low-confidence predictions should be sent to the Anything Else node. Let's see how to implement these two features in the assistant.

2.4.3   *Implementing confidence detection and the two-strikes rule*

This functionality is implemented via the following steps:

1 Initialize the context variable `misunderstood_count` to 0 in the Welcome node. This variable will be used to track how many times the assistant misunderstands the user.
2 Create a new Misunderstanding node at the bottom of the dialogue with the fallback condition.
3 Increment `misunderstood_count` inside the Misunderstanding node. This variable tracks total misunderstandings by incrementing every time a conversation includes this dialogue node.
4 Add a child node to the Misunderstanding node to check the misunderstood count, and if `$misunderstood_count >= 2`, deflect the user with the message "I'm sorry I'm not able to understand your question. Please try our phone support at 1-800-555-5555."
5 Make the existing Anything Else node the last child of the Misunderstanding node, completing the two-strikes functionality.

6 Create a Low confidence prediction node before all the other intent nodes with the low-confidence conditional logic (`intents.size() > 0 && intents.get(0) .confidence < 0.5`). When this node fires, it should go to and evaluate the Misunderstanding node's conditions. This node extends the two-strikes functionality by treating low-confidence intent predictions as misunderstandings.

The code is visualized in figure 2.17. The code listings appear after the figure.

1. Catch-all node for any misunderstandings increments a context variable on each visit.

2. If this is the second strike, deflect the user.

3. Otherwise, ask the user to restate their utterance.

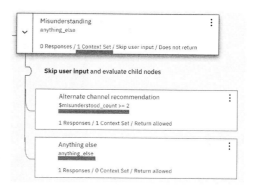

Figure 2.17 Visualization of two-strikes logic, which may look different in your platform of choice but should still be implementable

Listing 2.4 Initializing the misunderstanding counter

```
{
  "output": {
    "generic": [
      {
        "values": [
          {
            "text": "Hello. How can I help you?"
          }
        ],
        "response_type": "text",
        "selection_policy": "sequential"
      }
    ]
  },
  "context": {
    "misunderstood_count": 0
  }
}
```

Listing 2.5 Incrementing the misunderstanding counter

```
{
  "output": {
    "generic": []
  },
```

```
    "context": {
      "misunderstood_count": "<? $misunderstood_count + 1 ?>"
  }
}
```

Figure 2.18 demonstrates the two-strikes rule.

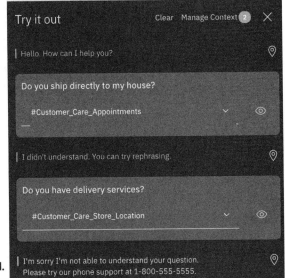

1. **An intent was recognized, but with low confidence. Strike one.**

2. **Another low-confidence intent is strike two, and the user is redirected.**

Figure 2.18   The assistant is asked two questions. For each question, it detects an intent with low confidence and visits the catch-all node. After two misunderstandings, the user is deflected to call customer service.

In figure 2.18, the assistant selected an intent for each user utterance. The first utterance, "Do you ship directly to my house?", was classified as `#Customer_Care_Appointments` but with low confidence. The second utterance, "Do you have delivery services?", was classified as `#Customer_Care_Store_Hours`, again with low confidence. Because of the Low confidence response dialogue node, the low-confidence condition fired before any of the intent-based nodes; thus, the system does not respond based on a (possibly wrong) intent selection.

How can you know that the intents were recognized with low confidence?

Watson Assistant will show you the confidence behind an intent when you hover over the "eye" icon next to the identified intent. The algorithms used by AI providers change continuously, but if you try this example, you should see low-confidence values, probably between 0.4 and 0.5.

Your platform will provide a way to see the intent confidence through a testing interface or API.

2.5   *Try to build this conversational AI yourself*

The principles demonstrated in this chapter will work in most conversational AI platforms. I have provided screenshots, terminology guides, and the reasoning behind each concept and example so that you can implement the examples in your platform of choice. Some of the low-level details are specific to Watson Assistant, but I am confident that you can implement Fictitious Inc.'s assistant in any platform.

The Watson Assistant source code is available on this book's GitHub site at https://github.com/andrewrfreed/ConversationalAI. The file is skill-Customer-Service-Skill-Ch2.json, and you can import it into your Watson Assistant instance. The JSON format used is not human-friendly and is best read from the Watson Assistant interface.

Try expanding the capabilities of the assistant on your own. For a first exercise, try responding to #Customer_Care_Contact_Us questions by giving out a phone number and an email address. Next, work on a multistep response to #Customer_Care_Open_Account inquiries. What other capabilities would you like to add to the assistant?

Summary

- User input to a conversational AI is an utterance. An utterance contains an intent (centered on a verb) and/or entities (centered on nouns).

- A conversational AI assistant responds to a user by extracting meaning from the user's utterance and then mapping that meaning to a response.

- The simplest response is to provide an answer to the user's utterance and wait for the user to send another utterance.

- A conversational AI can execute a process flow based on a user's utterance. That process flow will dictate additional questions or steps in the conversation that need to take place before an answer can be provided to the user.

Part 2

Designing for success

Y ou've decided what kind of AI assistant you need. Now you need a plan to build it.

Benjamin Franklin said, "An ounce of prevention is worth a pound of cure." An effective design process can save weeks or months (or years) of heartache. It's not enough to decide to use an AI assistant: you must tailor the technology to your particular use case and scenario. This part will help you design an assistant that meets the needs of both the business and the customers.

AI assistants automate processes, often through a conversational interface, which implies that you have processes to automate. In chapter 3, you'll learn how to select the right practices to automate through your AI assistant based on user needs and process complexity. You'll also learn how to assemble a dream team for building an AI assistant and see how the members of this team can best work together.

Chapter 4 covers how to design dialogue that improves your users' experience. Bad dialogue can ruin an otherwise-useful conversational AI. You'll learn dialogue practices for both voice- and text-based assistants.

AI assistants are ultimately created to serve a business need. Chapter 5 teaches you how to select the right metrics to evaluate your assistant against that business need. The business need and its associated metrics are foundational to all other aspects of the build cycle.

When you complete this part, you'll be ready to start building your own AI assistant.

Designing
effective processes

This chapter covers

- Organizing user needs by complexity and frequency for a milestone plan
- Identifying requirements for a minimum viable product
- Assembling your dream team to implement a conversational AI
- Addressing challenging parts of a process flow
- Assembling appropriate responses for web and voice channels

A conversational AI is more than a classifier and some orchestration logic, in the same way that a graphical user interface is more than lines and styling. A conversational AI is a complete user experience channel; it requires a careful and thoughtful design for end users. The quality of your design sets an upper limit on how successful your conversational AI assistant can be.

This chapter focuses entirely on conversational AI design, setting aside almost all machine learning and coding considerations. After reading this chapter, you will be able to design process flows for your conversational AI, optimized for your preferred deployment channel, and you will be able to decide what processes you should implement first. You'll be ready to learn how to write the dialogue supporting your new processes. Figure 3.1 shows the parts of your assistant that the user sees, but the invisible parts need to work well for a good user experience.

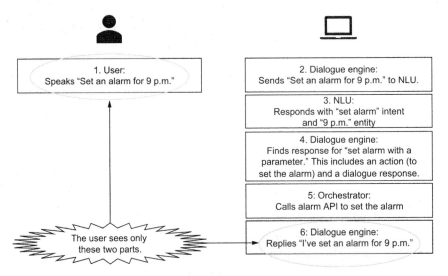

Figure 3.1   Motivating example. The user experiences only what they say and how you respond; they cannot see the internal parts. The parts invisible to the user need to be well designed so that the user has a good experience.

A conversational AI should be optimized for the channel on which it is delivered. Assistants are commonly deployed in voice channels (such as telephone) and web channels (such as websites). Voice and web have different strengths and weaknesses, and your design should account for those strengths and weaknesses. A good response for voice may not be a good response for web chat, and vice versa.

Regardless of channel, it is important to design a conversational AI that can be useful without requiring a "boil the ocean" approach. (*Boiling the ocean* refers to an impossibly large scope. Consider how much energy it would take to boil the ocean versus to boil a gallon of water.) You should brainstorm all the things that your assistant could do and then build an iterative plan to implement them. High-frequency and low-complexity requests are the first things an assistant should cover. ("What time do you close?" is a high-frequency, low-complexity question in retail.) As the frequency of a request decreases or its complexity increases, you need to decide on an appropriate strategy. (Is there a simple strategy for the request, or should it be escalated out of the assistant?)

In this chapter, I will demonstrate how to prioritize a list of user requests into a phased implementation plan. Then I will help you assemble your dream team to build your own conversational AI solution. Next, I will demonstrate key differences between the voice and web channels, and show you how to optimize your assistant to respond with questions and answers that will work well for a given channel.

3.1 What processes will the assistant handle?

To build a conversational AI assistant that delights your users, you must have a solid understanding of what your users want from the assistant and how you can provide it. You need to have business processes that your assistant should follow, and if these processes don't exist, you will be creating them. If you don't have a repeatable business process for resetting a user's password, for example, how can you automate it in a conversational AI?

As you design business processes and adapt them for a conversational AI, you may find challenges that require you to use a phased approach in delivering functionality. Processes often have a shortcut version (tell the user where they can go to reset their password) and a fully automated version (ask a series of questions verifying the user and then reset their password for them). When you work out a plan for which processes to implement in your assistant first, make sure to keep the user in mind.

3.1.1 Designing for the most common user needs

When building a conversational AI, you should try not to boil the ocean; rather, focus on high-volume and high-value activities, particularly for your first venture into conversational AIs. You should do an assessment of what information and processes you already expose to your users through other channels.

You can review call logs, search queries, interview subject-matter experts (SMEs), and so on. If you have a call center, shadow the staff for a day to see what kinds of calls they receive. Your business may already keep track of the top customer demands, and if so, you can use that information repository to guide this exercise. Many companies do not keep detailed records of what types of customer interactions they have and how frequently, so for them, a major benefit of conversational AIs is to start collecting that information. Note that the closer you are to real user data and the farther you are from opinions, the better you will do in this exercise. Chapter 6 introduces an additional methodology for gathering user input.

In this section, we'll develop an implementation plan for a customer service conversational AI for Fictitious Inc. We'll reference the Watson Assistant Customer Care Content Catalog, which contains a list of intents covering frequent customer service request types, shown in table 3.1. These intents are fairly generic for a retail customer service use case.

Now that we have the list of the most common request types, we must approximate the complexity of satisfying each type of request. We can use a simple low-medium-high scoring system, for example, or a T-shirt sizing system (small-medium-large). The goal

Table 3.1   Frequent Customer Care intents

Schedule/Manage Appointments	Reset Password
Add/Remove Authorized Users	Change Security Questions
Cancel Account	Get List of Programs
Get Contact Information	Redeem Points
Apply for a Job	Report Fraud
Check Loyalty Status	Store Hours
Adjust Notification Preferences	Store Location
Open Account	Transfer Points
Get List of Products	Update User Profile

is to quickly sort the types of requests into a 2×2 grid where the dimensions are formed by complexity and frequency. Figure 3.2 shows an empty grid. Try placing each of the request types from table 3.1 in the grid.

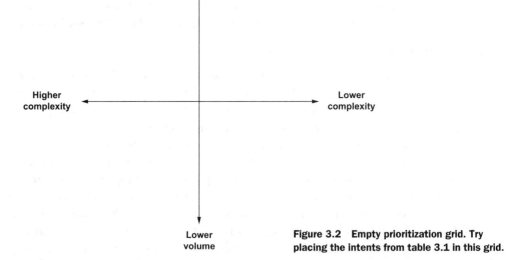

Figure 3.2   Empty prioritization grid. Try placing the intents from table 3.1 in this grid.

Gauge complexity by what it would take to satisfy the request completely and automatically according to your business processes. Many request types can be satisfied with a simple question-and-answer response or a complete process flow. Consider different versions of the Open Account flow.

Listing 3.1   Simple (redirection) flow for Open Account

```
Question: "I'd like to open an account"
Answer: "Please call our service line at 1-800-555-5555 and press 2 to open
    an account, or go to our account creation site at
    fictitiousinc.com/accounts"
```

Listing 3.2 Fully automated flow for Open Account

```
Question: "I'd like to open an account"
Answer: (A process flow with these steps)
1. Gather identifying information.
2. Determine account type.
3. Use account query API to see whether an account already exists.
4. Use account creation API.
```

You can always start by addressing a request via redirection or giving a purely informational response; later, you automate more of the response in future versions of your assistant. A conversational AI that always redirects may not provide the best user experience, but it can still be helpful to users. For the sake of this planning exercise, let's focus on the fully automated response first.

Open Account requests are among the most common request types for most retailers. This request type definitely belongs in the top half of the grid. As listings 3.1 and 3.2 show, creating an account requires several follow-up questions and several API calls, which is enough complexity to earn a spot in the top-left quadrant of figure 3.2 (high volume, high complexity).

Requests for your contact information—such as your phone number, mailing address, or email address—are also high-volume requests. These requests are simple to address: return a static answer, and the request is satisfied. We can place Get Contact Information in the top-right quadrant of figure 3.2 (high volume, low complexity). Try placing all the requests from table 3.1 in a grid. When you're done, review figure 3.3, which contains my analysis of the Fictitious Inc. intents.

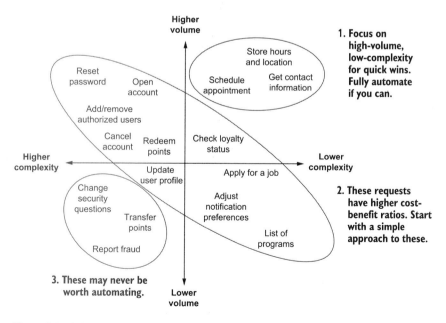

Figure 3.3 Volume and complexity analysis of Customer Care request types from table 3.1. An implementation plan must be based on cost-benefit analysis. Focus first on high-volume, low-complexity tasks.

Based on the plot of volume and complexity, you can perform a cost-benefit analysis. That analysis shows you what to implement first in your conversational AI. The highest return on investment comes from the high-volume, low-complexity requests, and you should handle as many of these requests as you can.

Next are the high-volume, high-complexity request types. For these requests, you need to determine whether a useful quick win can satisfy the requests (can you provide a link or general answer?) or whether you need to escalate these types of requests to an alternative channel, such as a human-staffed call center. You will need to train your assistant to recognize these requests even if it does not service them.

As time permits, you can address the easiest requests in the low-volume, low-complexity segment of figure 3.2. Take care not to spend too much time and introduce too much development work for these requests.

Low-volume, high-complexity requests may never be appropriate for an automated solution; you can use a generic escalation strategy for those requests. Figure 3.4 shows a generalized plan.

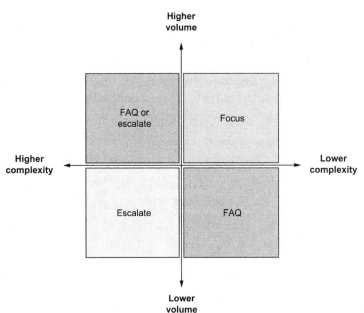

Figure 3.4   A generalized plan for requests based on volume and complexity

3.1.2 *Assembling a plan and a dream team*

When you review the request types on the volume/complexity graph, you can subdivide each request type into the processes and APIs that support it. The first common process may be authenticating a user. Other commonalities may include high-volume requests for store hours and store locations, as both are likely to reference a store locator API (because each store likely has different operating hours). You can also plot any APIs on your graph to influence what you implement first, as shown in figure 3.5.

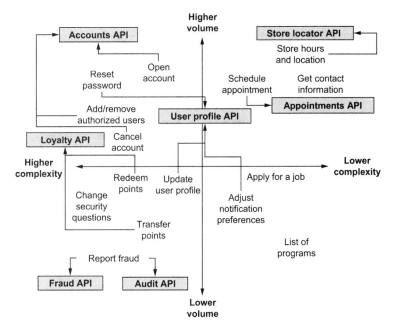

Figure 3.5 Overlaying the APIs required to fully automate an intent. The more intents that use an API, the more valuable it can be to integrate with that API. The User Profile API is a good candidate to integrate with because it supports so many common request types.

For your first conversational AI, a good plan is to implement a maximum of two or three process flows and a series of question-and-answer responses, as in frequently asked questions (FAQ). You should train the assistant to recognize the high-volume request types even if it will not answer them directly. You should use an incremental development process to build and expand the conversational AI. Each significant milestone can focus on a small number of process flows and on expanding the number of request types recognized. Table 3.2 shows what Fictitious Inc. might plan for its first two delivery milestones.

Table 3.2 Example delivery milestone plan

Milestone	Features delivered in the assistant
1	Gives store hours and location answers for the user's local store
	Provides FAQ-style answers for ~10 more intents, including account management, loyalty program, appointments, and job listings
	Redirects all other inquiries to another channel
2	Provides fully automated appointment scheduling
	Fully automates password resets
	Detects intents about fraud and redirects those requests to a special fraud hotline

For production-grade AI assistants, you'll need a multidisciplinary team to implement this plan. The team will design your conversational AI and the process flows it will use. The team will also develop and deliver the assistant according to time and budget. Figure 3.6 shows what your dream team might look like.

Business process SME

"I understand how the business works."

User experience designer

"I represent the voice of the user."

Developer/technical SME

"I can write the code."

Legal

"I'll make sure we don't get sued."

Marketing

"I want to make sure the assistant's voice is consistent with our brand."

Project sponsor

"I'm making sure we deliver a coherent solution."

Figure 3.6   **The dream team for delivering a successful conversational AI assistant**

That's a huge team; can't I build an assistant myself?

You can certainly build a prototype or proof of concept by yourself, sometimes in a matter of hours, but there's more to conversational AI than throwing together some technology. Most commercial-grade assistants require insight from a multidisciplinary team for both the sake of the project and the company. But if you are willing to perform multiple roles, there's no reason why you can't build an assistant by yourself.

Depending on your use case and business processes, your team should include the following skills and roles:

- *Business-process SMEs*—You need people who understand the business and the current as-is scenario. These experts should have a deep understanding of current processes, and ideally, they will have been involved in creating and shaping those processes. They provide critical guidance on how conversations can and should flow within a business process.
- *User experience (UX) designer*—A UX designer is the chief advocate for the user and makes sure that the experience works well for users. The designer provides valuable advice on how users will interact in a given channel. They will make sure that the conversation design delivers what the user wants, not only what you want.

- *Developer/technical SMEs*—The developer will code the dialogue rules into the conversational AI. Many assistants include some sort of technical integration in existing resources, such as a website, a telephony system, an authentication mechanism, or any number of APIs. Technical experts are needed to make sure that the conversation is technically possible, such as gathering any parameters required for API calls during a conversation.
- *Legal*—This team makes sure that legal and regulatory concerns are addressed in the assistant. You may need to present a disclaimer before providing sensitive or rapidly changing information through the assistant, for example.
- *Marketing*—Members of the marketing team help manage the tone and some of the content of the conversational AI. Because the assistant can be another public-facing channel for your company, it should stay in line with the existing tone, branding, and textual copy of other channels.
- *Project executive sponsor*—The sponsor should provide clear direction on the desired future state and keep team members focused and working together. The sponsor can also adjudicate any conflicts.
- *Analytics experts* (optional)—If you are running analytics on your other business processes, you will want some insight on designing the conversational AI assistant to support similar analytics. This insight will allow you to make an apples-to-apples comparison of your new assistant with the existing process. Analytic experts are optional, so you may not need them from day one, but it is easier to design in the analytics from the beginning than to bolt them on at the end. Your business-process SMEs may be able to cover this role.

3.1.3 Managing the design process

The members of the multidisciplinary team should work together to document and build the process flows that the conversational AI will follow. If your organization has a call center, it may have a decision tree or call script that agents follow. Your first goal is to document all the steps in the process. You'll need multiple team members to contribute. One team member may know every last detail of the process; another may know which systems and APIs support a given step; yet another may see how the new assistant channel can improve the user experience.

Let's revisit the password-reset process flow example from chapter 1. The team may note that password resets have the following requirements:

- Determine who needs the password reset by user ID.
- Authenticate that user by date of birth and the answer to a security question.
- Reset password only after successful authentication.
- No other authentication options are provided, so if authentication fails, do not reset the password.

These requirements can be converted to a process flow, as depicted in figure 3.7.

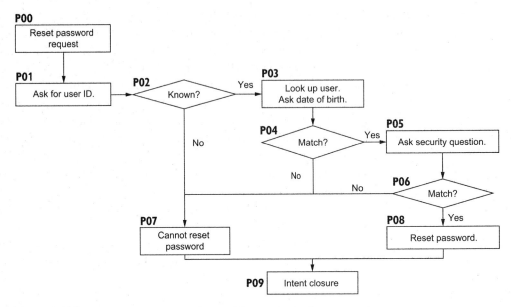

Figure 3.7   Example business process for resetting a password

In the process flow, it is useful to label each point in the process flow with an identi-fier, as shown in figure 3.7. An identifier makes it easier for each team member to be explicit about what part of the process flow they are working on. The team imple-menting the assistant can label the nodes with the identifier, for example, and the copy editor can supply text for each identifier. Overall, it's much easier to say "P04" than "the dialogue node after we ask for the date of birth."

You can diagram your process flow in any software you want to use. Some teams prefer to use an old-fashioned text editor or a spreadsheet tool. I prefer to use a draw-ing program, in which you can see the flow right in front of your eyes. With a drawing program, you can even print the process flow and hang it up in your team room or on a whiteboard.

Whatever software you use to create the process flow, you should treat the design artifact as first-class output. Make sure that the latest approved copy is readily available in a shared location to which the entire team has read access.

The first version of the script should be developed and approved by the entire team. No matter how good that first version is, you will need to make updates, and it's important to have a good change management process in place. Figure 3.8 shows a sample process.

You should use a locking or checkout process so that everyone knows who is mak-ing changes, especially if your script is written in software that does not allow collabo-rative editing or has poor merge capability. When you use locking or checkout

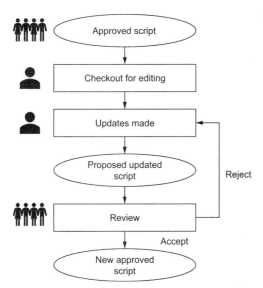

Figure 3.8   Example dialogue-script update process for a team

practices, everyone on the team can make suggestions about the script, but there should be only one editor at a time. The editor should always do the following:

- Work from the latest approved script.
- Notify team members that the script is being edited.
- Make one or more changes.
- Summarize the changes made.
- Distribute the updated script for review.
- Store the approved script in a location that's accessible by the team.

By following this process, the editor makes sure that team members are on the same page. Ideally, the updates are made during a collaborative design session, which ensures that the updates will not cause a business-process problem, a technical-implementation problem, a UX problem, or a legal problem.

Additionally, this process helps keep version control sane. Most process flows are created in drawing programs and stored in binary file formats. For all but the simplest file formats, merging and reconciliation is arduous or impossible. You may never get back to a single copy that contains everyone's changes. Figure 3.9 shows how process flows can get out of sync.

One significant source of process-flow changes comes when you start using or testing the process flows. While you are diagramming a process flow, be sure to ask "what if" questions that test the robustness of your processes. The earlier you think about "what if" questions, the stronger your process flow will be.

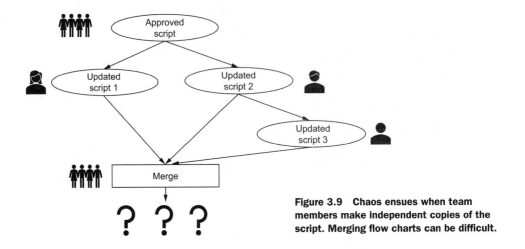

Figure 3.9   Chaos ensues when team members make independent copies of the script. Merging flow charts can be difficult.

Exercise: Test your process flow

It is much cheaper to change your process flow while it is only a diagram. After you put a process flow together, try it out. Does it work?

The password-reset flow chart in figure 3.7 may work well for the majority of cases, but it raises several questions:

- Can we help the user find their user ID?
- What if we can't find the user in our backend system by their user ID? (How many times should we ask them to try again?)
- What if the user has not set up security questions?
- Do we need to log failed (or successful) attempts?

Have your dream team review all process flows before you implement them.

3.1.4   *Cross-cutting design aspects*

You have design aspects to consider besides volume and complexity when you expose business processes through a conversational AI channel. Cross-cutting aspects include concerns that cut across all request types, such as authentication, CRM, and legal or regulatory. Cross-cutting design aspects may need to be built into your assistant from day one. If so, you may have to reduce the number of process flows to implement in the first version of your assistant.

AUTHENTICATION

The most common cross-cutting concern is authentication. Many business processes can be executed only when you know who the user is and have validated that they are who they say they are. Many APIs that you want to call from your assistant also require the user to be authenticated.

Integrating a conversational AI into your organization's security and authentication routines may be a complex task. You may need to build in long lead times to get the right IT resources and approvals together.

Many organizations do not include authentication in the first version of their assistant. Their milestone 1 includes only unauthenticated process flows or static question-and-answer responses; in milestone 2, they add authenticated process flows.

CUSTOMER RELATIONSHIP MANAGEMENT

Related to authentication may be a corporate dictate to store all customer interactions in a CRM software system. In the minimum CRM integration, when the assistant finishes a conversation with a user, the conversation transcript is stored in the CRM system and associated with that user.

A CRM system generally tracks additional structured fields. Fictitious Inc. may have a CRM system that tracks every call, recording the user who called, their reason for the call, and a summary of the call. The assistant could integrate with the CRM software by storing the fields in table 3.3 as structured data.

Table 3.3 Example mapping between CRM fields and conversational AI data

CRM field	Conversational AI data
User	User ID
Reason for Call	Name of first intent
Call Summary	Entire chat transcript

CRM software can help you design your assistant

The Reason for Call or Request Type field in your CRM software is a great clue to what types of requests your AI assistant should handle. You can use your CRM data to determine empirically which request types are most common.

Further, if your CRM software has required fields for data, your conversational AI is probably required to collect that data as well.

LEGAL OR REGULATORY

If some request types have legal or regulatory ramifications, you may decide that your assistant should never handle those requests directly. Instead, the assistant can redirect the user to another answer source, such as a website or telephone hotline.

The Fictitious Inc. legal team weighed in on the Report Fraud intent and noted more than three dozen regulatory nuances that must be met during an interaction about fraud. The team decided that automating the Report Fraud intent is too complex and risky and that the AI assistant should immediately redirect all fraud-related requests to a human-staffed call center.

WARNING   If you work in a heavily regulated domain, be sure that your legal team weighs in on your design. You want to find out as early in your design process as possible what rules and regulations your assistant needs to abide by.

3.2   Choosing the channel to implement first

The choice of a channel has far-reaching considerations that affect how your conversational AI assistant works. Each channel has pros and cons, and you will likely need to customize your assistant to exploit the benefits of a channel while avoiding the pitfalls. The specific channel you already use—voice or web—can also influence what you can go after first. Additionally, some business processes may be friendlier to adapt to voice or web. You can give driving directions with a map in a web channel, for example, but how would you give directions over a voice channel? Today's consumers are used to getting the information they want when they want it, in the mode that they prefer (figure 3.10).

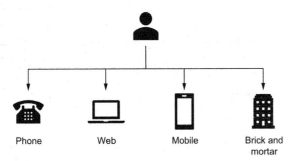

Figure 3.10   Consumers are used to picking the channel that works best for them.

Which channel has the closest affinity to most of your users? If your users are on the phone all day, they will be more likely to prefer a voice channel. If your users interact with you primarily through your website, app, or email, they will be more likely to prefer a web-chat option. Phones are ubiquitous, and nearly everyone knows how to make phone calls; whether they like using the phone is a different story. Similarly, instructing users to "Go to our website" may be a welcome relief or a daunting challenge, depending on your user base. Nothing is stopping you from supporting both channels, of course—only time and money.

All else being equal, it is easier to start with web chat than with voice. Voice introduces two additional AI services—conversion of speech to text and text to speech—that require additional development and training work. Training a speech engine is continuing to get easier, however. (I have published a quick guide to bootstrapping speech-to-text training from Watson Assistant training data with Marco Noel; see http://mng.bz/Wrpw.) I will dive deeper into voice training and voice solutions in chapter 9.

Table 3.4　Comparison of web and voice channels

Web benefits	Voice benefits
Fewer moving parts in technical implementation	Ubiquity (because almost everyone has a phone)
No need to train speech recognition	Friendly to non-tech-savvy users
Easily deployed on websites and mobile apps	Ease of transferring users in and out of assistant via public telephony switching

Let's explore more deeply the differences between voice and web channels. The key differences are how users receive information from the assistant and how the assistant receives information from users.

3.2.1　How users receive information in voice and web

The first difference between voice and web is the way the user receives information from the solution. In a web solution, the user will have the full chat transcript on their screen—a complete record of everything they said and what the assistant said. Although many users don't like scrolling, they have the option to scroll back to view the entire conversation at any time and reread any part they like. They can print their screen or copy/paste parts or the entire transcript at any time. A lengthy response can be skimmed or read in full at the user's discretion. The user may multitask while chatting, with little impact on the broader solution. A web assistant can return rich responses, including text, images, buttons, and more. Figure 3.11 shows some of the differences.

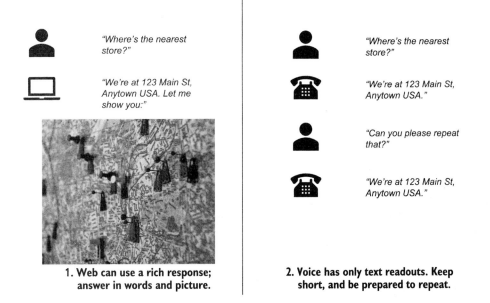

"Where's the nearest store?"

"We're at 123 Main St, Anytown USA. Let me show you:"

1. Web can use a rich response; answer in words and picture.

"Where's the nearest store?"

"We're at 123 Main St, Anytown USA."

"Can you please repeat that?"

"We're at 123 Main St, Anytown USA."

2. Voice has only text readouts. Keep short, and be prepared to repeat.

Figure 3.11　The web channel allows rich responses such as images. Voice solutions should be prepared to repeat important information. Map photo by Waldemar Brandt on Unsplash (https://unsplash.com).

Conversely, in a voice channel, the user's interaction is only what they hear. If the user misses a key piece of information, they do not have a way of getting it again unless you code "repeat question" functionality into your assistant. Figure 3.11 shows how web and voice channels can best handle a question like "Where's the nearest store?"

Further, a long verbal readout can be frustrating for a user: they may need a pencil and paper to take notes, they may have to wait a long time to get what they want, and they probably have to be quiet for fear of confusing the speech engine. (I practically hold my breath while talking with some automated voice systems!) Also, directly sending rich media responses like images is impossible over voice, though you may be able to use side channels such as SMS or email to send information for later review.

You must be aware of the cost to the user when you have a long message. As shown in figure 3.12, a web user can skim long messages, but a voice user cannot. Beware the temptation to cram every last piece of information into a message, especially in voice. The average adult reading speed is around 200 words per minute, and speaking speed is around 160 words per minute, though automated speech systems can be tuned to speak more quickly.

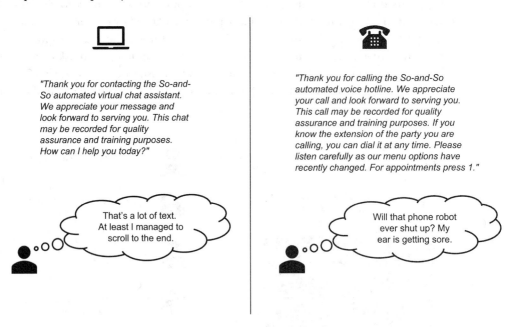

Figure 3.12   Different channels have different user experiences

Consider a hypothetical greeting:

> *Thank you for calling the So-and-So automated voice hotline. We appreciate your call and look forward to serving you. This call may be recorded for quality assurance and training purposes. If you know the extension of the party you are calling, you can dial it at any time. Please listen carefully, as our menu options have recently changed. For appointments, press 1.*

I timed myself reading this 62-word message. It takes 20 seconds of audio to get to the first useful piece of information. (I hope that you wanted an appointment!) Perhaps the lawyers insisted on including it, but look how much "junk" is in that message from the user's point of view. Figure 3.13 breaks down the greeting.

Text	Feeling	Internal monologue	Time
"Thank you for calling the So-and-So automated voice hotline."		"I appreciate the thanks. I know this is an automated hotline just from listening to the voice."	0–3 seconds
"We appreciate your call and look forward to serving you."		"Please don't waste my time with this corporate-speak."	3–6 seconds
"This call may be recorded for quality assurance and training purposes."		"I'm sure you are recording this and doing everything you can with this recording. Please let's get to what I need."	6–10 seconds
"If you know the extension of the party you are calling, you can dial it at any time."		"If I knew their extension I wouldn't be here! I never know the extension when I call these things!"	10–14 seconds
"Please listen carefully as our menu options have recently changed."		"I've been listening carefully for an eternity and you have yet to tell me anything useful!"	14–18 seconds
"For appointments press 1."		"Finally some useful information! But I don't want appointments!"	18–20 seconds

Figure 3.13 User's thought progression through a long greeting

Contrast that greeting with the following one:

> *Thanks for calling So-and-So. Calls are recorded. How can I help you?*

This new message takes 4 seconds to get to value while still covering the basics of greeting, notification, and intent gathering. You get only one chance to make a great first impression; don't waste your users' time on your greeting. It takes work to be concise, but your users will appreciate you for it. Take to heart the following quote:

> *I have only made this letter longer because I have not had the time to make it shorter.*

> —Blaise Pascal, *The Provial Letters* (Letter 16, 1657)

3.2.2   *How the assistant receives information in voice and web*

Another key difference between voice and web is how you receive input from the user. In a web channel, you can be sure of receiving exactly what was on the user's screen. You may provide a pop-up form to collect one or more pieces of information at the same time (such as first and last name and the full address). The user may have clicked a button, and you will know exactly what they clicked. The user may have misspelled one or more words, but conversational AIs are reassuringly resilient to misspellings and typos, as demonstrated in figure 3.14.

In a voice channel, you will receive a textual transcription of *what the speech engine interpreted.* Anyone who has used voice dictation has seen words get missed. The assistant can be adaptive to some mistranscriptions (just as it can be adaptive to misspellings in chat) when the words are not contextually important. Figure 3.15 shows a voice assistant adapting to a pair of mistranscriptions: *wear* for *where* and *a* for *the.*

Aside from simple mistranscriptions, another class of inputs gives speech engines trouble; any input that is hard for humans will be hard for speech engines as well. Proper names and addresses are notoriously difficult for speech engines in terms of both recognition (speech to text) and synthesis (text to speech). When I'm talking to a person on the phone, and they ask for my last name, I say, "Freed. F-R-E-E-D." But many people hear "Free" or try to use the old German spelling "Fried." Common names are not that common; you should be able to rattle off a couple of "uncommon" names within your personal net-

"Wheres teh nearst sotre?"

Automatic spelling correction: "Where's the nearest store?"

"We're at 123 Main St, Anytown USA. Let me show you."

Figure 3.14   Most major conversational AI platforms are resilient to misspellings.

"Where's the nearest store?"

Transcription may have errors: "Wear is a nearest store"

"We're at 123 Main St, Anytown USA."

Figure 3.15   Voice assistants can adapt to mistranscriptions in general utterances as long as the key contextual phrases are preserved, such as *nearest store.*

work rather quickly. Speech engines work best with a constrained vocabulary, even if that vocabulary is the English language; most names are considered to be out of vocabulary.

What's a vocabulary?

Speech-to-text providers refer to a *vocabulary*, which is a list of words. A speech model is trained to recognize a set of words. A generalized English model may have a dictionary that includes all the most common words in the English language.

Your assistant will probably need to deal with uncommon words and jargon. The name of your company or the products your company offers may not be included in that vocabulary of words, in which case you will need to train a speech model to recognize them.

Addresses are harder than names. I found a random street name on a map: Westmore-land Drive. If you heard that name, would you transcribe *Westmoreland Drive, W. More-land Drive,* or *West Moorland Drive*? Figure 3.16 shows a challenge in mapping similar phonetics to words that sound similar.

The difficulty in receiving certain inputs from users affects the way you build a dia-logue structure, perhaps most significantly in authenticating users. In a web chat, you can collect any information you need from a user verbatim. In fact, you may authenticate

Figure 3.16 **Transcription challenges on unusual terms**

On spelling out words and the difficulty of names and addresses

Spelling out a difficult name can be helpful for humans, but it does not help machines much. Letters are easily confused; B, C, D, E, G, P, and T sound similar without context. Humans may require several repetitions to interpret a proper name correctly, even when the name is spelled out.

There is rich literature on the difficulty of names and addresses. One such article is "The Difficulties with Names: Overcoming Barriers to Personal Voice Services," by Dr. Murray Spiegel (http://mng.bz/8WYB).

on your regular website and pass an authenticated session to the web chat. In a voice channel, you need to be more restrictive in what you receive. During authentication, a single transcription error in the utterance will fail validation, as it would if the user mistyped their password (figure 3.17).

In the best cases, speech technology has a 5% error rate, and in challenging cases such as names and addresses, the error rate can be much, much higher. (Some voice projects report a 60–70% error rate on addresses.) With alphanumeric identifiers, the entire sequence needs to be transcribed correctly, as shown in figure 3.17. A 5% error rate may apply to each character, so the error rate for the entire sequence will be

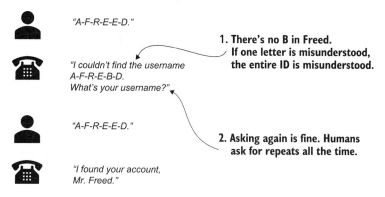

Figure 3.17 **For most data inputs, a single transcription mistake prevents the conversation from proceeding. Voice systems need to take this fact into account by using reprompts or alternative ways to receive difficult inputs.**

higher. For this reason, a six-digit ID is much more likely to transcribe accurately than a 12-digit ID (table 3.5).

Table 3.5   Summary of data types by how well speech engines can transcribe them

Data types that transcribe well	Data types that do not transcribe well
Numeric identifiers (such as Social Security numbers) Dates Short alphanumeric sequences (such as ABC123)	Proper names Addresses

For accurate transcriptions, constrained inputs such as numeric sequences and dates work best. If you encounter a transcription error, you can always prompt the user to provide the information again. Keep in mind that you will want to limit the number of reprompts (more on that coming up in chapter 4). You may implement a three-strikes rule; if three consecutive transcriptions fail, you direct the user to alternative forms of help that will serve them better.

Voice authentication can use an alternative channel such as SMS. You can send a text message to a number on file for a user with a one-time code and use that code in authentication, instead of collecting information over voice. If you absolutely must authenticate over the speech channel via an option that is difficult for speech, be prepared to work hard at both speech training and orchestration layer postprocessing logic. You will need a good call-hand-off strategy in this scenario.

Summary

- Users will have a variety of request types with a range of frequency and complexity. You need to carefully prioritize a subset of these request types to implement in the first version of your assistant.
- It takes a village to build a successful conversational AI. You need to consider many perspectives, such as business, technical, and legal. A diverse team should contribute to the solution.
- Review each request type, and determine all the steps required to automate it fully in a process flow. Identify steps that can be removed or replaced so that you can deploy a minimum viable product.
- There are different requirements for effective dialogue over web and voice channels. Web allows rich responses, and users can scroll, whereas voice responses usually must be shorter and may need to be repeated. In a web channel, you are always sure what the user typed, but in a voice channel, you receive what the speech engine transcribed—not necessarily what the user said. Some parts of a process flow will need to be altered based on the specific channel.

4

Designing effective dialogue

This chapter covers

- Writing dialogue that supports your process flows
- Creating dialogue with tone, empathy, and variety
- Asking questions that increase your chances of getting a useful response
- Responding to conversational mishaps

In chapter 3, you learned how to design effective processes that your conversational AI assistant will implement. After you design all the flow charts and user-to-system interactions, you need to breathe life into them by writing the dialogue text your assistant will read or speak.

The assistant can respond in several ways to a user who needs to reset a password, as shown in figure 4.1. A response of "I need your user ID so I can reset your password" is direct but has a nearly accusatory tone. A response of "I'm sorry you can't access our system. I'll try to help you. To start, what's your user ID?" conveys a softer tone and lets the user know what's happening next. From a programming

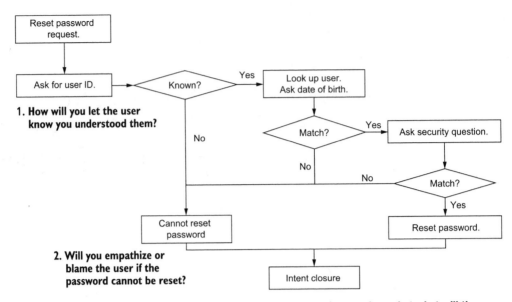

Figure 4.1   Motivating example for the chapter. This process flow is a good one, but what will the assistant actually say at each of these prompts? How can we prime users to answer questions in a way that moves us through this process? What tone will the assistant use at each prompt?

standpoint, both of these responses are identical, but users will not perceive them the same way.

Any given process flow has multiple types of nodes. Sometimes, the assistant will be passive, answering questions directed by the user. Sometimes, the assistant will take a more dominant approach, directing a user through a process flow. Each of these response types requires dialogue that conveys empathy and a consistent tone while getting the job done.

The assistant can ask for any required information from the user in several ways. It could get the user's zip code, for example, by asking for an "address," a "zip code," or a "five-digit zip code." You can surely imagine which one will generate the most consistently usable responses.

In human-to-human conversations, we know that meaning is not just what you say, but also how you say it. Some people even formulize it. Albert Mehrabian's 7-38-55 Rule of Personal Communication is that spoken words are 7% of verbal communication, voice and tone are 38%, and body language is 55%. Read more at http://mng.bz/EVBj.

Words matter, but so does tone. A difficult message can be softened with empathy. Just as you shouldn't blurt out the first thing that comes to mind, you shouldn't be thoughtless about what goes into your assistant's dialogue.

In this chapter, you will learn how to write dialogue with tone, empathy, and variety so that a user is not constantly reminded that they are talking to an unfeeling bot. You will learn how to keep dialogue on track (or bring it back on track) without being rude, increasing your chances of a successful process flow. You will learn how to respond when the assistant doesn't understand the user or when you need to transfer the conversation from the assistant to a human-to-human interaction.

By the end of this chapter, you'll be able to write dialogue that supports your process flows, and you'll be ready to train your assistant to recognize the intents that will initiate these process flows.

4.1 Writing dialogue

Writing the dialogue copy is a first-class skill in building a conversational AI. If you use a professional copywriter for your website and marketing materials, you should apply the same level of skill and polish to the textual dialogue within your assistant. Your AI assistant is out on the front lines, interacting directly with your customers and representing your brand. The text your assistant returns on the screen or speaks over the phone is as important as the technical functionality you enable in your assistant. Users will remember a cold, impersonal assistant negatively and will dislike it even more if they feel that the assistant is wasting their time. Conversely, a pleasant bot delivering the right amount of information in a timely manner will be remembered fondly.

It is important to get the structure of the dialogue tree right. The introduction to this chapter outlines several considerations for building a robust process flow that dialogue will sit in. After you and your team have done all this precision work, it is important to breathe life into the process with well-designed dialogue copy. Your full team should design the process tree to include a description of each step (this node is where we ask for the date of birth, for example); a smaller group of writers can refine the specific wording.

A war-room approach
You may find it advantageous to lock everyone in a room and get immediate consensus on the dialogue. This approach certainly reduces the number of back-and-forth sessions and review cycles for edits. Some teams have implemented self-help conversational AI assistants after a single all-day writing session to design their process flow.

Regardless of the approach you take to writing the dialogue copy, you need to take the task seriously, including the writing considerations described in the next three sections.

4.1.1 Take a conversational tone

In chapter 2, we talked about the infinite number of ways that users can express the same intent with different word variations. Do you recall all the ways people might express the need to reset a password, for example? The infinite variations of language apply to the text you send back to your users as well. In any phase of a conversation, you have nearly infinite ways to express what you want to say, but following some best practices will definitely help you provide a good user experience.

The first thing to consider is the general tone that your AI assistant will use. Whether or not you intentionally inject a tone into your assistant, users will perceive one. Many people hate talking with bots because they are impersonal, and the bot responses feel disembodied. Figure 4.2 demonstrates two extreme tonal variations.

Figure 4.2   The tone used by your assistant influences how users feel about it.

Your assistant does not need to pass the Turing Test. (A computer application that behaves in a manner indistinguishable from a human is said to pass the Turing Test, which Alan Turing devised in 1950.) But you should be mindful of the way the bot's language will be perceived by users. It's good to be proactive and define a target tone.

Does your organization already have a brand? If so, your users will expect your assistant's tone to have some affinity with that brand. Does your brand have a serious nature, for example, or is it perceived as being informal? If your assistant is 180 degrees different from your existing branding, your users will find the difference jarring. If you have a marketing team, they need to be in the room to make sure that the tone of your assistant is in line with the rest of your branding. As briefly discussed in chapter 1, the tone should line up with the persona your brand uses, if it uses a persona.

When you have a target tone in mind, it is important to use an appropriate tone for each situation. If a user is bringing you a problem like "I can't log in!!!!", you do not want to react in a callous manner. Your assistant should respond with empathy. Acknowledging a user's problem with a simple "I'm sorry" is a useful, empathetic step. If empathy does not come naturally to you, you should have the assistant dialogue written or revised by someone to whom it does. Figure 4.3 shows how the assistant's dialogue can affect the user.

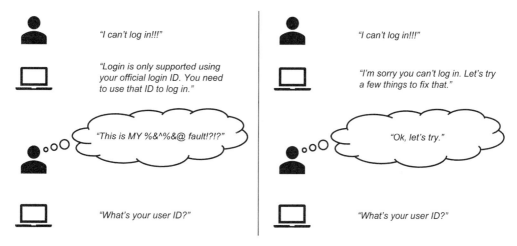

Figure 4.3 A little empathy goes a long way. Both dialogues use the same process flow, but the cold, technical approach on the left implies "blame the user" language.

4.1.2 *Don't repeat yourself (much)*

Users will sense robotic tone if every interaction with your assistant has a templated, formulaic feel. Variety is the spice of life and is particularly useful in the areas of the dialogue that users will encounter most often:

- *The greeting message*—The first message your users encounter when they interact with the assistant. Some components of the message may need to stay the same (such as a disclaimer), but others can be varied.
- *List of capabilities*—Assistants often tell users what capabilities are available, either directly (in a greeting) or only when asked. Consider varying the order in which the capabilities are listed, at least for separate interaction sessions.
- *"I don't understand"*—It's frustrating for users to hear "I don't understand" over and over. Humans naturally vary the way they say that they don't understand, and you remove a little of the robotic feeling when your assistant varies its responses too.

Your conversational AI platform will let you vary dialogue responses for any part of your dialogue tree. Figure 4.4 shows one such example from a Watson Assistant implementation.

Check the documentation on your AI platform to see how you can vary the responses given by a dialogue node. This feature is a common one, and some platforms even offer multiple message selection policies in addition to random selection. Message variation is a simple way to improve the way your users perceive the assistant, so use this feature.

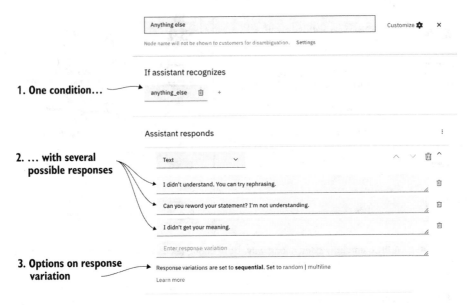

Figure 4.4   Most AI platforms let you set multiple possible responses for a given dialogue node. The platform will randomly select one of these responses each time the dialogue node is visited.

4.1.3   *Acknowledge the user*

The way to be a better communicator is to listen carefully to the other side, empathize with the other side, reflect back what you are hearing, and only then move on in the conversation. This generalized advice holds true for interacting with AI assistants. Consider the two hypothetical dialogue flows in figure 4.5.

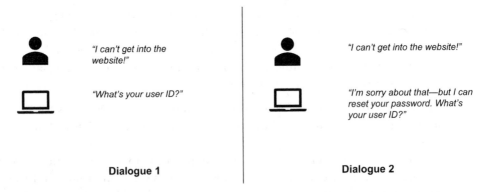

Figure 4.5   Acknowledge that you understood the user (and use empathy while you're at it).

Figure 4.5 shows two different dialogues that implement the same process flow. Dialogue 1 is concise, but the user has no indication that they were understood. Dialogue 2 acknowledges the user with a simple reflection of the understood intent (reset password) and shows empathy to the user as well. When Dialogue 2 requests the user ID, the user has good situational context for why the assistant asks this question. Dialogue 2 is more likely to lead to a good outcome than Dialogue 1.

Additionally, it is good practice to give a user something before asking them for additional information. At the start of the conversation, we put the onus on the user with something like "How can I help you?" They have provided some information in their utterance in the form of an intent. We can give the user something—a message that we understand their initial request—before requesting additional information. A user generally understands that more information will be required from them as the conversation goes on, but it is still good to give them something when you can.

Reflecting back your understanding is particularly important in the case of open-ended input, when you are attempting to extract the user's intent. Intent detection is by its nature a probabilistic exercise, and there is a chance that you will misunderstand the user's intent. You can acknowledge the intent and move on, as in the preceding example, or you can ask the user to confirm your understanding ("You'd like to reset your password, correct?").

A confirmation prompt will improve overall solution accuracy. If the confirmation is negative, you can easily handle it in your dialogue flow, but doing so will necessarily lengthen the conversation. Using a confirmation prompt is a good idea when your classifier is not performing well and you have not been able to improve it. Allowing the user to know what you think their intent is gives them useful information that they can act on. In the password example, the user could interrupt your flow with "That's not what I want!" or (worst case) restart the conversation. At least they have the choice.

Acknowledging the user is also good even when the expected input is constrained. When you ask for a user ID, for example, you generally have a pattern in mind; let's assume an alphanumeric sequence with a minimum and a maximum length. When the user provides the input that you expect, you should give a clue that you've received it before moving on with the next step of the conversation. Consider the dialogue examples in figure 4.6 for our password-reset flow.

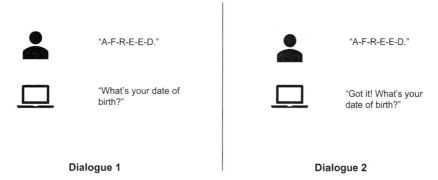

"A-F-R-E-E-D."

"What's your date of birth?"

"A-F-R-E-E-D."

"Got it! What's your date of birth?"

Dialogue 1   Dialogue 2

Figure 4.6   A simple acknowledgement lets the user know that the conversation is proceeding well.

Figure 4.6 contrasts two approaches. In Dialogue 1, the user might assume that the assistant collected the user ID correctly, but they can't be sure. Is the system going to validate all the input at the end, or has the user ID already been validated? The answer is unclear, and the user can't be sure where they stand. In Dialogue 2, it is clear that the user ID has been received and probably validated as well. Upon clear acceptance of the user ID, it makes sense to advance the dialogue to the next input question: date of birth. Dialogue 2 can be shortened further to "And what's your date of birth?" This short acceptance message doesn't create a pause between the statement and the question.

There's a lot more to conversational design

Conversational design is a rich field. Entire books have been written on the process, including *Conversational UX Design*, by Robert J. Moore and Raphael Arar (ACM Books, 2019) for general conversational design, and *Practical Speech User Interface Design*, by James R. Lewis (CRC Press, 2016) for voice solutions.

Humans interact differently with one another than they do with machines. Human–computer conversation generally involves taking turns, with each party saying one thing and waiting for the other to respond. Human–human conversation is a bit more free-form, often including digressions and meandering conversations. Humans are remarkably adaptive in this way.

It's common for a human–human conversation to start with "How are you doing today?", "How's the weather?", or a friendly greeting like "I hope you're healthy and happy." Some people even like to start conversations that way with an AI assistant. They may be trying to find out whether they are talking to a bot (or they may want to mess with it). Any conversational messages not directly related to serving a goal are generally referred to as *chitchat*.

Your conversational AI should be prepared to deal with a little bit of chitchat. Ironically, the more chitchat your assistant engages with, the more chitchat it will get. A kind of arms race can occur: if you start responding to requests like "Tell me a joke," you'll soon get requests like "Tell me another one." This type of response is generally not a good use of your time in training the assistant or constructing the dialogue it will use. Rather than engaging these requests directly (by telling a joke), it is a good idea to turn the chitchat back to the specific goals and training embedded in your assistant.

If your conversational AI greets users with "How can I help you?" and a user responds with "Hi there," you can respond with a greeting of your own and a small list of capabilities to start a goal-oriented conversation. In our sample assistant, a good response could be "Hello, and thanks for your interest. I'm able to help with several things, including password resets, store locations and hours, and making appointments. How can I help you?"

By default, most AI assistants do not recognize chitchat unless they are trained to do so. In these cases, the assistant will respond with the default or catch-all condition.

This user experience is not the best—if the user says "Hello" and the assistant says "I don't understand," that response is machinelike—but you can use it in initial assistant construction. This response may be all you need if you have a task-oriented user group. You can also address this situation by putting additional information, such as a list of capabilities, in the "I don't understand" node to help put the conversation back on track.

4.2 Asking questions

The concept of nearly infinite variations applies to asking questions as well. Your conversational AI is driving or steering the conversational flow, and the questions and statements it makes can help keep the conversation on track. Although you cannot predict the direction in which a user will go, you can increase the probability of an expected response through gentle nudges in the dialogue. Dialogue contains two primary types of questions:

- *Open-ended*—To a question like "How can I help you?", the user could respond with nearly anything. An open-ended question generally tries to determine the user's intent.
- *Constrained*—Questions like "What's your date of birth?" have an expected outcome; the response generally includes a date.

As you design your conversational flow, you should be aware of what type of question you are asking and what kinds of responses you are scripting for. You will get better responses during conversations with users if you know the question type for each section of your dialogue flow. A poorly worded constrained question can generate open-ended responses and could confuse your assistant.

Users say the darnedest things

No matter how well you script your processes, users may still surprise you. When you ask "What's your date of birth?", a user may opt out by responding "I want to speak to a human." Conversational AI providers will give you a way to provide a default response in these cases. Be prepared to use it.

Open-ended questions can be constrained if you provide a list of suggestions. The first question in most assistants is generally some variation on "How can I help you?"—a perfectly open-ended question. You can help users by including a brief list of the assistant's capabilities, such as "I can help you with several things, including finding a store near you and setting up an appointment. How can I help you?" Alternatively, you can choose to list the assistant's capabilities when the assistant doesn't understand the user's response to this first question. By providing the user a hint, you have effectively narrowed the range of possible responses.

One question that sits on the border between open-ended and constrained is a common question situated at the end of a dialogue flow, when the assistant has finished servicing one intent and is ready to start on another. The question often resembles "Can I help with anything else today?" As worded, this question is ambiguous: it could be a constrained question (which the user answers "Yes" or "No"), or the user might directly start a new intent ("I also want to make an appointment"). You can lightly nudge this interaction to be a constrained question by saying "Yes or no, can I help with anything else today?", or you can provide a stronger nudge by displaying Yes and No buttons. Alternatively, you can code the dialogue node to expect a "Yes," "No," or intent-based response. A nudge cannot guarantee that a user will do what you expect, but it primes their brain in the direction you desire. Figure 4.7 shows an example nudge that helps a user understand what a model number is.

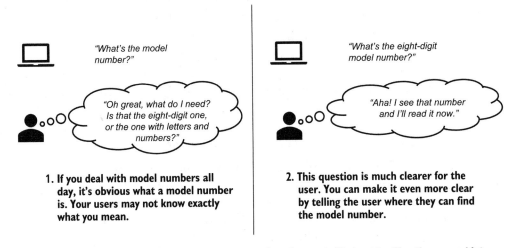

1. If you deal with model numbers all day, it's obvious what a model number is. Your users may not know exactly what you mean.

2. This question is much clearer for the user. You can make it even more clear by telling the user where they can find the model number.

Figure 4.7   If you ask an unclear or ambiguous question, the user will struggle. Give the user a hint whenever possible.

Constrained questions have an implied response type. A date-of-birth question should have a date response, for example. Many times, however, it is appropriate to be more specific about what you want. You may integrate with an API that expects information to be in a certain format, or you may be asking for a piece of data that users are unfamiliar with. Asking a question precisely, with consideration of your constraints, will yield more responses that move the conversation forward.

The last example in table 4.1 is particularly useful for information that users don't reference often. When I call a support line and am asked for the serial number of some product, I am often squinting at the bottom of the product, trying to figure out which of the alphanumeric sequences I'm being asked for. Knowing the format and length of the input helps me figure out what information is needed. Depending on your use case, you may want to supply additional context ("What's the nine-digit number in the top-left corner of your ID card?"). To save time on dialogue readout, you may want to save the lengthier instructions for a failure scenario. You need to balance the time and cost of providing the additional context versus the time and cost of getting invalid input.

Table 4.1 Improving unclear questions by adding precision

Imprecise question	Precise question
"What's your date of birth?"	"What's your month, day, and year of birth?"
"What's your zip code?"	"What's your five-digit zip code?"
"What's your employee ID?"	"What's your nine-digit employee ID number?"

Constrained questions should also have a mechanism for recognizing statements like "I don't know" and "I don't have it," in addition to recognizing expected responses.

4.3   What if the assistant doesn't understand?

Despite all your planning, design, development, and test efforts, there will still be times when the assistant does not understand the user. These times are wonderful opportunities to learn about unexpected user behavior and can help inform future improvements. You need to have a plan for these situations; it's frustrating for a user to deal with an assistant that does not understand them (figure 4.8).

Figure 4.8   A conversational AI may have no idea what the user means.

Do not assume that an AI assistant can, or even must, always understand the user. Misunderstandings happen in human–human conversations as well, and you can take a cue from how we humans resolve misunderstandings.

There are several ways to respond when the assistant does not understand the user:

- *Reprompting*—Admit that you did not understand, and ask the user to clarify.
- *Disambiguation*—Give the user a list of possible interpretations of what they said, and ask them to pick one.
- *Escalation*—The assistant admits defeat and sends the user to an alternative channel.

4.3.1   Reprompting

The simplest response when the assistant does not understand is to be completely transparent, responding with some flavor of "I don't understand." Most conversational AI platforms provide the capability for a default response when no other dialogue response satisfies the conditional logic within the dialogue flow. If you tried the demo in chapter 2, you probably saw and tested this response node. Reprompting means asking the question again, usually with different wording.

An unfortunate consequence of new conversational AIs is that the first direct response the user receives from the assistant may be an "I don't understand" message. This response is a necessary side effect of giving users free rein on what they can say—both a blessing and a curse compared with strict menu options and numeric call trees. Thus, it is good to handle this response with care.

A good "I don't understand" message should convey empathy or at least not blame the user. Take the stance that it's the assistant's fault for not understanding. "I don't understand" places responsibility on the assistant. "You provided an invalid input" places responsibility on the user. This advice also applies to constrained questions. When you ask the user for a particular input (say, a numeric identifier), and the response is in the wrong format (say, too many digits), a response like "You provided too many digits" sounds accusatory compared with "I couldn't find that ID; could you provide the nine-digit ID again?" This approach is particularly important in voice solutions, in which it's more likely that the voice system missed or misheard a digit than that the user provided the wrong number of digits.

In addition to accepting responsibility for the misunderstanding, it is good to nudge the conversation back on track by providing additional guidance. The phrase "I didn't understand. You can try rephrasing." accepts responsibility ("I didn't understand") and gives a suggestion to move the conversation forward ("You can try rephrasing"). Without a nudge, the user may decide to repeat themselves, which will not get them any farther in a web-chat solution. (It might help in a voice solution if the misunderstanding was due to a speech-transcription failure.) Positive suggestions for next steps include a request to reword/rephrase or to give additional clarifying instructions. For open-ended questions, you might suggest a couple of common questions that you support. For constrained questions, you might provide additional guidance on how to provide the information you are seeking ("The employee ID is on the back of your corporate badge").

An "I don't understand" node should be triggered when the user response is not understood with high confidence. Watson Assistant selects an intent only if that intent is predicted with confidence greater than 0.2, for example. (Other platforms use different threshold levels.) Depending on your use case and training, you may want to use a different confidence level. In chapter 2's demo, I used a confidence threshold of 0.5. A low-confidence intent has a probability of being wrong, and it is better for your users to respond with "I don't understand" than to respond based on the wrong intent. (In chapter 7, we will explore the meaning of confidence further.)

In figure 4.9, the utterance "When will your points program open?" triggered a low-confidence intent. The #Customer_Care_Store_Hours (with 0.30 confidence) barely beat the more correct #Customer_Care_Program_Inquiry intent (with 0.27). If the dialogue had not been coded to consider intent confidence, the response would have been to provide the store hours—a completely unsatisfying response for the user.

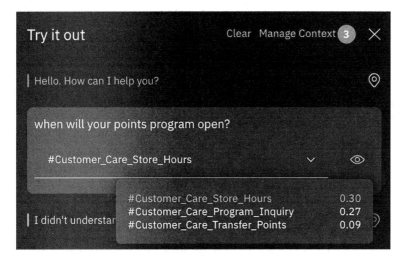

Figure 4.9 An AI assistant may weakly understand an utterance, detecting intents with low confidence. The highest-confidence intent `#Customer_Care_Store_Hours` is still a low-confidence intent. When the intent confidence is low, you are often better off responding that you didn't understand the user.

User utterances that trigger a reprompt should be reviewed periodically to see whether the assistant's dialogue rules or intent training need to be updated to capture more user utterances. Table 4.2 lists some best practices for reprompting. We will discuss analyzing user utterances further in chapter 6.

Table 4.2 Best practices for reprompting

Do	Do not
Convey empathy ("I'm sorry, I did not understand").	Give specific advice on how to move the conversation forward ("Please give me your nine-digit member ID").
Reprompt if your assistant has low confidence in the detected intent.	Blame the user ("You provided an invalid input").
State a problem with no solution ("You provided the wrong number of digits").	Assume that it is bad to reprompt when you are uncertain.

4.3.2 Disambiguation

Sometimes, the AI assistant will not be able to choose a single intent based on the user's utterance. The utterance may trigger multiple intents with medium to high confidence, and in this case, it can be appropriate to ask the user what they meant. Well-defined intents are trained with general boundaries, but an utterance can still sit near multiple boundaries.

Consider the case of "What time can I come in to visit?" (figure 4.10). This utterance is an ambiguous one for the Fictitious Inc. assistant; it sounds a little like a request for an appointment and a little like a request for store hours. It's ambiguous because it has a time component ("What time"), but the ending language ("visit") does not neatly fit into appointments or store hours. Disambiguation is best invoked when two or more intents have similar confidence values.

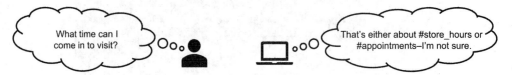

Figure 4.10   When multiple intents could be correct, disambiguation is appropriate.

In this case, it's appropriate to offer the user a list of suggestions reflecting your partial understanding. The assistant's confusion is not total, only partial, and it's reasonable to reflect this fact. Give the user a clear path forward by presenting a short list of choices, one of the choices generally being "None of these," which invokes the standard misunderstanding flow.

If you followed the chapter 2 demo, try asking your assistant "What time can I come in to visit you?" In my assistant, the intents with the highest confidence were `#Customer_Care_Store_Hours` and `#Customer_Care_Appointments`, with 0.58 and 0.57 confidence, respectively. This scenario is perfect for using disambiguation. Both intent confidences are above our low-confidence threshold, and they are similar. The assistant can respond with a clarifying question such as "Did you mean store hours, appointments, or none of the above?"

The major AI platforms give you enough information to determine when disambiguation is needed and help you implement the disambiguation. You can implement disambiguation in application logic, as follows:

- Trigger disambiguation when multiple intents have similar confidence values and those values are above your low-confidence threshold.
- Disambiguation choices should include an option for each intent that had similar confidence and a "None of the above" option.

Some platforms offer a disambiguation feature that automates this logic for you.

Disambiguation is also a good idea when the user makes a one-word utterance. In the case of the Fictitious Inc. assistant, consider whether the user utterance is "Account," which could reasonably mean `#Customer_Care_Open_Account` or `#Customer_Care_Cancel_Account` or `#Customer_Care_Loyalty_Status` or even `#Customer_Care_Products_Offered`. You may be tempted to update training in such a way that this utterance is forced to go to one of the intents, but this solution is a reflection of what you want, not what the user wants. One-word utterances are frequently ambiguous, and in this context, "Account" is certainly ambiguous. A disambiguation flow is useful for most one-word utterances that have affinity with multiple intents.

User utterances that trigger a disambiguation flow should also be reviewed periodically. These utterances can show unclear boundaries or unexpected relationships among different intents, and they may form useful new training data. Review disambiguation results in your assistant's logs periodically to see whether you need to improve training on any ambiguous intents. Table 4.3 summarizes some best practices for disambiguation.

Table 4.3 Best practices for disambiguation

Do	Do not
Use disambiguation when multiple intents are returned by the classifier with high confidence.	Use disambiguation when a user utterance is a single word that relates to several different intents.
Review your assistant's logs to see when disambiguation was needed.	Ignore intents with high, but not the highest, confidence for an utterance.
Pick a single intent for a single-word utterance when multiple intents are reasonable.	

4.3.3 Escalation

At times, a conversational AI should stop trying to handle the conversation and hand it off to another channel. As in a human–human conversation, sometimes the conversational participant should be escalated to a manager.

There are three primary reasons for escalation:

- *Opt-out*—The first escalation reason is *opt-out* (figure 4.11), which occurs when the user decides that they do not want to converse with a conversational AI anymore. Statements like "I want to speak to a real person" or "Get me out of here" are problems that an automated solution cannot solve and should not try to solve. A user should have this level of agency in their conversation. Some assistants implicitly use a tone analysis of the user's utterances and interpret a negative sentiment or angry tone as being an opt-out request. Telephonic assistants treat a touchtone entry of 0 as being an opt-out as well.

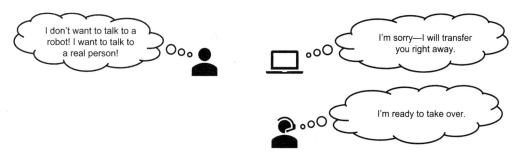

Figure 4.11   An opt-out flow

- *Misunderstandings*—It is appropriate for the assistant to use reprompting and disambiguation on occasion; remember that humans use them too. But if the assistant is repeatedly not understanding, the user will get frustrated with the experience. It is common to implement a three-strikes rule (or a two-strikes rule; see chapter 2), so that if the assistant misunderstands the user a given number of times in a row or across a conversation, the user will be escalated out of the conversation.

- *Business process*—In this case, the assistant understands enough about the user's request to know that it cannot service the request. This escalation path is frequently coded to divert complex or sensitive business process flows away from an automated solution and toward a dedicated channel (figure 4.12).

Figure 4.12   Business processes can dictate that certain conversations should be handled by a human.

Regardless of the escalation reason, you have multiple ways to implement escalation. The most satisfying experience for users is to stay within the same channel. If the conversation is happening over web chat, an escalated conversation invokes a web chat backed by a human. If the conversation is happening over the telephone, the call is automatically transferred to a human or call center. Less satisfying is ending the conversation with instructions to the user to go somewhere else; a web chat ending with "Call our support line" or "Email us" puts an extra burden on the user. Whatever channel the user chose to interact with you in is probably the channel they prefer, so you should make an effort to stay in that channel.

Note that many conversational AI providers have built-in integration layers to automate escalations. You can use these layers to hand off a chat to a human agent seamlessly. You should plan where your assistant will send users when it cannot satisfy those users. Table 4.4 summarizes some best practices for escalation.

Table 4.4 Best practices for escalation

Do	Do not
Let the user ask to leave the assistant (opt-out).	Fail to recognize an opt-out request.
Help the user leave the assistant when the assistant consistently misunderstands them.	Fail to keep track of how many misunderstandings occurred in a conversation.
Assume that some business processes will not be handled by the assistant.	Keep the user in the assistant forever.

Summary

- Dialogue should be written with an intentional tone. The tone affects how users perceive your assistant. You should be proactive about the tone your conversational AI uses.
- Show empathy for the user when they have a problem, and let the user know that you understand them. Give cues that reflect your understanding of their intent, and intentionally move the dialogue forward.
- There are many ways to ask a question. It is important to include enough specificity in your questions to get the responses you need from users.
- The assistant will not always fully understand the user, and you need a plan for it to follow when that happens. You can handle misunderstandings with reprompts, disambiguation, or escalation.

Building
a successful AI assistant

This chapter covers

- Avoiding the most common AI assistant failures
- Selecting appropriate success metrics for your assistant
- Knowing which metrics are commonly used for which types of assistants
- Instrumenting your assistant to measure the right metrics

So far in this book, we have covered why you would build an AI assistant (chapter 1) and how to build an AI assistant (chapters 2–4). In this chapter, we take a different approach, examining the practices that make AI assistants succeed. Specifically, we will focus on how to tell whether an AI assistant is making a positive impact on your bottom line.

When I started writing this chapter, I typed *why do AI projects fail* in a search engine. There was no shortage of relevant results! Avoiding failure is clearly important when creating an AI assistant. But we should aim higher than not failing and consider how to make our AI projects succeed.

In chapters 1–4, we used Fictitious Inc. as a motivating example. Fictitious Inc. is trying to improve its customer service department by using a conversational AI assistant; the company is getting overloaded with routine customer service questions. It heard that many AI ventures fail and doesn't want to be one of them.

In this chapter, we will examine how Fictitious Inc. can succeed with their assistants. Further, we'll look at a variety of AI assistant types in a number of industries. Specifically, we'll look at the key business objectives for each type of assistant and at the most common metrics used to assess whether an assistant is successful.

5.1 AI assistant use cases

Table 5.1 shows some AI assistant use cases.

Table 5.1 AI assistant use cases sorted by AI assistant type

AI assistant type	Industry/use case
Conversational AI (self-service)	Retail customer support
Conversational AI (agent-assist)	Insurance sales
Command interpreter	Smartphone
Command interpreter	Consumer electronics (smart TVs)
Event classifier	Customer support
Event classifier	Email classification

As described in chapter 1, there is overlap in the technology used in each assistant type, but all use classifiers. There is some commonality in how these assistant types are developed, but each assistant type has different use patterns. These differences lead to using different success metrics for each assistant type.

When you deploy your AI assistant to production, you'll want to have your success metrics easily accessible to all your stakeholders. The most common approach is to create a dashboard that displays your metrics in real time. Many AI platforms come with built-in analytics and dashboards. You can start with these dashboards, but you may need to do some custom work to track the success metrics that are important to you.

Success metrics differ by AI assistant type. The assistant types we will review are

- *Conversational AI*—This assistant type uses a fully conversational interface, using text or voice input. The users may be end users (who are helping themselves, in a self-help scenario) or agents (who are helping other users, in an agent-assist scenario). Users are likely to ask several questions in one session. You may also call this type of assistant a *chatbot* or *voicebot.*

- *Command interpreter*—This assistant is generally used to invoke a single command ("Set an alarm for 9:30" or "Turn on the lights"). The assistant gathers a set of information required to execute a command, executes that command, and then leaves the user alone.
- *Event classifier*—This assistant type is often embedded in another tool. Users may not interact directly with the classifier. The assistant analyzes user input and makes inferences about that input. Those inferences are used to assess or route user input.

Regardless of which assistant type you are using, it's a good idea to have SMART goals for the success metric(s) you use. There are slightly varying different definitions for the acronym, but I will use the following:

- Specific
- Measurable
- Achievable
- Relevant
- Time-bound

Each of the metrics in this chapter is fully compatible with a SMART-goal mindset. For each assistant type, I will give Specific metrics and show how to Measure them. I will discuss Achievable targets (and I promise that each is Relevant). The Time-bound metric will vary depending on your project, but I advise using a span of less than a year. Let's start by exploring how conversational agents succeed.

5.2   *Conversational AI success metrics*

Conversational AI assistants are perhaps the most AI assistants created today. They are deployed because the problems they solve cost companies a lot of money.

Fictitious Inc. deployed a conversational AI assistant so that it could deflect calls from its human-staffed customer service department. Every customer service inquiry costs money to handle (not to mention the effect of complaints on revenue). Self-service conversational AIs are used in many industries, especially retail and insurance, to reduce total customer service expense. It is not unusual for a human-handled call to cost several dollars and for an AI-handled call to cost one dollar. The savings can add up quickly. Further, an AI assistant can provide answers faster than a human agent, especially because it can handle requests from multiple users at the same time.

Agent-assist conversational assistants are used in industries with high turnover, such as customer service, sales, and technical support. It can cost thousands or tens of thousands of dollars, and weeks or months, to train a new employee to full self-sufficiency; then the employee might leave. Agent-assist assistants can dramatically reduce the time to self-sufficiency, which reduces training costs and improves customer satisfaction.

Conversational agents commonly use the following success metrics:

- *Containment*—How many requests the assistant completes (start to finish) without transferring the user to another system
- *Time to resolution*—From start to finish, how quickly the user got the information they needed
- *Net promoter score (NPS)*—A 0–10 rating of the user's experience, with higher numbers being better
- *Coverage*—How many requests the assistant attempted to answer without transferring the user to another system

Let's explore each of these metrics in detail.

5.2.1 Containment

A *contained* session is one in which the user never leaves the assistant. Containment is the most popular metric for self-service conversational agents. The simplest definition of containment is "how often requests were not directed to another channel." Figure 5.1 demonstrates the concept.

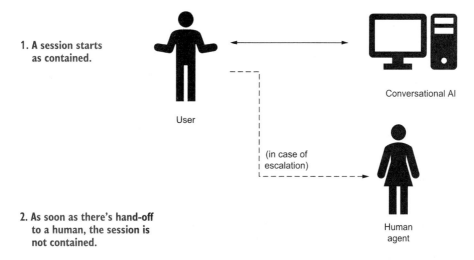

1. A session starts as contained.

User

Conversational AI

(in case of escalation)

2. As soon as there's hand-off to a human, the session is not contained.

Human agent

Figure 5.1 A session with a conversational AI starts as contained. If an escalation occurs, the session is not contained.

Containment is commonly used in call centers and interactive voice response systems. Containment is important when the cost disparity between resolution channels is high. Before AI assistants were popular, call center employees would be measured on containment (how often they resolved a call without escalating to a manager). Measuring an AI assistant on containment is a natural extension of this practice. Table 5.2 demonstrates how several conversations rate on containment.

Table 5.2   Containment analysis of two conversations

Contained	Not contained
System: "How can I help you?" User: "When are you open today?" System: "We are open from 9 a.m. to 9 p.m." User: (Hangs up)	System: "How can I help you?" User: "When are you open today?" System: "I'm sorry; I'm not trained to answer that question. Let me transfer you to customer service."

Total costs vary by containment. The higher the AI's containment is, the lower the costs are. The reasoning behind containment is simple. Every phone call or chat session completely handled by your AI is by definition not using your human agents. Each of those sessions can be claimed as savings on the human cost. If it costs $5 for a human to handle a call and $1 for an AI assistant to handle a call, the assistant breaks even at 20% containment. Table 5.3 demonstrates the effect of containment on a company's bottom line. Assume that there are 100 calls; an AI assistant costs $1 to handle a call, and a human costs $5.

Table 5.3   Total costs by containment

Contained	Not contained	AI assistant costs	Human costs	Total costs
10	90	$100	$450	$550
20	80	$100	$400	$500
30	70	$100	$350	$450

This table should be compared with the baseline scenario, in which no AI assistant exists. In this scenario, 100 calls cost $500. When an AI assistant is the first point of contact, it receives all the calls (or chats) first. Thus, the break-even point in table 5.3 is 20% containment. If the AI can exceed 20% containment, it will start saving you money.

From a SMART-goal perspective, it's a good goal to target a high-enough containment rate to save money. You should not abuse or cheat this metric, however.

Table 5.4 shows additional containment scenarios. These scenarios show why containment is not the end-all success metric but should be combined with other metrics to measure the success of your assistant.

Table 5.4   Containment analysis of additional conversations

Contained	Not contained	Contained	Not contained
System: "How can I help you?" User: (Hangs up)	System: "Let me transfer you to customer service."	System: "How can I help you?" User: "When are you open today?" System: "Sure, I can help you reset your password." User: (Hangs up)	System: "How can I help you?" User: (Repeatedly presses the 0 button on their phone) System: "Let me transfer you to customer service."

It may surprise you to know that if either party disconnects the session, the session is contained. You've probably had a bad customer service experience in which the system was trying to get you to hang up. In figure 5.2, Dialogue 1 shows that user disconnections are always counted as contained, and Dialogue 2 shows artificial containment by ignoring an opt-out request. Neither dialogue is containment you should feel good about.

"I can't hear you. I'll call you back."
<CLICK>

"Yes! Contained call!"

Dialogue 1

"I need to speak to a human."

"I'm sorry, I don't understand."

Dialogue 2

Figure 5.2 Don't cheat containment, which is an imperfect metric.

The simplicity of containment and its direct impact on the bottom line make it an important metric for evaluating the success of a conversational AI. Table 5.5 lays out the pros and cons of containment as a success metric.

Table 5.5 Pros and cons of containment as a success metric for conversational AIs

Pros	Cons
Easy to measure Aligns directly with the bottom line Industry standard	Susceptible to gaming May not align with user needs

Containment cannot be the only metric, though, especially because it does not truly measure user satisfaction. Let's move on to metrics that consider the user's perspective.

What if the session has some success before the session is transferred?

Sometimes, a session has one or more successful interactions before an interaction causes a transfer. How is a call like that one measured?

In the strictest definition of *containment*, *any* transfer means that the session is not contained. Full stop. Several practitioners, however, use partial containment or a similar metric that gives the system credit for any requests fulfilled before a transfer occurred.

5.2.2   *Time to resolution*

Time to resolution is a popular metric in both self-service and agent-assist scenarios. Simply put, time to resolution is the time between a user initiating a session and the user getting resolution. Corporations frequently build AI assistants to decrease time to resolution for their users. Figure 5.3 illustrates the concept.

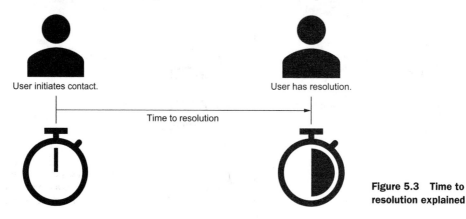

Figure 5.3   Time to resolution explained

A good AI assistant can greatly reduce average time to resolution. This result may seem to be counterintuitive; human experts can provide answers pretty quickly when you ask them. How much better could an AI assistant be?

In the case of a self-service assistant, the AI assistant gets a head start. When you open a session with an AI assistant, it's ready to respond right away. When you open a session with a human agent, you often have to wait in a queue or be placed on hold before you ever speak to a human. If your AI assistant can resolve a session without any human involvement, the time to resolution can be quite low. Figure 5.4 demonstrates the head start that self-service AI assistants have over human agents.

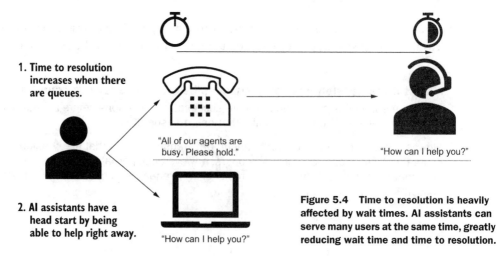

Figure 5.4   Time to resolution is heavily affected by wait times. AI assistants can serve many users at the same time, greatly reducing wait time and time to resolution.

For agent-assist AI assistants, time to resolution is decreased because the human agent works with the assistant to resolve issues. How many times have you been on the phone with customer support and been placed on hold? Agents place customers on hold so that they can look up the answer online, ask a colleague, or mutter to themselves while they thumb through a manual. With an agent-assist assistant in the picture, the agent will have more answers at their fingertips and will be able to resolve issues more quickly. Figure 5.5 shows how agent-assist AI assistants reduce time to resolution.

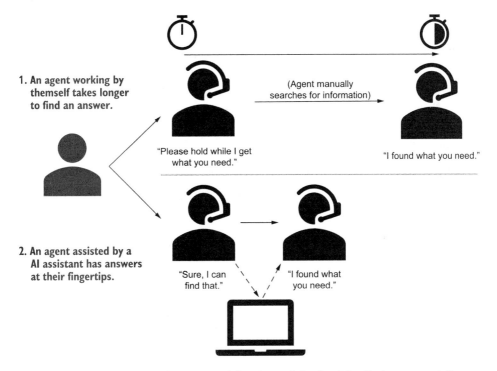

Figure 5.5 Agent-assist AI assistants speed time to resolution by giving the human agent the information they need, when they need it.

It's important to note that you get decreased time to resolution only if your assistant is smart enough to resolve user requests, or at least smart enough to gather the information required to resolve those requests. An AI that constantly responds with "I'm sorry; I didn't understand" is not helping the user.

Time to resolution is a useful metric and resilient to attempts to game it, as long as you pick a good resolution marker. A simple marker, but one that's easy to game, is how long until the user disconnects. (Don't game time to resolution by trying to make the user hang up.) A more appropriate marker for time to resolution is when the assistant provides useful information to the user or the user states that their request is satisfied.

One shortcoming of time to resolution is that it can be difficult to decide when a request is truly resolved. You can use implicit resolution markers (the user disconnects, or the assistant sends some information), or you can ask the user directly ("Does this resolve your request?"). Explicit markers are more precise, but users often disconnect before confirmation questions are asked.

For a SMART goal, you should aim to decrease the current average time to resolution. The assistant will resolve some calls without a transfer; other users will use your assistant and then transfer (and potentially sit in a queue). The callers who get transferred will have a longer time to resolution. Be sure that enough calls are resolved without transfers that the average time to resolution decreases.

Table 5.6 lays out the pros and cons of time to resolution.

Table 5.6   Pros and cons of time to resolution as a success metric for conversational AIs

Pros	Cons
Easy to measure Fast resolution aligns with user needs.	May require using an implicit marker in conversation to determine when resolution is achieved Users may disconnect before you know whether an issue is resolved,

If users are having their requests resolved quickly, they should be happy. Next, we will look at a metric that determines how pleased (or displeased) they are.

5.2.3   *Net promoter score*

NPS is based on responses to the following question: "How likely is it that you would recommend our company/product/service to a friend or colleague?" Users respond with a score between 0 and 10. High scores (9 and 10) are the gold standard; your service is so great that users will brag to their friends about it. The lowest scores indicate that your service is so bad that users will tell their friends to avoid it.

A variation on NPS is an arbitrary satisfaction survey offered at the end of the AI interaction. The precise scale is less important than gathering direct feedback from your users.

Corporations frequently do NPS surveys of their customers independently of their AI assistants. Corporations often launch AI projects to help with NPS. If a company has long wait times for customer service, field agents take too long to resolve issues, or human agents don't know the right answers, that company may already have an NPS problem. AI assistants can improve NPS by resolving issues quickly; thus, NPS pairs nicely with time to resolution as a success metric.

When the user provides an NPS, there's no need to guess whether the user is satisfied; they've told you. The direct connection to the user and the difficulty of gaming NPS make it a valuable success metric.

There are two primary criticisms of NPS:

- *Users rarely answer surveys.* Perhaps only 5-10% of your users will answer a survey question, and this sampling may not be representative enough to draw good conclusions from. (If you average a 0 NPS, however, you can certainly draw conclusions from that score!)

   ■ *You may not be able to tell why the user is unhappy.* If the user asks, "Am I covered to see a specialist?", and the assistant accurately answers, "No, your plan does not cover specialists," the user may provide a low NPS score even though the assistant performed well.

Finally, it is only appropriate to ask the NPS question after the assistant has resolved at least one issue. As shown in the following sample dialogue, the survey should be the third question you ask the user at earliest:

1   "How can I help you?" (intent capture)
2   "Can I help with anything else?" (intent resolution)
3   "On a scale of 0 to 10, how satisfied are you with your service today?" (survey)

The implicit contract between user and assistant should be that the assistant can ask for something from the user only after it has given something to the user. It's best to ask the survey question when the user is done providing information.

Further, it does not make sense to ask a satisfaction question if the assistant will be transferring the user to a human agent—partly because it's highly unlikely that the user is satisfied, and partly because the agent can ask a survey question after resolving the user's issue. That survey can cover both the agent and the assistant. If you are measuring containment in addition to NPS, the assistant will be sufficiently punished by the containment score. For a SMART goal, aim to improve your current NPS in the first few months after deploying your assistant.

Table 5.7 summarizes the pros and cons of NPS.

Table 5.7   Pros and cons of NPS as a success metric for conversational AIs

Pros	Cons
Easy to measure Direct reflection of how users feel Difficult to game	Users frequently disconnect without answering surveys, leading to small sample sizes. Users may give you a bad score for a "right" answer that they don't like.

Both self-service and agent-assist AI assistants can improve a company's NPS rating. In the next section, we look at one last common metric used to evaluate conversational AIs.

5.2.4 Coverage

The last metric commonly used to evaluate success is coverage. Coverage can be used to evaluate both self-service and agent-assist types of conversational AIs. Simply put, coverage is a measurement of how many requests the assistant tries to answer. In figure 5.6, Dialogue 1 is covered, and Dialogue 2 is not covered, giving our assistant a 50% coverage score.

An assistant with low coverage is not providing much value to users. When coverage is low, the user is likely to keep getting responses like "I'm sorry; I didn't understand"

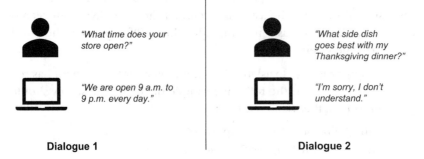

Figure 5.6   Demonstration of coverage. Dialogue 1 is covered because the assistant tried to answer. Dialogue 2 is not covered because the assistant did not try to answer.

until the assistant decides to transfer the user to an alternative channel. In this case, the user would probably prefer to go straight to that other channel without having to go through your assistant first!

High coverage can be guaranteed by giving a targeted response to every single request. The more requests you answer, however, the more likely you are to give an incorrect answer. Figure 5.6 showed an assistant with 50% coverage. If we made that assistant less conservative about when it responds to a user, we could end up with figure 5.7. The assistant might classify "What side dish goes best with my Thanksgiving dinner?" as a #Store_Location intent with low confidence. If the assistant responds based on that low-confidence intent, the coverage will go up, but the user will have a worse experience.

Coverage is achieved by answering a lot of questions, but effectiveness is measured by how many responses are useful. In figure 5.7, the assistant provides a useful answer to Dialogue 1; this conversation counts toward both coverage and effectiveness. Dialogue 2 gives a wrong answer; the response increases coverage but decreases effectiveness.

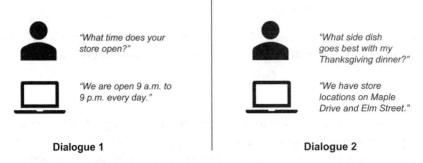

Figure 5.7   Cheating the coverage metric by responding even if the assistant is not sure about the intent. Dialogue 1 is covered and effective. Dialogue 2 increases coverage but is not effective.

Solving the tension between coverage and effectiveness

Coverage and effectiveness have a natural tension. The more questions you answer, the more likely you are to give wrong answers. Each question you answer increases coverage, and each wrong answer decreases effectiveness.

Chapter 6 discusses how to train your assistant (to optimize coverage), and chapter 7 discusses how to test your assistant (to optimize effectiveness).

In chapter 2, we implemented a low-confidence response filter for Fictitious Inc. so that its assistant responded only when intents were recognized with high confidence. This approach decreases coverage but increases effectiveness and improves the user experience.

For agent-assist conversational AIs, there is less downside to having high coverage. The agent can always choose to ignore any advice from the AI. But if the assistant gives too much irrelevant advice to the agent, the agent may tune it out.

Coverage is most useful when it is used to determine how to improve the assistant. When you analyze the performance of your AI assistant, look at all the user requests that were not covered. This set of data shows you what kinds of requests your users really want. If you find a lot of meal-planning questions like "What side dish goes best with my Thanksgiving dinner?", you could plan a new `#recipes` or `#guided_shopping` intent.

In chapter 3, we discussed how to plan the implementation of your assistant. During your planning phase, you'll probably identify more intents you want to service than you can easily implement. My advice was to choose and start with high-value intents. When your assistant goes into production, the uncovered conversations can be more helpful for prioritizing new functionality in your assistant than your original plan was.

For a SMART goal, follow the Pareto Principle, also known as the 80/20 rule. Generally, you can solve 80% of a problem in 20% of the time, and the remaining 20% of a problem will take 80% of the time. You may never cover 100% of user requests, but if you can identify and respond intelligently to the most common requests (the easy 80%), you will provide value to yourself and your users. You may need to adjust this target, but it's a great place to start for both coverage and effectiveness.

Table 5.8 summarizes the pros and cons of coverage as a success metric.

Table 5.8 Pros and cons of coverage as a success metric for conversational AIs

Pros	Cons
Easy to measure	Cannot be used as the only success metric
Shows where bot capability may need to be expanded	Does not measure whether responses are useful (effective), only whether they are given
	May not be aligned with user goals
	Susceptible to gaming

5.2.5   *Instrumenting your conversational AI*

Your AI platform may gather some of these metrics for you automatically. Some metrics can be determined generically, without any knowledge of your assistant; other metrics require detailed understanding of your specific assistant. For these metrics, you'll have to help the assistant by writing some code.

Containment, for example, can be measured generically by many AI platforms, especially if they provide built-in integrations to escalation channels. Transfer or escalation scenarios are often handled by a single dialogue node. Containment can be measured by counting the number of visits to that dialogue node divided by the total number of conversations.

Figure 5.8 demonstrates a manual instrumentation of containment. (Your platform will offer similar capability.) In this figure, any transfer will add the `context_connect_to_agent=true` flag to a conversation. If you also update the "conversation start" dialogue node to include `context_connect_to_agent=false`, you can use the `context_connect_to_agent` variable value to count how many conversations are, or are not, contained.

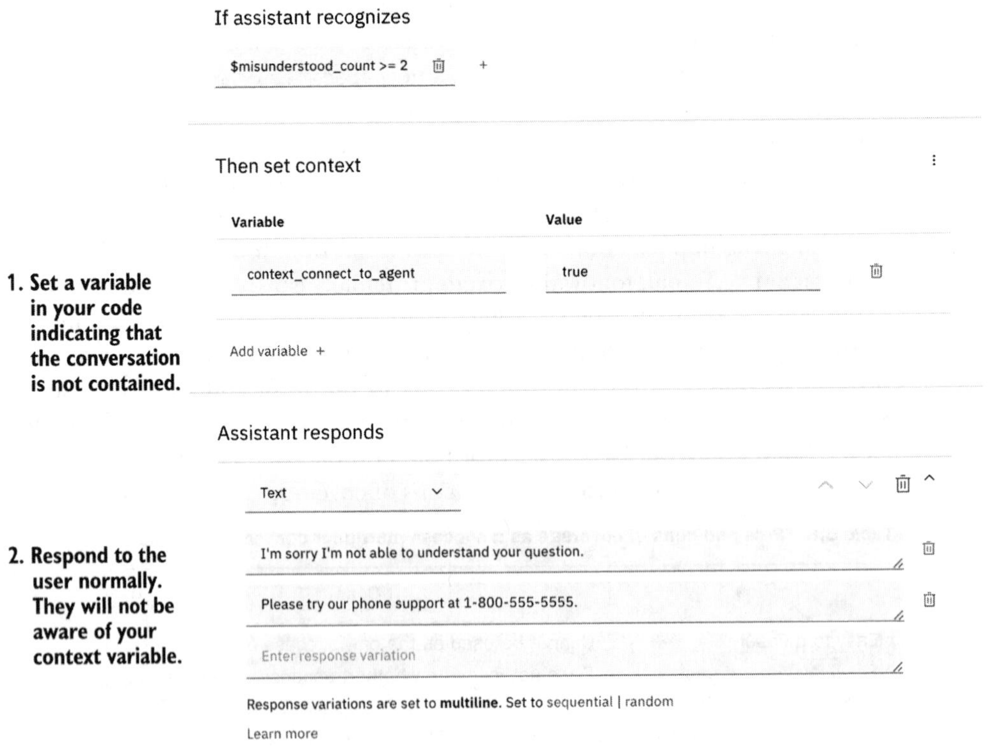

If assistant recognizes

$misunderstood_count >= 2   🗑   +

Then set context   ⋮

Variable	Value	
context_connect_to_agent	true	🗑

1. Set a variable in your code indicating that the conversation is not contained.

Add variable +

Assistant responds

2. Respond to the user normally. They will not be aware of your context variable.

Text   ∧ ∨ 🗑 ∧

I'm sorry I'm not able to understand your question.   🗑

Please try our phone support at 1-800-555-5555.   🗑

Enter response variation

Response variations are set to **multiline**. Set to sequential | random
Learn more

Figure 5.8   Manually instrumenting a conversational AI to measure containment

Instrumenting your conversational AI to measure the most common success metrics generally requires only one of the following actions, though you can mix and match them depending on your platform:

- Recording which dialogue nodes or dialogue responses align with success metrics
- Adding variables associated with events to your dialogue
- Adding code to emit events to a reporting tool

Table 5.9 shows some common techniques for instrumenting the common conversational agent success metrics.

Table 5.9 Instrumentation methodologies for common conversational AI success metrics

Metric	Common instrumentation techniques
Containment	Define a transfer or escalation node. Set a variable for containment status. Emit "conversation started" and "conversation transferred" events.
Time to resolution	Define which dialogue nodes equate to resolution. Compute the time between starting a conversation and visiting a resolution node. Emit "conversation started" and "conversation resolved" events.
NPS	Set a variable for a numerical survey result. Emit an event with an NPS response.
Coverage	Define a fallback or default dialogue response. Emit "coverage failure" and "coverage success" events.

5.3 Command interpreter success metrics

Conversational agents are frequently deployed to reduce costs for corporations, either by improving self-service options for consumers or by augmenting the intelligence of users in agent-assist deployments. Conversational agent success metrics focus directly on cost savings and time to value. Conversational agents are often backstopped by human experts, and success is measured partly by how rarely that backstop is used.

Command interpreters, on the other hand, don't lead to direct cost savings. Instead, a good command interpreter makes you excited to use a product or a series of products. A command interpreter rarely exposes new capability; it only makes that capability faster to use.

Table 5.10 shows how some capabilities were achieved before and after command interpreters.

Table 5.10 Accessing capability without and with command interpreters

Scenario	Without command interpreter	With command interpreter
Set an alarm for 9 p.m. on your phone.	Find the Clock app. Find the Alarm setting. Use a slider to set an alarm time.	Press the wake button. Speak "Set an alarm for 9 p.m."

Table 5.10 Accessing capability without and with command interpreters *(continued)*

Scenario	Without command interpreter	With command interpreter
Turn up the volume on your smart TV from 15 to 20.	Figure out which of the many, many buttons on your remote is Volume Up. Press the button several times.	Press the wake button. Speak "Set volume to 20."
Order paper towels online.	Open a browser or app. Search for paper towels. Select the product you want. Click Buy.	Press the wake button. Speak "Order more paper towels."

The capabilities in table 5.10 are nothing earth-shattering. We've long been able to set alarms, increase television volume, and order paper towels online. What makes the command interpreter exciting is how quickly the capabilities can be enabled when the appropriate device is in hand. Table 5.11 shows a dramatic reduction in time to value for these same scenarios.

Table 5.11 Time to value without and with a command interpreter

Scenario	Time without command interpreter (expert user)	Time with command interpreter
Set an alarm for 9 p.m. on your phone.	18 seconds	5 seconds
Turn up the volume on your smart TV from 15 to 20.	10 seconds	5 seconds
Order paper towels online.	30 seconds	5 seconds

Voice-enabled command interpreters are fast. As fast as you can say what you want, it can happen. In table 5.11, I did an apples-to-apples test by timing each action while having a device in my hand. Many popular command interpreters can be set to "always listening" mode, helping them further reduce time to value.

Should a device always be listening?

A device that is always listening can respond to user requests more quickly than a device that needs to be awakened first. But there are considerable ethical and privacy concerns about a device that's always listening, even if a user opts into that service. Tread carefully if you create a command interpreter that's always listening.

5.3.1 Usage

Time to value is an important design consideration for conversational AIs, but it is difficult to draw a direct connection between time to value and your bottom line. If I use a voice command to set a lot of alarms on my phone, that action does not make my phone manufacturer any money, and it doesn't save the manufacturer any time either.

My smart TV manufacturer is not directly affected by whether I change the volume by voice command or by button press.

The closest connection to bottom-line effect comes from the order-paper-towels scenario. If I can quickly order paper towels via a home assistant, I'm going to be ordering from the same retailer that created the assistant. For this specific type of command interpreter assistant, the connection to real money earned is clear. For all other command interpreters, the value is still indirect.

Usage is perhaps the best success metric available for any command interpreter. As a producer of command interpreters, you can infer that your users like the command interpreter if they use it—a lot. My phone lets me set alarms through a dedicated app or a voice-enabled command interpreter. When I set multiple alarms per day through the voice option, the manufacturer can assume that I'm happy with the command interpreter. For measuring usage, you can use either the total number of times the command interpreter is used or the relative percentage of how often the command interpreter is used versus other methods.

Further, the way the command interpreter is used (or not used) can give a hint as to how well it is performing. I set a lot of alarms and reminders on my phone; clearly, the command interpreter works well on those features. I rarely use the command interpreter on my phone to play music, open apps, or to send text messages. This data is useful for my phone manufacturer, which can use it to further improve its command interpreter.

It's challenging to describe a one-size-fits-all SMART goal for usage. You will want to see an increase over time in the number of people who use the assistant, as well as the number of times they use it. Usage has a natural upper bound. Recall setting an alarm on a phone; there are only so many alarms that one needs to set every day. You may convert users to setting all their alarms via your command interpreter (instead of via app), but you probably won't increase the number of alarms they set.

Table 5.12 shows the pros and cons of usage as a success metric.

Table 5.12   Pros and cons of usage as a success metric for command interpreters

Pros	Cons
Easy to measure	Usually does not tie directly to the bottom line
Shows where bot capability may need to be expanded	Does not tell you why a feature is not used
Directly aligned with user value	

5.3.2   *Stickiness*

Stickiness is the only other success metric that I associate with command interpreters, and it's hard to measure directly. Stickiness is directly correlated with income, however; thus, it's worthy of discussion.

If your command interpreter has a lot of usage, that fact suggests that its users like to use your products and services. Most cellphone users in the United States get their phones through multiyear contracts, so it behooves the manufacturers to have a good command interpreter on their phones. The more I use the voice assistant on my current phone, the less likely I am to want to switch phone manufacturers at the end of my contract. This phenomenon is often called *stickiness*, either because users are more likely to stick around or because they are figuratively glued to their phones.

Stickiness applies to more than phones. Consider any smart device in your home, such as a TV remote, thermostat, or security system. If you get used to and really like the command interpreter interface on one device, you're likely to want to buy more devices from that manufacturer, especially if those devices are compatible with the interface you already know.

You may consider *stickiness* to be a fanciful term for vendor lock-in, which may be true. It is true that if you provide users plenty of value now, they are likely to have a positive impression of you in the future.

Stickiness is hard to measure because it can occur over a long-time scale and the data required to measure it may not be directly available. The opposite of stickiness is almost impossible to measure. (If someone stops using your product and buys a competitor's product, how would you know?) Ideally, you would segregate sales or subscription data by how often consumers used your command interpreter and determine whether the command-interpreter users are buying more or less of your product.

Improvements in your command interpreter will take a long time to influence stickiness. If my phone manufacturer releases a fantastic new feature today, and I love it, it'll still be a few years before I'm ready to buy my next phone. This lag time can be even worse in other industries; I may like my smart TV, but it'll be several years before I buy another one. Stickiness is perhaps best thought of as a method of connecting usage with revenue.

If stickiness is your success metric, your SMART goal needs to include an increase in sales or revenue in the time following your assistant's deployment. Table 5.13 lists the pros and cons of using stickiness as a success metric.

Table 5.13 Pros and cons of stickiness as a success metric for command interpreters

Pros	Cons
Connects usage to the bottom line	Difficult to measure
	Takes a long time for correlations to show up

5.3.3 *Instrumenting your command interpreter*

The command interpreter is an interface for invoking commands. The usage metric is measured mostly by counting how many times the interpreter was used. The only question is where to do the counting. Figure 5.9 lays out the alternatives: measure usage of the command interpreter or of the commands.

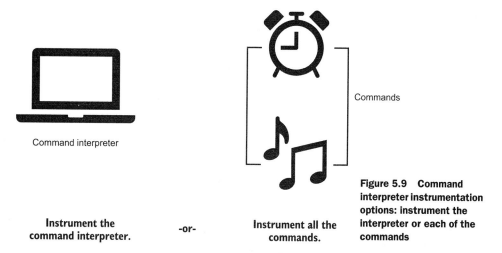

Command interpreter

Instrument the command interpreter. -or- **Instrument all the commands.**

Figure 5.9 Command interpreter instrumentation options: instrument the interpreter or each of the commands

Instrumenting the command interpreter is the simplest option. Every time you execute a command, you can emit an event to a reporting solution showing which command was executed. The positive side of this approach is that you can write a few lines of code and be done. The negative side of this approach is that you will be able to measure only absolute usage, not relative usage. If my phone manufacturer uses this approach, it can tell how many alarms I create by voice, but not what percentage of all alarms I create by voice.

My phone manufacturer could infer some relative metrics by comparing me with other users. If the average user sets six alarms a week, and I use voice to create six alarms per week, I'm probably setting all my alarms by voice. Or the relative usage may not matter. My manufacturer may learn enough about me by looking at what features I bother to activate via voice and what features I don't.

If measuring relative usage is important for an analysis of your command interpreter, the only way you can be certain is to instrument each of the commands you enable. The instrumentation is simple: each command should report every time it was invoked and state whether it was invoked by the command interpreter. The downside of this approach is that you need to make this instrumentation change in every one of the commands you support. Worse, this approach has a heavy maintenance cost if you ever need to change the instrumentation.

Regardless of which method you choose, instrumenting for your command interpreter generally involves emitting a single event at the right time.

5.4 *Event classifier success metrics*

An *event classifier* examines input data and classifies it into some target. Throughout this book, I provide several examples of classification, usually classifying a user utterance against a set of intents. Classifiers are frequently deployed outside conversational systems. They are used to classify email (is it spam or not spam?), for example, and to route customer support requests to the appropriate expert (is the issue a hardware or software issue?).

Figure 5.10 shows an exemplary classifier use case. A classifier can be assigned to a generic email address like info@fictitiousinc.com and can direct any mail it receives to the appropriate department. Fictitious Inc. might use the classifier to send mail to sales, legal, human resources, and customer support.

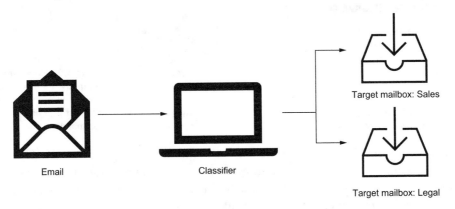

Email   Classifier   Target mailbox: Sales

Target mailbox: Legal

Figure 5.10   Example email classification flow. A classifier can listen to a functional email address like info@fictitiousinc.com and route the email to the person who's best suited to handle it.

When you're developing a classifier, the most useful metric usually is accuracy (how often the classifier picked the correct classification target). But the classifier is deployed to serve some broader goal, often connected to monetary metrics and the bottom line. Accuracy influences those metrics, but it's more important to focus on the goal and the direct metrics in that goal. Let's explore a couple of these metrics.

5.4.1 *Time to resolution*

Time to resolution is defined for classifiers as it is for conversational assistants. A clock starts ticking as soon as the user makes a request and stops when they get a useful answer.

Figure 5.11 shows how a classifier can decrease time to resolution. In the first example, Bob may pick up an email from the info@fictitiousinc.com functional mailbox, but he may not know how to answer the email and may forward it to Susie. The email could sit in Susie's inbox for a few hours (or days) before she sees it, realizes that she can't answer it, and forwards the message to Joe. Fortunately, Joe can answer the email. In the second example, a classifier is used, and the correct recipient is identified the first time.

In either scenario, the time spent waiting for the first person to see the email is the same. The nonclassifier scenario has a higher time to resolution when the email sits in a wrong mailbox, waiting again to be routed. During this wait time, the user is not getting any resolution and will slowly but surely get frustrated.

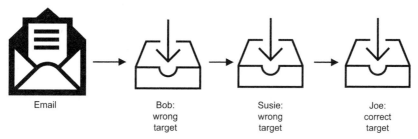

Without a classifier, an email may be forwarded several times until it's sent to the right destination. Each hand-off causes wait times and delays.

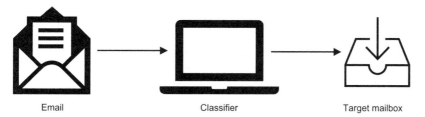

A classifier is likely to route the email to the right destination the first time, reducing delays.

Figure 5.11 Comparing email routing with and without classifiers

Alternatively, a classifier can be used to make sure that enough information is present before a human touches the input and starts the clock. Figure 5.12 reminds us of the example from chapter 1. The classifier can review input from a user and immediately give them feedback about how their input will be classified and whether any information is missing from their request. Without that help from the classifier, the human receiving

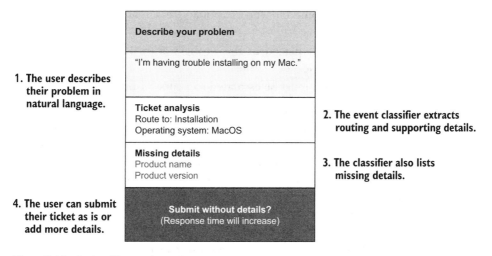

Figure 5.12 A classifier can immediately notify users of missing details in their requests. The users won't have to wait for a human recipient to respond to the request with "I need more details."

the input might immediately return it to the user, saying "I need more details"—a frustrating response, especially if the user has already been waiting for days.

Finally, an automated classifier can save time because it's always on and never gets tired. Many companies use humans as classifiers—Level 1 support, for example. When I call customer support, I have to wait on hold before I even get to Level 1. A classifier, by contrast, can handle many requests at a time and starts my resolution process more quickly.

Your SMART goal for time to resolution will depend on how long your average resolution time was before. Classifiers can often shave hours or days off average resolution time, and you may see an orders-of-magnitude reduction in time. Try to reduce resolution time by half.

Table 5.14 outlines the pros and cons of time to resolution as a success metric.

Table 5.14   Pros and cons of time to resolution as a success metric for event classifiers

Pros	Cons
Easy to measure Aligns with user value	Appropriate only for certain classifier use cases

5.4.2   *Number of hand-offs*

As alluded to in section 5.4.1, the average number of hand-offs is a useful metric for determining how well your resolution process is working. As shown in figure 5.11, each hand-off is an opportunity to lose time waiting for a response. Extra hand-offs due to misroutes are expensive in both time and reputation. Your service looks worse to a user the longer they have to wait for a useful response.

There are multiple ways that a process could have multiple hand-offs. Here are a few:

- Email is sent to someone who cannot address it, and they must send it to someone else.
- A trouble ticket is placed in the wrong work queue, and the receiving team must place it in another queue.
- A support request must be escalated to a supervisor.

You can assume an average cost in time to resolution for every hand-off. Further, each hand-off is a waste of your company's money when personnel are looking at issues they cannot resolve. Finally, hand-offs can lower employee satisfaction and morale. Who wants to be spending their time looking at "wrong things"?

Measuring the number of hand-offs may require some work on your part. This work may involve finding out how many times an email is forwarded, for example. (How will you measure this automatically?) Trouble-ticket systems often maintain an audit trail to show who owned or worked on a ticket, but this audit trail may be difficult to parse. Depending on what process your classifier is addressing, the number of hand-offs may still be worth measuring.

Your SMART goal for number of hand-offs will depend on how many hand-offs you averaged before the classifier. The 80/20 rule is a good guideline. Aim to have zero additional hand-offs for 80% of your cases that use the classifier.

Number of hand-offs and time to resolution are closely related, but tracking them both is worthwhile. Table 5.15 shows the pros and cons of number of hand-offs as a success metric for classifiers.

Table 5.15 Pros and cons of number of hand-offs as a success metric for classifiers

Pros	Cons
Aligned with user value Aligned with the bottom line	Tracking number of hand-offs may require special reporting logic.

5.4.3 Other customer satisfaction metrics

Several of the metrics described in this chapter can also apply to classifiers. If you are injecting a classifier into a process, you may still want to measure NPS, customer retention, or similar metrics.

The challenge with using these metrics to evaluate your classifier is that your users probably don't interact with the classifier directly. NPS makes sense for a conversational agent because a user has probably spent several minutes talking with it, having a series of back-and-forth interactions. With that length of interaction, the user can form an instructive opinion about the assistant.

With a classifier, the user's interaction is brief or invisible. As a user, I don't know whether you're using a classifier; I only know whether you're taking a long time to respond to me. If you misroute my email, I'm unhappy; you don't even need to ask. Every time you send my trouble ticket to someone who can't help, I get more frustrated.

Even so, user feedback is valuable. You can still collect NPS or measure customer retention, but you should apply that metric to the entire process—not only the classifier. A customer satisfaction metric should be one of your success metrics.

Table 5.16 lays out the pros and cons of using customer satisfaction metrics to evaluate your classifier.

Table 5.16 Pros and cons of customer satisfaction metrics for evaluating your classifier

Pros	Cons
Aligned with user value and the bottom line Difficult to game	Evaluates your entire process, not only the classifier Should be paired with another success metric

5.4.4 Instrumenting your classifier

Like a command interpreter, a classifier is usually embedded in another tool or process. Therefore, the instrumentation often happens outside the classifier itself. The process needs to be instrumented with the following timestamps:

- When user input was received
- Every time user input was routed
- When the user's request was resolved

If you are using a classifier in an email-based process, this information already exists in most email headers. If your classifier is embedded in a trouble-ticket system, this information is probably encoded in a history or an audit trail. Similarly, most customer relationship management (CRM) systems keep track of this information.

Depending on your system, you may not need to instrument your system to add this tracking data, but you might have to write reporting code to extract it.

Summary

- To avoid AI failure, you must plan for success and decide how you will measure it. You should use SMART goals to ensure that you are heading in the right direction with your metrics.
- Conversational AI success metrics include containment, time to resolution, NPS, and coverage.
- Command interpreter success metrics include usage and stickiness.
- Event classifier success metrics include time to resolution, number of hand-offs, and assorted customer satisfaction metrics.
- You may need to add code to your AI assistant or to its associated infrastructure to measure success metrics.

Part 3

Training and testing

You've selected a use case requiring an AI assistant and designed all aspects of the experience. Now it's time to start constructing the assistant.

AI assistants are built on top of machine learning classification algorithms called classifiers. These classifiers learn through a training process. The classifier is trained by example. Given a set of data, the classifier infers patterns and learns to differentiate the data.

In chapter 6, you will learn how to train your assistant. Training starts with finding a suitable data source; several possible sources are described. Then this data must be curated and organized in a way suitable for the classifier to train on. Training data must have variety, volume, and veracity. Each of these "three Vs" has a big impact on the classifier.

Testing AI assistants requires two different disciplines. A data science discipline is required to test the accuracy of the assistant. A software engineering discipline is required to test the remaining functionality, particularly the dialog flows. These disciplines are isolated into separate chapters.

Chapter 7 covers the data scientist testing aspect. In this chapter, you'll learn methodologies and metrics for testing how accurately your assistant identifies user intents. You'll learn how to identify the most important mistakes your assistant makes.

Chapter 8 covers the functional testing aspect. This includes verifying that the assistant faithfully implements the dialog flows you so carefully designed. This chapter also introduces automated testing methodologies that accelerate your testing cycle and give you confidence in the conversational AI's performance.

After completing this part, you'll be ready to put your assistant into production.

Training your assistant 6

This chapter covers

- Training an assistant to recognize intents from user input
- Collecting a viable training data set for your AI assistant
- Analyzing how training data affects an assistant's performance

Training is an important part of building an AI assistant. Good training increases the intelligence of the assistant and enables it to be more useful to your users. Training influences almost every single success metric and is important no matter which type of assistant you are building. This chapter will teach you what you need to start training your assistant.

Fictitious Inc. prototyped its first conversational AI using sample data from its AI provider. This data trained the assistant to be proficient at recognizing generic customer service intents. But what if a suitable sample data set did not exist? How could Fictitious Inc. build a training data set and use it to teach its conversational AI? Let's explore a scenario in which Fictitious Inc. was not given a precreated training set and had to build its own.

AI assistant platforms come with samples or starter kits for rapid prototyping. You may be able to get started building your assistant with this sample data, but you will eventually need training data that is customized to your specific use case. Whether you are starting from scratch or extending a sample data set, the steps in this chapter will help you train your assistant. We will use Fictitious Inc.'s conversational AI assistant as an example, but the steps are mostly the same for command interpreters and event classifiers, with minor terminology differences.

6.1   *Training an AI assistant*

When we created a new AI assistant for Fictitious Inc., that assistant did not know anything about customer service. A new AI assistant comes with little knowledge built in. It had some basic knowledge of the English language, including grammatical constructs and some spell-checking. At the end, the assistant knew a few things about customer service, but only what we trained it on.

Fictitious Inc. needs to build a training data set so that the assistant can recognize and serve the most common requests. The company has identified the most significant intents that its customer-service-based conversational AI needs to handle, including store hours, store location, and password reset; now it needs to train the AI assistant to recognize these intents. The generalized process for training an AI assistant is shown in figure 6.1.

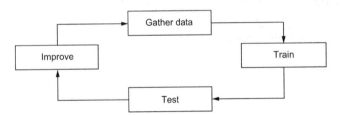

Figure 6.1   Training an AI assistant is part of a continuous cycle.

For this conversational AI, two things are needed to start training:

- *Gather data.* What do users say? What textual utterances will they send to the AI? Fictitious Inc. needs to find both what intents users will have and how they will textually phrase them.
- *Train.* What do the utterances mean? The assistant will be trained on pairs of utterances with their associated intents. From this training data, the assistant will reverse-engineer how to find the intent in user utterances.

Training data is always a pair of input and expected output. For this example, the input is an utterance, and the output is an intent. Table 6.1 shows example training data for the assistant.

You train a conversational AI by defining intents and providing several examples of each intent. The AI assistant's classifier uses machine learning to analyze the training data, extracting patterns that it can use to identify the categories in future input data.

Table 6.1 Example training data for a conversational A

Utterance	Intent
"Where are you located"	`#store_location`
"What time do you open?"	`#store_hours`
"How can I reset my password?"	`#reset_password`

(AI assistants generally use supervised learning classification algorithms. For an example of how these algorithms work, see chapter 11.)

A training analogy

The process of training AI is similar to teaching students. Students are given homework and provided an answer key to check their work. The students learn concepts from the homework and can confidently solve problems they have seen from that homework. Students do homework until they can consistently produce correct answers.

From the teacher's point of view, it is tough to tell how much students have learned; are they mastering the concepts or simply working back from the answers? Teachers assess student performance by giving exams with problems that were not in the homework. Grading performance on these unseen problems tells the teacher how well a student has learned. This analogy is demonstrated in table 6.2.

Table 6.2 Comparing AI training and student education

Task	AI assistant	Student education
Preparation for learning	Collect a set of utterances and their associated intents as candidate training data.	Create problem sets with an answer key. Teacher assigns some of the problems as homework.
Practice and learning	Give some training data to the assistant.	Student does homework and checks the answer key.
Assessment	Create a test set from the candidate data not included in training.	Teacher creates an exam from problems not included in homework.
	Test the assistant on data it was not trained on.	Student takes an exam.
Declaration of mastery	High accuracy when you test the assistant with data it has not been trained on	Student performs well on the exam.
Remediation if no mastery	Additional training of the assistant	Additional homework and new exams

Why don't we train and test with the same data?

Just as a teacher does not put homework questions on the exam, we should not use the same training data to test the AI assistant. The true test of the training process is how well the assistant classifies input it has never seen before. Most assistants correctly classify the exact data they were trained on, so testing with that data is not informative.

It's OK to have some overlap in the train and test data sets, especially when the inputs are short, as they are in many voice-based conversational assistants, but don't overdo it.

The conversational AI-building team is ready to teach the assistant. Let's help them start by finding data they can use to train it.

6.2   *Finding training data*

The training process starts with finding a good source from which to build training data. This source helps determine what users want and how they ask for it. Fictitious Inc.'s customer service team does a lot of password resets for users. The team might assume that users will typically ask to reset their passwords, but as they review data, they may find that users prefer to ask to unlock their accounts. An assistant will perform much better when it's trained based on how users actually say things than on assumptions of how users might say things.

AI learns everything it knows from training data. The data used in the training process should be as close as possible to what the assistant will encounter in production. The quality of the training data determines how accurate this assistant will be at recognizing what real users ask of it. How can the team find the best possible training data? It ultimately needs to find out three things:

- The intents, or categories of questions, that users will ask
- The relative frequency, or distribution, of those intents
- How those intents are worded

The team has already explored the first two questions. As a reminder, figure 6.2 shows how the intents were plotted based on their relative frequencies and the complexity of automating them.

Fictitious Inc. had several potential data sources from which to create figure 6.2. Each of the sources has pros and cons. Like many conversational AI builders, the company can use a mixture of some or all of these training sources. The primary sources include production logs, mock user interfaces, and subject-matter experts (SMEs).

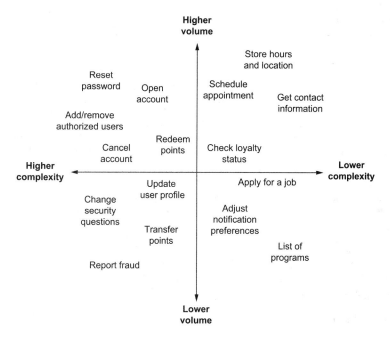

Figure 6.2 **Example distribution of intents. The assistant still needs to be trained on how these intents are phrased. What wordings are given by users?**

6.2.1 Production logs

The best place to find real user utterances is a real conversational AI in the same use case. Fictitious Inc. would love to get training data from another customer service text-based conversational assistant. But for most people, this situation presents a chicken-and-egg problem: needing a production AI assistant so that you can build an AI assistant. Still, this approach is workable in several cases, or a reasonable alternative exists.

When you don't have an existing assistant for the same use case in production, ask whether you have something close. Table 6.3 shows some candidate training data sources.

Table 6.3 **Production data sources suitable for training AI assistants**

Data source	Good for	Reason	Caveat
Human-to-human chat logs	Conversational AI	Will closely mirror utterances sent to an automated text-chat conversational AI	Will need adaptation for voice assistants; the intents will match but not the wording.
Human-to-human call transcripts	Conversational AI	Will closely mirror the distribution of intents received by a conversational assistant	People speak differently to other humans compared with how they talk to machines.

Table 6.3   Production data sources suitable for training AI assistants *(continued)*

Data source	Good for	Reason	Caveat
Search logs	Conversational AI	Will closely mirror the distribution of intents received by a conversational AI	Search queries tend to be much shorter than conversational utterances.
Emails	Event classifiers Conversational AI	An email classifier should be trained on real email.	An email is longer than a conversational utterance. But the subject line or first sentence can be close to a conversational utterance.
Customer relationship management (CRM) event records	Any	Will closely mirror the distribution of intents	Will not provide any insight into how these intents are phrased by customers

The best part of using production data is that it is hard, verifiable data. Rather than theorize about what users might do, you can consult production data to find out exactly what they do, which is much better than guessing or theorizing.

> *Most of the world will make decisions by either guessing or using their gut. They will be either lucky or wrong.*

—Suhail Doshi, chief executive officer, Mixpanel

In the ideal scenario, your production data would line up exactly with your new AI assistant use case. In these cases, no caveats are required on the data source. If you are converting a human-to-human chat channel to an automated chat powered by a conversational AI assistant, you can reasonably assume that users will ask the assistant the same questions that they ask the humans.

Most times, you will not be so lucky as to have an exact alignment of data sources. You can still use production data to guide your training, but you'll have to be careful. Generally, the distribution of intents will be similar across channels, but the wording from users will differ.

Let's assume that Fictitious Inc. has access to transcripts from its human-to-human call center. This example is not in perfect alignment with text-chat use case. Humans talk differently to other humans than they talk or type to machines; human conversations are often more wordy and indirect and may stray off topic. Figure 6.3 compares a typical human-to-human conversation with a human-to-machine conversation.

Dialogue 1 comes from production data. Dialogue 2 imagines what the same user might say if they spoke to an automated solution on the telephone. The same user who spoke 63 words to another human might type only four words to a bot. We can't be sure how they will phrase their utterance to the bot. We expect that some of the language will be similar and that the overall intent will be the same. We should not train the conversational AI on the full 63-word utterance.

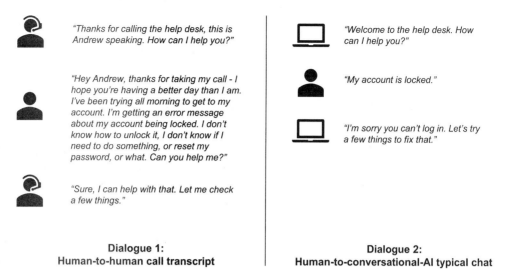

Dialogue 1:
Human-to-human call transcript

Dialogue 2:
Human-to-conversational-AI typical chat

Figure 6.3 Comparing an **actual human-to-human call transcript** with a hypothetical human-to-conversational-AI log

I would use the following **statements extracted from Dialogue 1** to train my assistant:

- "I'm getting an **error message** about my account being locked."
- "I don't know how **to unlock my account**."
- "Reset my password."

Each of those statements **describe the reset password intent** with no ambiguity. Each of those statements was **extracted directly** from the user transcript, with one exception: in the second statement, I **replaced** "it" with "my account." Figure 6.4 breaks the transcript into fragments and **identifies the role each fragment plays** in the conversation.

The remaining **statements in figure 6.4** are not useful for training. "I've been trying all morning to get to **my account**" is close but is a bit ambiguous by itself. "I don't know if I need to do **something**" and "Can you help me?" are so ambiguous that they

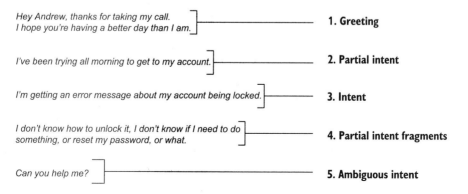

Figure 6.4 Breaking down the **63-word opening of a human-to-human conversation**

could apply to any intent. Similarly, no part of the greeting unambiguously hints at an intent.

Why not train on ambiguous statements?

In production, users will give ambiguous statements. Why can't we train the assistant on those statements?

AI assistants learn to recognize intents through unambiguous statements. Ambiguous statements will be identified as not closely matching a single intent or loosely matching multiple intents. Ambiguity is best handled at run time by asking the user to disambiguate.

Fictitious Inc. will be able to use human-to-human transcripts and emails to train the conversational assistant by slicing and dicing the data in this way. These data sources are great to use because they contain textual phrases from real users. The users are verbose, and it's easier to trim verbose data than to augment terse data.

The best production logs include the user's actual phrasing. We can also look at Fictitious Inc.'s CRM records, but these records usually include only a summary of the user interaction, not the user's direct phrasing. In figure 6.5, we see a CRM record in which the user asked a question related to a locked account and the representative recorded the call as a password reset issue. In this case, the intent was preserved, but the user's wording was lost.

"Thanks for calling the help desk; this is Andrew speaking. How can I help you?"

"Hey Andrew, thanks for taking my call. I hope you're having a better day than I am. I've been trying all morning to get to my account. I'm getting an error message about my account being locked. I don't know how to unlock it, I don't know if I need to do something, or reset my password, or what. Can you help me?"

"Sure, I can help with that. Let me check a few things."

CRM case:
Password reset

Figure 6.5   Beware of logs in which the user utterance is lost; they help you find intents but not the phrasing of those intents. Here, the user asked a verbose question full of nuance, and the representative recorded only "password reset."

Still, it is useful to verify which intents are the most common in the CRM records, which will help prioritize which intents are most useful for the conversational AI to handle.

The best way to find out what users might say is to review what users have said before. Production logs are a great source of real phrasing from users, even if they require some adaptation. If you don't have production logs, you still have ways to get representative utterances from users. If you can't find out what users have said before, you can still find out what they would like to say. A mock user interface is one possible way.

6.2.2 A mock user interface

If Fictitious Inc. did not have access to production data, it could gather some simulated data from a mock user interface. A *mock user interface* is a prototype or dummy interface with no intelligence except the ability to log questions asked of the assistant. The interface looks like (or for voice sounds like) the real thing, but it does not understand the questions. A mock interface is functionally equivalent to a survey or user interview, but it puts the user in a context closer to the intended use and thus will gather more representative (and less fabricated) questions.

Many AI platforms can help you build a mock user interface. An example mock interface is shown in figure 6.6. A good mock user interface should

- Greet the user and set expectations that answers will not be given.
- Allow users to ask questions.
- Log the questions and invite users to ask additional questions.

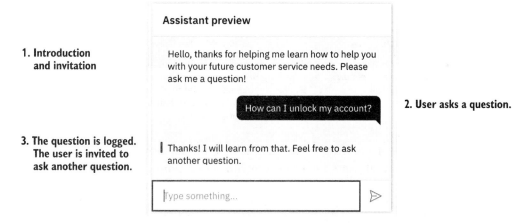

Figure 6.6   A sample mock user interface, which has the look and feel of a real conversational AI. It does not understand anything the user says, however; it only logs utterances for future training.

Be polite with your mock user interface. Expose it only to volunteers. Do not violate a social contract by letting users discover this fact on their own; they may have false expectations of getting help from the assistant. Users should explicitly opt into your mock user interface. You can send a link to your assistant through email or include it at the end of any survey that your users can opt into. Figure 6.7 shows an exemplar introduction to a mock user interface.

When you're asking for input through a mock user interface, introduce users to the interface, give a call to action, and conclude with thanks. The introduction should manage expectations properly. The call to action must strike a delicate balance. If you are too vague, the questions you collect may not be useful. If you are too prescriptive,

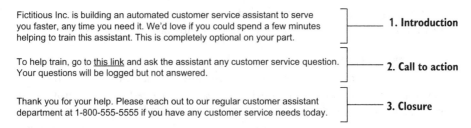

Fictitious Inc. is building an automated customer service assistant to serve you faster, any time you need it. We'd love if you could spend a few minutes helping to train this assistant. This is completely optional on your part. — **1. Introduction**

To help train, go to this link and ask the assistant any customer service question. Your questions will be logged but not answered. — **2. Call to action**

Thank you for your help. Please reach out to our regular customer assistant department at 1-800-555-5555 if you have any customer service needs today. — **3. Closure**

Figure 6.7   A mock user interface. You are asking users to do work for you, so be polite.

you may bias your users and skew the way they ask questions. Table 6.4 shows some variations Fictitious Inc. could use as its call to action.

Table 6.4   Variations of a call to action that invites participants to a mock user interface

Call to action	Usefulness	Reason
"Ask me anything."	Too vague	This call to action is an open invitation for off-topic questions such as "What's the weather like?" and "Tell me a joke." It's fun for the participants but doesn't help train your assistant.
"Ask me any customer service question."	Just right	Users are given an appropriate scope. The bot will not be open-ended; it will focus on customer service.
"Ask me any customer service question, such as how to reset your password."	Too biased	The users will be primed to include your words in their questions. You will get mostly meaningless wording variations such as "Please reset my password" and "Help reset my password" rather than a varied and representative distribution of questions.

The strength of a mock user interface is that it interacts with real users. The reason to interact with real users is to find out the actual phrasing they use, rather than the hypothetical or synthetic phrasing you think they will use. When you are using production logs, there is no question that the phrasing you see is actual user phrasing. A mock user interface is trying to be the next best thing.

Fictitious Inc. must be aware of biasing participants in the mock interface. If users were asked "How would you ask to have your password reset?", their brains would be primed (biased) with the words "reset" and "password." Without that bias, they may be more likely to ask about locked accounts or login problems.

Build your own mock user interface

A mock user interface can be built in most AI platforms. You need to configure only two pieces of dialogue: the welcome node and the fallback node. (Terminology may vary slightly across platforms.) The welcome node includes the greeting and initial call to action. The fallback node should thank the user and invite them to ask another question. Sample code for a mock interface built in Watson Assistant is provided in the book's GitHub repository at http://mng.bz/qeGN.

It can be difficult to get **enough** training data from a mock user interface alone. Fictitious Inc. can supplement **the data** it gathered from production logs with data from the mock interface. There's **one** more potential source of training data: SMEs.

6.2.3 *Subject-matter experts*

If you can't access user utterances directly, the next best data source is someone who knows about users. SMEs are skilled in their domains and often interact with real users. Fictitious Inc. can **ask its senior-level customer service agents** how they interact with users in the call center. Production logs and mock interfaces provide firsthand insight into users; interviewing SMEs provides secondhand insight. Secondhand is still better than none.

The company can ask the SMEs what questions users ask and how those questions are phrased, but it should **be cautious** because this approach is the most heavily biased approach of all. This **approach relies** on human memory, and human memory is not reliable. The SMEs generally **will** know the most common intents, though not with mathematical rigor.

The challenge in **getting** training data from the SMEs comes when they are asked how users phrase their **questions.** SMEs may be overconfident in their ability to recall what users say. (It's hard **to** know your own bias.) An SME might describe the password reset intent phrasing **as follows:** "Mostly, users ask about password, reset, locked accounts, and that's about it." When pressed for additional variations, they may start reordering the keywords **given** previously, such as "Reset my password" and "My password needs to be reset." They are unlikely to remember the full variety of user phrasings when asked.

Fictitious Inc. can **ask** the SMEs how they train new customer service representatives. Documentation for **new employees** can be used to gather training data. Figure 6.8 shows an annotated **excerpt from** a call-center playbook.

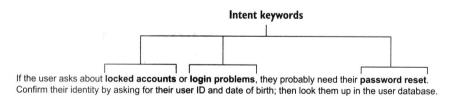

Intent keywords

If the user asks about **locked accounts** or **login problems**, they probably need their **password reset**. Confirm their identity by asking for **their user ID** and date of birth; then look them up in the user database.

Figure 6.8 Training materials for customer service agents may include keywords for the intents your assistant will receive. From this material, we can infer that "locked account" and "login problem" are synonymous with "password reset."

The training material in **figure 6.8** gives us keyword suggestions for the "password reset" intent. The keyword **phrases** "locked account," "login problems," and "password reset" are treated synonymously. These keywords will not line up exactly with how users ask their questions (they **may instead** say "Unlock my account"), but this level of variation is a good place to start. From figure 6.8, we can infer several training utterances:

- password reset
- reset my password
- locked account

- my account is locked
- login problem
- can't login

The process of inferring user utterances from keywords is heavily biased. No matter how clever you are, you can't help but include the words you've already seen. You are unlikely to come up with variations like "Unlock my account" or "I get an error when logging in." The latter has zero overlap with the previous keywords, as well as having a different grammatical structure. A keyword-based approach is likely to have training gaps like these. We'll explore the effects of these gaps later in this chapter.

After reviewing production logs, collecting data from a mock user interface, and interviewing SMEs, Fictitious Inc. has gathered a great set of user phrases that can become training data. Each utterance needs to be associated with a single intent to become training data for the AI. Let's look at how to find intents in data.

6.2.4   *Organizing training data into intents*

Fictitious Inc. has collected a variety of actual and potential user utterances from each of its data sources and is ready to organize them by intent. Initially, the company did top-down intent creation based on historical user needs. In this section, it will do bottom-up intent creation based on the utterances real users use.

> **Bottom-up intent discovery versus top-down**
> Discovering user needs is a critical part of the planning process. These needs will align with the intents but may not match one to one. Beware of biasing yourself when you create the intents. Try to find the intents present in the data rather than force-fitting the data into the intents.

Table 6.5 shows a sample of the utterances the company collected. Take a few minutes to review the utterances and to organize them into intents.

Table 6.5   Example utterances collected from mock user interface

reset my password	i'm locked out of my account
my account is locked	close my account
where are you located	sign up for fictitious inc rewards
what time are you open	directions to fictitious inc
store hours	i need a job
when do you close tonight	can i have a password reset
i need to open an account	i need your schedule
how many points do i have left	do you have a store downtown
can't login	is this thing on
i forgot my password and need to reset it	

Please note that there are no perfect answers. Every time I do an intent-mapping exercise like this one, I am amazed by the variations and alternatives that people come up with. I've included my mapping of these utterances in figure 6.9. Don't peek until you've at least thought about the intents.

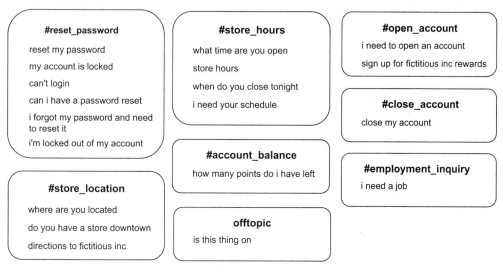

Figure 6.9 One possible organization of the utterances from table 6.5

Compare this organization with your own. What differences did you see? Here are a couple of differences I've gathered from performing this exercise with various audiences:

- *Reset password versus locked account versus login problems*—It's reasonable to define these intents as separate even if they share an answer.
- *Hours versus open/close times*—Requests for opening and closing times are different requests. I combined them because the most common hour requests are ambiguous; "store hours" and "schedule" do not fit cleanly into an open or close intent.

There's no one correct way to organize data into intents. Reasonable people can and will differ on intent definitions. The precise criteria are not so important as the fact that your whole team agrees on the definitions and that these definitions lead to satisfied users. A conversational AI trained with data in disagreement will not perform well. Whenever your team does not agree on a definition, have them work together until a consensus can be found; then train your assistant on that consensus data.

Although there are no perfect answers in the intent-mapping exercise, some mappings work less well than others. The distribution of intents generally follows a power-law distribution. You may be familiar with this idea as the Pareto Principle, or the 80/20 rule (chapter 5). The core idea as it relates to assistants is that 80% of the utterances fall into 20% of the intents. Fictitious Inc.'s data fits this pattern, as demonstrated in figure 6.10.

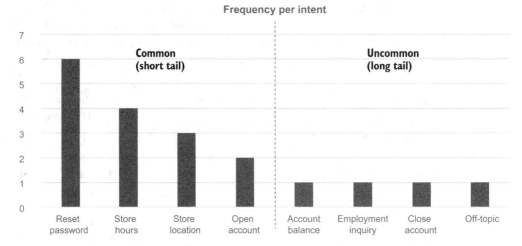

Figure 6.10   Distribution of the number of examples per intent in an intent-mapping exercise. There will be common and uncommon intents. Focus on the most common intents first.

In some literature, the common intents are called the *short tail*, and the remaining intents are the *long tail*. The sweet spot for value is to focus on the short-tail questions. In figure 6.10, the short tail covers somewhere between the first six and eight intents. Focus on training these common intents first.

> ### Exercise
> Take the conversational AI from chapter 2, export the training data, and delete all the intent labels. Then shuffle the data and organize it into intents. If you are pressed for time, feel free to use a subset of the data.
>
> When you are done, compare your intents with the original intents. The odds are that you'll have both some different intents as well as some different utterances within the intents.
>
> The larger your data set is, the more likely you are to have differences of opinion when labeling the data with intents.

6.3   *Assessing whether you have the right training data*

The quality of the training data sets an upper limit on the accuracy of an AI assistant. Fictitious Inc. should inspect the quality of its training data before training its assistant. Training data must meet three criteria to produce optimum results, and I refer to these criteria as the three Vs:

- Variety
- Volume
- Veracity

The training data is a ground truth for the model and must follow all these characteristics for the model to be successful. If your training data is missing one or more of these three Vs, your assistant will not be as accurate as it could be. These inaccuracies will lead to a poor experience for your users and increased costs to your organization.

Let's assess Fictitious Inc.'s training data against each of the Vs in turn.

6.3.1 Training data variety

An assistant should be trained on data with variety representative of what the assistant will see in production. Fictitious Inc. has a wide demographic range of customers, each of whom may phrase their requests differently. This variety should be captured in the training data; otherwise, the assistant may not recognize common phrasing patterns, which will lead to bad outcomes.

> ## A famous example of a nonrepresentative sample with negative consequences
>
> If a sample is biased, not representative of the whole, it can have disastrous consequences. One famous example is the 1948 U.S. presidential election. The *Chicago Daily Tribune*'s polls predicted a decisive victory for the Republican challenger, Thomas Dewey. Instead, incumbent Harry Truman won in a landslide. A retrospective analysis showed that the *Tribune*'s polls were done entirely over the phone; phones were not present in every household yet and were most often in wealthy Republican households (http://mng.bz/7jrV).
>
> There is extensive literature on avoiding sampling bias. Suffice it to say that you should carefully inspect your sampling process for any potential biases. A good sample has a similar distribution of characteristics as the broader population. A truly random sampling can achieve that. As demonstrated in the *Tribune* example, "random" and "convenient" are two different things. The *Tribune* surely thought it was doing random sampling.

Let's compare the variety in two data collection strategies. To keep the example simple, we'll focus on a single intent: password resets. In the first strategy, Fictitious Inc. will skimp on data collection time and ask SMEs how users ask for password resets. We'll call this data set *fabricated*. In the second strategy, the company will collect actual user utterances from production logs and a mock user interface. We'll call this data set *representative*. These two data sets are shown in table 6.6.

There is some nominal variety in the fabricated examples, but they are largely identical from the classifier's point of view. Every statement includes "my password," and almost all include "reset my password." There is almost no variety in the verbs. (Did you notice that the SME was biased by the wording in our question?)

By contrast, the representative data set has rich variety; it has twice as many unique words (23 versus 13), and each example uses a different verb. What if Fictitious Inc.

Table 6.6   Comparing what users might say with things users do say

Fabricated data set (Strategy 1)	Representative data set (Strategy 2)
I need to reset my password	I'm locked out of my account
I want to reset my password	I can't remember my login info
Password reset	I have a pw issue
How do I reset my password	I forgot my password
Help me reset my password	Reset password
Need help resetting my password	Can't get past the login screen
I forgot my password	

trained two different conversational AIs: one on the fabricated data set and one on the representative data set? Which do you think would perform better?

Try it out. There's no need to trust your intuition on this one.

I performed this experiment. I created two copies of an existing assistant and added a #reset_password intent. (Full experiment setup: I created a new skill in Watson Assistant, imported the Banking intents from the Content Catalog, and tested by using the version parameter value 2020-04-01. I added the training examples one by one in the order in which they are listed in the data table. Other AI platforms and classifiers learn at different rates.) I performed two different experiments of the new #reset_password intent, using the different data sets:

- *Experiment 1*—Train on fabricated user utterances, test on real user utterances
- *Experiment 2*—Train on representative utterances, test on fabricated utterances

The experiment results are summarized in table 6.7.

Table 6.7   Summary of experiments

Experiment	Training data	Test data	Accuracy on test data	Average confidence on test data
Experiment 1	Seven fabricated utterances	Six varied and representative utterances	33%	0.39
Experiment 2	Six varied and representative utterances	Seven fabricated utterances	100%	0.91

Table 6.7 shows the power of variety in training data and underscores the need for a good data collection exercise. (This test is a little unfair; it's easy to predict the set of fabricated utterances correctly, precisely because they have so little variety.) If Fictitious Inc. had gone to production with only its fabricated #reset_password utterances, it would have missed almost two-thirds of user password reset requests, which would have had a disastrous effect on success metrics. The assistant with fabricated data performs so poorly that it's worth exploring in detail, as shown in table 6.8.

Table 6.8 shows how little the assistant learns from fabricated data. The utterance "I forgot my password" was classified with perfect confidence because it appeared in

Table 6.8   Experiment 1: Training an assistant with fabricated training and testing on actual training data

Test utterance	Top intent	Top intent confidence	`#reset_password` Confidence
I'm locked out of my account	other	0.37	n/a
I can't remember my login info	`#reset_password`	0.13	0.13
I have a pw issue	other	0.17	0.14
I forgot my password	`#reset_password`	1.00	1.00
Reset password	`#reset_password`	0.97	0.97
Can't get past the login screen	other	0.09	0.08

both the training and test data. The remaining training phrases included the words "reset" and "password," so it is not surprising that the assistant classified "Reset password" correctly. After those two phrases, the assistant was never even close. Without being trained on varied data, the assistant has little chance of correctly predicting the intent in varied utterances.

> ## Data collection from real users can be costly but generates excellent data variety
>
> The training data collection techniques shown in this chapter can be time consuming. There is a strong temptation among AI assistant builders to skimp on data collection and have SMEs fabricate example data. Many SMEs believe that they can generate a similar sampling of training data as would be found in a data collection process. These people are well intentioned but generally wrong. The distance between their fabricated sample and the real-life distribution is proportional to the size of the accuracy problem you'll have using their data.
>
> If you cannot find good training data, you can start with fabricated data and the insight of your SMEs, but make sure to set aside time in the near future to improve the variety in your training data. Keep track of which training samples are from actual users and which examples are fabricated. Over the life of the assistant, you should remove most of the fabricated examples and replace them with actual user examples.

Variety is clearly important to an accurate assistant. Fictitious Inc.'s assistant worked much better when trained with a variety of data

6.3.2   Training data volume

All classifiers require a volume of training data to train successfully. Given the nearly infinite ways that natural language can express an intent (in conversational assistants) or a classification (in event classifiers), we should not expect a classifier to be able to extrapolate all of them from one or two examples. How many training examples will Fictitious Inc. need?

Commercial AI platforms vary in their recommendations, but they generally work best with ten or more examples per intent. (AI platforms make differing recommendations on the specific data volume you need to train your assistant. Training data volume requirements have steadily decreased as platform builders have improved their algorithms.) The sample and built-in intents from commercial platforms are often trained on many more examples. The sample code used in chapter 2 was based on Watson Assistant's Content Catalog, which included 20 examples per intent.

In section 6.3.1, we saw how increasing the variety of training data affected the accuracy of the assistant. We can see how training data volume affects the assistant by running the same experiment in multiple iterations, starting with one piece of training data and adding one training in each successive iteration. The training data volume effect is shown in figure 6.11.

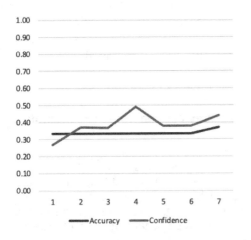

1. Accuracy and confidence are almost completely unaffected by training data that has volume but not variety.

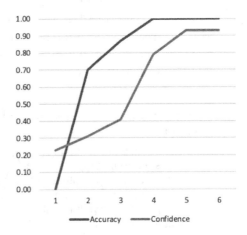

2. Accuracy and confidence increase, then plateau, when training data increases in volume and variety.

Figure 6.11   Accuracy on the #reset_password intent, based on the volume of training data. Diagram 1 uses a fabricated training set with little variety. Diagram 2 uses a training set with high variety.

Figure 6.11 shows that training data volume does not always have a significant impact on accuracy:

- In diagram 1, the training data had little variety. Each new piece of training data contributed little variety and thus had little impact on the assistant's performance.
- In diagram 2, the training data had high variety. Each new piece of training data added significant variety, and the assistant learned from every example. (The shape of the accuracy curve in this experiment is affected by the order in which the examples were added. When the first and only training example was

"reset password," the fabricated test set was predicted with 100% accuracy and 76% confidence. This example underscores how important it is for the training data variety to be similar to the test set variety.)

Figure 6.11 shows that training data volume is a means to an end. Artificially inflating training data size by adding many similar examples does not help the assistant. This experiment shows that a small volume of varied examples can outperform a large volume of nonvaried examples.

The most important part of training data volume is getting a high-enough volume to cover the variety you expect the assistant to encounter and so that patterns can emerge. Training generally improves with more examples (as long as they follow the other two Vs: variety and veracity).

Can different intents have different training volumes?

Yes. As shown in this chapter, capturing the right variety is more important than hitting a specific volume target. Some intents will have good variety with fewer examples than other intents.

Still, it's good to have approximate volume balance across your intents, meaning a similar number of examples for each intent. Each training example creates some gravity toward that intent. An intent with several times more examples than the average per intent will have too much gravity, causing overselection of that intent. Similarly, an intent with far fewer examples than average is likely to be underselected.

An intent with too many examples will have a large positive bias and cause a large negative bias in every other intent. The mathematics are outlined in chapter 11. In short, the number of examples in a given intent influences the positive bias toward that intent. For a selected intent, the number of examples in every other intent influences the negative bias toward the selected intent.

We've seen that training data variety and volume are both important drivers of accuracy. Let's look at the final V: veracity.

6.3.3 Training data veracity

Veracity derives from the Latin word *verax*, meaning *true*. You may have heard the phrase "Garbage in, garbage out." This phrase certainly applies to training data. The AI assistant learns directly from training data. If that data is not true (not correct), the assistant will not learn the right lessons from the training data.

An important aspect of veracity is that the training data is unambiguous. Every training data sample should match to one intent—no more and no fewer. The `#reset_password` utterances were all completely unambiguous in intent. Let's examine some ambiguous utterances from the production logs. These utterances are as follows:

- Account
- Oh, I'm so glad to talk to someone, I need to reset my password
- I need to reset my password and verify my points balance

Each of these utterances suffers from some ambiguity. Let's see whether and how we can use these statements when training an assistant.

AMBIGUITY: NO INTENT MATCHED

If a Fictitious Inc. user started their conversation with the single word "account," what should the assistant do? The user may ultimately want to open an account, close their account, modify the account, or check their account balance. There's no way to know which of these things they want to do based on the utterance alone. The first type of ambiguity is a statement that does not match any intent at all. This type of statement cannot be used as a training example for any intent because no intent can be inferred from the statement by itself.

Though the utterance "account" cannot be used as training data, we can create and use variations of that utterance that unambiguously indicate a single intent, as shown in table 6.9.

Table 6.9 How an assistant should treat short utterances

Ambiguous (handle at run time)	Unambiguous (use in training)
Account	Open account
	Close my account
	Account balance

Users will ask ambiguous questions. Ambiguity should be handled at run time, not during training. At run time, your assistant can respond to ambiguity by asking a disambiguation question. If the user says "account," the assistant can disambiguate by asking "What type of account service do you need?" An assistant is most accurate when it is trained on unambiguous examples. This training will help it deal with ambiguity at run time. You should not train with statements that don't clearly identify an intent and should instead let a disambiguation flow clarify them. (This approach is brilliantly explained in "Best Practices for Building a Natural Language Classifier," by Cari Jacobs, at http://mng.bz/myey.)

Do users really use one-word utterances?

Yes. These utterances are surprisingly common. Users are familiar with keyword-based automated telephone systems, in which a single word may advance you to the next menu option. In text-based AI assistants, some users treat the dialogue input like a search query box. Single-word utterances are often ambiguous.

AMBIGUITY: ONE INTENT MATCHED (LOOSELY)

The second ambiguous example was "Oh, I'm so glad to talk to someone, I need to reset my password." At first, this request seems like an unambiguous password reset request. But this statement has a lot of filler that does not contribute to the intent. It would be equally common to see an utterance "Oh, I'm so glad to talk to someone, I need to check my points balance" or "Oh, I'm so glad to talk to someone, I need to close my account." The opening "Oh, I'm so glad to talk to someone" provides no contextual information to the assistant.

Filler adds ambiguity and should be omitted from training data. The classifier in the assistant learns from every word in the training data, so precision is important.

> ## Sources of filler
> You are especially likely to find extraneous content in transcripts from human-to-human interactions. Humans are social creatures; we can't help ourselves. When training a conversational assistant, remove filler from the training data.

Fictitious Inc. can remove the filler before using these utterances to train its assistant. The modified ambiguous and unambiguous statements are shown in table 6.10.

Table 6.10   How an assistant should treat verbose utterances

Ambiguous (handle at run time)	Unambiguous (use in training)
Oh, I'm so glad to talk to someone, I need to reset my password	I need to reset my password
Oh, I'm so glad to talk to someone, I need to check my points balance	I need to check my points balance

Arguably, the segment "I need to" has some ambiguity, as it could be part of an utterance in multiple intents. "I need to" or even "I need" could be removed from the training examples, as long as you are consistent and remove them from every intent. I prefer to keep those phrases because different intents can have different levels of urgency.

AMBIGUITY: MULTIPLE INTENT MATCHED

The utterance "I need to reset my password and verify my points balance" demonstrated the last form of ambiguity: when an utterance truly matches multiple intents. This user utterance describes two intents: #reset_password and #check_balance. Users may ask your AI assistant such compound questions, but the training phase generally is not the correct place to handle them.

The best way to use a compound utterance in your training data is to split it into two component utterances. The utterance "I need to reset my password and verify my points balance" can become "I need to reset my password" and "I need to verify my points balance," each of which is an unambiguous example for their respective intent. These unambiguous new examples are suitable for training the assistant. Compound

My AI platform lets me train on compound questions. Why shouldn't I?

Some platforms allow you to train compound classes like #reset_password_and_check_balance, but this solution generally is not scalable.

The first problem is that the new compound classes are going to be similar to each other as well as to the component classes.

The second problem is that the number of possible compound intents grows exponentially with the number of component intents. Providing enough training data for compound intents generally is a nonstarter.

statements are too ambiguous for training; break them up unambiguous training examples (table 6.11).

Table 6.11   Comparing ambiguous and unambiguous utterances

Ambiguous (handle at run time)	Unambiguous (use in training)
I need to reset my password and verify my points balance	I need to reset my password I need to verify my points balance

VERACITY SUMMARY

The training data for AI should always have veracity. Every piece of training data should unambiguously match one intent. Unambiguous training data provides clear patterns for your assistant to learn from. Users may ask an assistant ambiguous questions, but the correct way to handle ambiguity is at run time. You can always deal with an ambiguous user utterance by asking a follow-up clarifying question.

NOTE   If you cannot identify the right intent for an utterance in fewer than 15 seconds, that utterance is too ambiguous for use as training data.

Summary

- An assistant is trained by example, not programmed. The assistant is shown utterances that match each intent and then infers patterns from that data during the training process.
- Training data should be collected from a source as close as possible to the AI assistant. The best data source is production logs, which provide actual and representative user phrasing; the least accurate source is expert intuition.
- Training data must include a variety representative of actual user data. Getting the right variety of data is more important than creating a large volume of training data.
- Training data must be unambiguously correct.

How accurate is your assistant? 7

This chapter covers

- Collecting test data for your assistant
- Assessing the accuracy of your assistant
- Selecting the best accuracy metric(s) to use for your assistant

AI assistants make predictions based on the way they are trained. How can you tell whether this training is working well? You shouldn't release an assistant into the wild if you don't know how well it works. You need to be able to tell whether you are making the assistant smarter or dumber when you change the way you train it.

Fictitious Inc. wants to assess what the conversational AI assistant's accuracy will be when it goes into production. The best way to test an assistant's accuracy is to see how well it predicts intents in production, which poses an interesting conundrum. The company doesn't want to go to production without reasonable accuracy, but it won't know the assistant's true accuracy until it is in production.

The best way to handle this conundrum is to train and test your assistant iteratively, as shown in figure 7.1. The virtuous cycle (gather data, train, test, and improve) provides a repeatable methodology to build and improve your AI assistant.

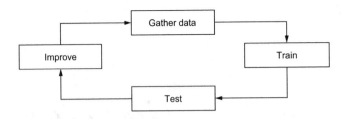

Figure 7.1 **The virtuous cycle of testing how accurate your assistant is**

It's OK for Fictitious Inc. to start with imperfect data because the data can be continually improved. You have to start somewhere!

In chapter 6, I covered how to gather data and train your assistant. In this chapter, I walk through how to test your assistant's accuracy. An accuracy test should tell you not only how accurate your assistant is, but also where and why it is inaccurate, including showing any error patterns. This chapter gives you the tools to assess your assistant's accuracy so that you understand its strengths and weaknesses. This information helps you identify focal points for improvement.

7.1 Testing an AI assistant for accuracy

An AI assistant session starts with user input. The assistant classifies that input, decides the appropriate response action, and responds to the input. The user may respond to the system, starting the cycle anew. Figure 7.2 shows how execution flows in an AI assistant.

Figure 7.2 Execution flow in an AI assistant

Figure 7.3 depicts an annotated conversation. A user may say, "I'm locked out of my account," and the assistant will classify this utterance to the #reset_password intent. The assistant uses the intent to select a dialogue response. The entire conversation cycle needs to be tested. In this chapter, we will focus entirely on testing the classification process so that we can determine how accurate the assistant is.

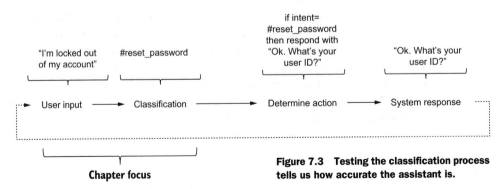

Figure 7.3 Testing the classification process tells us how accurate the assistant is.

Let's first define accuracy. The simplest definition of accuracy is the ratio of correct predictions to total predictions:

```
accuracy = correct predictions / total predictions
```

When the assistant classifies the utterance "I'm locked out of my account" as a `#reset_password` intent, it is correct. When the assistant classifies the utterance "Where can I apply for a job?" as the `#store_location` intent, it is incorrect.

Accuracy is an equation of right and wrong. The assistant is right when it predicts the correct intent for a user utterance and is wrong when it predicts an incorrect intent for a user utterance.

Fictitious Inc. wants a detailed picture of the assistant's accuracy. It wants to know which parts of the assistant work well and which parts do not work well, assumes that some intents will be more accurate than others, wants to be able to find intents with major accuracy problems so that they can be fixed, and wants specific insights into any accuracy problems that are found. The following sections explore how to test the accuracy of the assistant.

7.1.1 Testing a single utterance

The accuracy of a conversational AI can be tested one utterance at a time. Some AI providers let you access the classifier independently of the dialogue engine, and some do not. The classifier can be tested independently of the rest of the assistant, even if the classification is coupled to the dialogue, by looking only at the classification and ignoring the dialogue. (Some of the major platforms bundle these two functions together, especially those with a "low-code" model. Other platforms keep these functions separate. Your platform's API documentation will tell you whether these functions are bundled or separate.) In figure 7.4, a testing interface shows how the assistant classifies the utterance "What time are you open?"

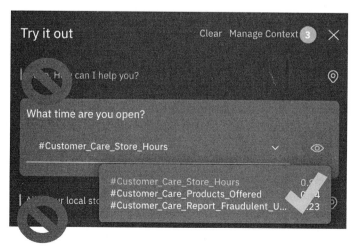

Test classification accuracy by inspecting the intent and ignoring the dialogue response.

Figure 7.4 If your AI platform couples the classification and dialogue response, you can still test the classifier manually by ignoring the dialogue response.

Fictitious Inc. can test the classifier manually in a testing interface, testing one utterance at a time. This approach is fine for quick tests, but the company can expect to test thousands of utterances over the life of the assistant and will want to automate these tests by using an API.

Every AI platform I surveyed for this book exposes an API for testing the assistant's classifier. The API requires an utterance for input and provides an intent as output. Depending on your platform, you may need to provide additional configuration parameters, such as username, password, or version. The next listing demonstrates an exemplary API call.

Listing 7.1 Using an API to test the classification of "What time are you open?"

```
curl -X POST -u "{your_username}:{your_password}" --header "Content-
    Type:application/json" --data "{\"input\": {\"text\": \"What time are
    you open?\"}}" "{your_url}/message?version=2020-04-01"
```

The input and output from this API call are shown in figure 7.5.

API Input
Provide the <u>utterance</u>.

```
{
  "input": {
    "text": "What time are you open?"
  }
}
```

API Output
Extract the <u>intent</u>.

```
{
  "input": {
    "text": "What time are you open?"
  },
  "intents": [
    {
      "intent": "Customer_Care_Store_Hours",
      "confidence": 0.9874794483184814
    }
  ],
  "entities": [],
  "output": {
    "text": [
      "All of our local stores are open from 9am to 9pm."
    ]
  }
}
```

Figure 7.5 Using an API to test a classifier one utterance at a time

Your platform may provide a software development kit (SDK), which makes it easier to interact with its classification APIs. If the platform doesn't provide an SDK, you can write your own scripts to interact with these APIs. Having code that calls the classification API is the first step in automating classification tests. The second step is calling the API in a repeatable fashion. Fictitious Inc. created a shell script, classify.sh, to make a single classification call. The contents of this script are highly dependent on the AI platform, but the script should do the following:

1 Take two input parameters: an utterance and its expected intent.
2 Initialize a connection to the AI assistant.
3 Call the assistant's classification API to classify the utterance.

4 Extract the predicted intent, and compare the predicted intent with the expected intent.

5 Output four parameters: the utterance, the expected intent, the predicted intent, and the correctness of the predicted intent.

The desired output from this script is shown in table 7.1. The four pieces of information in the table form the basis of all accuracy measurements for the AI assistant.

Table 7.1 Example output format for an automated classification test

Utterance	Actual intent	Predicted intent	Prediction assessment
What time do you open?	`#store_hours`	`#store_hours`	Correct

Fictitious Inc. can get some specific insights by testing one utterance at a time. This approach is a great stepping stone to achieving accuracy testing goals. Testing one utterance at a time is not a scalable solution, but it helps automate accuracy testing.

7.1.2 Testing multiple utterances

Fictitious Inc. wants to find patterns of errors. To do so, it needs to test many utterances at the same time. Now that the company has automated a process to test a single utterance, it can expand that process to test multiple utterances—that is, it can revise the classify.sh script to test multiple utterances at a time by essentially inserting a for loop into the script. The pseudocode of this script takes the following steps:

1 Take one input: a comma-separated-values (CSV) file with two columns, each row containing an utterance and its expected intent.

2 Initialize a connection to the AI assistant.

3 For every row in the CSV file, call the assistant's classification API to classify the utterance; extract the predicted intent and compare the predicted intent with the expected intent; and output the utterance, the expected intent, the predicted intent, and the correctness of the predicted intent.

With this new script, Fictitious Inc. can run an accuracy test on an entire spreadsheet's worth of data at the same time. For the first multiple utterance test, the company creates an input file with four rows, each row with an utterance and its intent, and passes this file to this new script. The output from the script is shown in table 7.2.

Table 7.2 Testing four utterances in a single test with an automated script

Utterance	Actual intent	Predicted intent	Prediction assessment
I'm locked out of my account	`#reset_password`	`#reset_password`	Correct
Where is the Elm store?	`#store_location`	`#store_location`	Correct

Table 7.2 Testing four utterances in a single test with an automated script *(continued)*

Utterance	Actual intent	Predicted intent	Prediction assessment
Can I get a job?	#employment_inquiry	#employment_inquiry	Correct
Where can I apply for a job?	#employment_inquiry	#store_location	Incorrect

The ability to test a batch of utterances at the same time is more useful for assessing the assistant's accuracy than testing one utterance at a time. By reading this tabular report, you can extract the following insights:

- The assistant was 75% accurate in this small test.
- The assistant never made a mistake on #reset_password.
- When the correct answer was #store_location, the assistant did not make any mistakes.
- When the correct answer was #employment_inquiry, the assistant seemed to be confused, sometimes correctly selecting #employment_inquiry and sometimes incorrectly selecting #store_location.

Perhaps the most useful insight from this data is the potential confusion between #employment_inquiry and #store_location. For AI assistants, *confusion* is defined as a pattern of errors between a group of two or more intents. Knowing that the assistant is 75% accurate in this test is interesting, but knowing the source of the errors is actionable. When Fictitious Inc. improves the assistant, it needs to address the biggest sources of confusion first. By reading the result data carefully, the company can extract useful insights, including potential confusion, which gets increasingly difficult as the test gets larger. More test samples will add more rows to the table. The number of potential confusions explodes as more intents are added. Because any pair of intents can be confused, the number of potential confusions is proportional to the square of the number of intents. Fortunately, one method of visualizing confusion is even easier to read than a table: a confusion matrix. A *confusion matrix* is a grid with the following characteristics:

- The first dimension lists the correct intents.
- The second dimension lists the predicted intents.
- Each square in the grid is the number of times the correct and predicted intent combination occurred.
- Any number off the main diagonal represents confusion.

Optionally, the squares are color-coded such that the opacity matches the relative frequency of that occurrence, which makes the sources of confusion easier to spot. Figure 7.6 shows an initial confusion matrix.

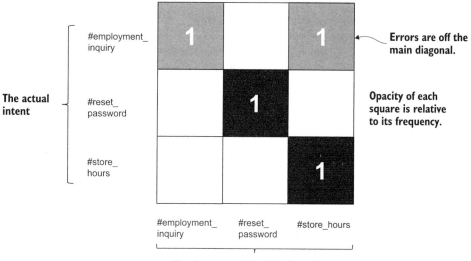

Figure 7.6   A confusion matrix visualizes accuracy testing results.

With the confusion matrix, insights jump right off the page. The matrix is easily scannable. Most of the color opacity is on the main diagonal, and it's easy to find the intent pair with confusion.

Fictitious Inc. can now test multiple utterances, create a table of the test results, and visualize the results with a confusion matrix. These tools are foundational in the quest to assess the accuracy of the assistant. This first test data set included only four utterances, which are not nearly enough to give a reliable estimate of the assistant's accuracy. The company needs to build a good test data set so that it can understand how accurate the assistant will be when it is deployed to production.

7.1.3   Selecting a test data set

The most useful data set for testing an assistant is data from that assistant in production. With production data, you can extract a set of data that has both volume and variety representative of what the assistant receives.

Fictitious Inc. has not yet gone to production and can only simulate a production test using data that it thinks will be representative of production data. The accuracy from this test will be as predictive of their eventual production performance as synthetic data is reflective of the eventual production data. (Both the training data and test data sets should evolve over time. Data from production will be introduced into the training and test data sets.) Collecting good test data is as important as collecting good training data.

The true test of classifier accuracy is how well it classifies data it was not trained on. A classifier requires two data sets: a training data set and a test data set. Fortunately, these data sets can be drawn from the same source with the same methodology.

Can the test data overlap the training data?

Some overlap in the two data sets is OK, but it is best if you can minimize the overlap. One of the most important outcomes from a blind test is understanding how well it classifies data it was not trained on. (We can generally assume that it will classify training data well.)

One notable exception is voice-driven conversational assistants. In these assistants, many user utterances are short (possibly one word), because users are frequently terse with automated voice assistants. Such an assistant is likely to include the most common short phrases in both training and test sets.

Fictitious Inc.'s first test used only four utterances, of which the assistant predicted three correct intents. Can we assume that the assistant is 75% accurate? Probably not. The assistant has 18 intents, most of which were not included in the test. With only four pieces of test data, we cannot make strong assumptions about the assistant's accuracy.

In production, the assistant might be 95% accurate or 20%. Because of the small test set size, we cannot rule out either score. The more representative test data is added, the more likely the accuracy score will be to reflect production accuracy. At the very least, the company needs to add test data for each intent. Figure 7.7 demonstrates the trustworthiness of a test's accuracy score based on a volume of representative data.

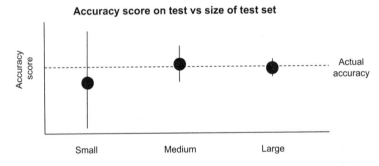

Accuracy score on test vs size of test set

1. The accuracy score from a small test may vary significantly from the true accuracy, especially in case of sampling bias.

2. A large test set with representative variety gives an accuracy score close to the actual accuracy.

Figure 7.7   Assuming representative variety in the test set, the larger the test set, the more precise the accuracy score is. This plot shows accuracy scores for three test sets and a confidence interval for each score.

To measure how accurate an assistant will be when it goes to production, we need to test on data that it will see in production. Having enough test data volume is critical. Figure 7.7 showed us how test data volume affects the trustworthiness of the test score. Because test data can be gathered the same way as training data, we can gather one set of data and divide it into two sets.

In a perfect world, the test data set would be much larger than the training set or at least equal in size. Assuming that the test data set is representative of the data the assistant will encounter in production, the larger the test data set is, the more confident you can feel in the test results. Small test sets are susceptible to sampling bias. Figure 7.8 demonstrates the trade-off between relative test set and training set sizes. (A common practice for machine learning is to put 80% of your data into the training set and 20% into your test set—a good compromise for typical data volumes.)

Excellent. The large volume of test data will give precise results.

Good. The test data has as much variation as the training data.

Fair. Minimal test variety means the results may not reflect reality.

Uh-oh. How can you know how the classifier will perform?

Figure 7.8   The more test data you have, the less likely the test data set is to be susceptible to sampling bias, and the more you can trust the results from an accuracy test. You can create a test set by holding out examples from the training set and moving them to a test set.

Most AI builders, however, struggle to find enough data for the training set alone. A good heuristic for training data volume is to have 10 to 12 examples per intent. Fictitious Inc.'s assistant has 18 intents, which requires at least 180 training data samples. An equivalent test data set would have another 180 data samples, bringing the total to 360 data samples (20 per intent). Ideally, none of these examples should be fabricated; all should be collected from users or production logs. Most initial data collection exercises don't achieve this volume. Having 20 representative, nonfabricated examples per intent is a lot for creating a new conversational AI.

> **NOTE**   Data is king when you're testing your assistant. The quality of your test data set directly influences how much you can trust your accuracy measurement.

You can trust the accuracy score from an accuracy test only if the test data is representative of the eventual production data. In figure 7.9, I've plotted several examples of `#reset_password` utterances, organized by similarity. If Fictitious Inc. runs an accuracy test based on the examples in Box 1, the results from the test will not be informative. The examples in Box 1 are clumped together with minimal variety and do not represent production variety. By contrast, the examples in Box 2 capture a wide variety. Box 2 is representative of all the ways users will ask for their passwords to be reset.

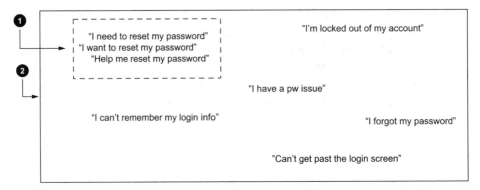

Figure 7.9   A synthetic test set (Box 1) may not capture the full range of variety from users (Box 2). Accuracy scores based on nonrepresentative variety will be misleading.

An accuracy test based on data in Box 2 will be much more useful than a test based on Box 1 data because it will more precisely reflect the assistant's true accuracy.

We can start with an imperfect test set and expand it over time. The first time we build a conversational AI assistant, we may not have a large test set when we first try to assess the assistant's accuracy. Even if we are not able to build a dedicated test set right away, we will still be able to test the assistant for patterns of confusion. Let's explore the testing methodologies we can use.

7.2   Comparing testing methodologies

Fictitious Inc. has two testing goals:

- Estimate how accurate their assistant will be in production as precisely as possible.
- Find the most common sources of confusion in the assistant, showing the most common patterns of errors.

The company has two test methodologies they can use, depending on the volume of test data:

- *Blind test*—Hold out a subset of the available data for use as a test set. The assistant is never trained with the test set data; the test data is used only for testing. Accuracy comes from how many correct predictions are made on the test set.
- *k-folds cross-validation test*—Have no dedicated test data set; have only the training data set. Train *k* temporary assistants, and for each one, hold out a different subset of data for a test set. Accuracy comes from averaging the results from each of the multiple classifiers.

Blind test results are predictive of production accuracy and show where the assistant is truly confused. A *k*-folds test can tell only where an assistant is probably confused and cannot be used to predict production accuracy. The simplest decision on which test to use is based on the volume of available test data, as depicted in figure 7.10.

The best case is that Fictitious Inc. has enough testing data to run a blind test. With the blind test, the company can achieve both testing goals. If insufficient data is

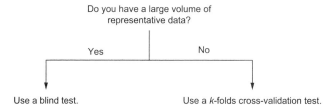

Figure 7.10 The volume of representative test data you have helps you select the test methodology to use.

available, the *k*-folds test is a backup plan. Finding probable confusion sources is a useful step in accuracy evaluation. The following sections explore these testing methods.

7.2.1 Blind testing

A *blind test* uses blind data, which means that the classifier did not see that data during the assistant's training. We can generally assume that the volume of training data is significantly smaller than the number of input variations the assistant will see in production and infer that most of the data the assistant encounters will not have been included in training. A blind test is valuable specifically because it shows how well the assistant predicts data it has not been explicitly trained on.

A blind test follows a few simple steps for each utterance in the test data:

1. Get the classifier's predicted intent for the utterance.
2. Get the actual intent for the utterance (sometimes called the *golden intent*).
3. Compare the predicted and actual intents to score the assistant.

Fictitious Inc. first trained a new intent when it added a #reset_password intent to an assistant populated with several intents from a sample data catalog. The assistant was accurate in predicting each of the sample intents, which let the company isolate the effect of training a single new intent.

The #reset_password intent was based on synthetic data. The company asked how users might ask to have their passwords reset and recorded several example statements for use in a training data set. A little later, some example #reset_password utterances from other data sources were used as a test set. The training and test data sets for #reset_password are shown in table 7.3. The company fabricated a training set based on intuition and then tested it against data collected from actual users.

Table 7.3 The data sets used in a first attempt at the `#reset_password` intent

Training set (fabricated)	Test set (from production logs)
I need to reset my password	Reset password
I want to reset my password	I'm locked out of my account
Password reset	I can't remember my login info
How do I reset my password	I have a pw issue
Help me reset my password	I forgot my password
Need help resetting my password	Can't get past the login screen
I forgot my password	

Fictitious Inc. trained the assistant by adding the new #reset_password data from the first column in table 7.3 and then ran a blind test using only the data in the second column. This test was useful for determining the accuracy of their #reset_password intent. After the assistant was trained, the company tested it on each utterance in the test set and then calculated how many times the correct intent was predicted. In that test, only two of the six test data were predicted correctly, yielding 33.3% accuracy. Table 7.4 gives details for this first blind test.

Table 7.4   Blind test results

Utterance	Top intent	Confidence	Assessment
I'm locked out of my account	other	0.37	Incorrect
I can't remember my login info	#reset_password	0.13	Incorrect (confidence is too low)
I have a pw issue	other	0.17	Incorrect
I forgot my password	#reset_password	1.00	Correct (was also part of the training data)
Reset password	#reset_password	0.97	Correct
Can't get past the login screen	other	0.09	Incorrect

The results offer several insights, leading to the conclusion that the #reset_password training data variety and volume are insufficient:

- The 33.3% accuracy tells us that the assistant is not accurate in identifying password reset requests.
- All the utterances that do not include the word *password* are classified incorrectly, which tells us that the training data needs more variety.
- The overall low confidence of the predictions (except those containing the word *password*) suggest that the training data needs more volume.
- Only one utterance that did not overlap with the training data was predicted correctly—another signal that the training data volume and variety are insufficient.

This blind test was small. The assistant was trained on many intents, but only one of those intents was tested, which demonstrates how the training process affects a single intent. For most blind tests, we prefer to look at all the intents at the same time.

Let's look at another blind test. For simplicity, the assistant is restricted to five intents: #appointments, #employment_inquiry, #reset_password, #store_hours, and #store_location. This test uses training and test sets of equal size: 50 total training utterances and 50 total test utterances.

Re-create this blind test

You can re-create this blind test by following these steps:

1. Load the chapter 2 demo code into Watson Assistant.
2. Remove all but five of the intents.
3. Export the training data into a CSV file.
4. Remove the rest of the intents from the assistant.
5. Split the CSV file into two equal parts, one for training and one for testing, each with 10 examples of each of the five intents.
6. Import the training data back into Watson Assistant.
7. Test the assistant, using the test data set.

This test scenario is ideal; the training data volume was adequate (10 examples per intent), and the test data was as large as the training data, suggesting that any insight from the blind test will be instructive as to how the assistant will perform in production. Because the test data has 50 rows, only the summary metrics from the blind test are shown in table 7.5.

Table 7.5   Accuracy metrics for each of the intents in the blind test

Intent	Accuracy score
#appointments	0.78
#employment_inquiry	0.89
#reset_password	0.90
#store_hours	0.89
#store_location	0.7
Total	0.82

The first thing we see in table 7.5 is overall accuracy; the assistant is 82% accurate in this test. (The individual intents are technically using an F1 score. For the sake of this exercise, you can think of the score as accuracy.) Further, three of the intents are quite high-performing, with accuracy of 89% or 90%. Overall accuracy is brought down by the performance of the #store_location intent, with 70% accuracy, and the #appointments intent, with 78% accuracy. Fictitious Inc. will want to investigate this intent first. The fastest way is to review the confusion matrix from this test, shown in figure 7.11.

The confusion matrix in figure 7.11 immediately shows some error patterns. Almost every error by the assistant is found in the #appointments and #store_location columns, meaning that the assistant is overpredicting these intents. Four of the errors occurred when #appointments was predicted, and three of the errors occurred when #store_location was predicted. This result suggests what went wrong in the test, but

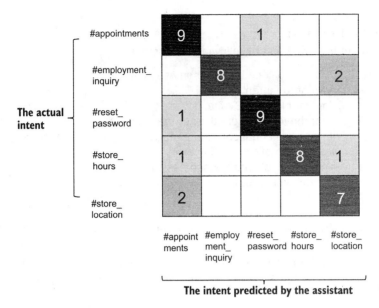

The actual intent — #appointments, #employment_inquiry, #reset_password, #store_hours, #store_location

The intent predicted by the assistant — #appointments, #employment_inquiry, #reset_password, #store_hours, #store_location

Figure 7.11 Blind-test confusion matrix, given five intents with an equal volume of training and test data

we don't have to guess. With table 7.6, we can inspect all nine errors from the blind test to search for additional insights.

Table 7.6 Errors made by the assistant in a blind test

Utterance	Actual intent	Predicted intent
Want to change my visit	`#appointments`	`#reset_password`
Where is your careers page?	`#employment_inquiry`	`#store_location`
Hire me please	`#employment_inquiry`	`#store_location`
I have had the same pin used to contact telephone customer support for a long time and would like to change it. Could you please help me to set this up?	`#reset_password`	`#appointments`
What are the business hours of the store nearest to me?	`#store_hours`	`#store_location`
At what hour can I swing by?	`#store_hours`	`#appointments`
I need help with find a store.	`#store_location`	`#appointments`
Restaurants nearby please	`#store_location`	`(no intent)`
I want to know about a store.	`#store_location`	`#appointments`

Fictitious Inc. achieved both of its accuracy testing goals. For these five intents, the assistant will have approximately 82% accuracy. Further, the bulk of their problems come from two of the intents. Reviewing these two intents is an actionable next step to improve the assistant. These testing goals were achieved only because there was enough data to create a test set and that test set was representative of production variety.

> ### Blind tests are only useful on representative data
>
> Any insight from a blind test is actionable when the test data comes from people using the assistant. Running a blind test on fabricated user utterances may be a waste of time (garbage in, garbage out). It is unlikely that your fabricated user utterances will resemble the distribution of actual utterances in production.
>
> The most valuable outcome from a blind test is understanding how your assistant performs against real user input.

A blind test gives you the best understanding of how accurate your assistant will be, particularly when you use production data in the test set. Because Fictitious Inc. is not in production, what will it do if it doesn't have enough data for a blind test? It can use a *k*-folds cross-validation test.

7.2.2 *k-folds cross-validation test*

A *k-folds cross-validation test* is an alternative way to simulate how an assistant may perform in production. If Fictitious Inc. did not have production data to do a real blind test, it could still examine the assistant with a *k*-folds cross-validation test. As with all simulations, there is a probability that findings will not be representative of the reality the assistant will see in production. *k*-folds testing is best suited to assessing how confusing the assistant's training data is. This estimate of confusion can be used to hypothesize whether the assistant will be confused in production as well.

k-folds testing shuffles all the training data into *k* separate segments. Every piece of training data appears in one of the *k* test sets and in *k*-1 train sets. For each of the *k* folds, a different segment is held out as a test data set, and the other *k*-1 segments are used to train a temporary assistant. In each fold, a blind test is executed on a temporary assistant. The *k*-folds result is the aggregated result of the *k* blind tests. Figure 7.12 demonstrates a *k*-folds test with *k*=5.

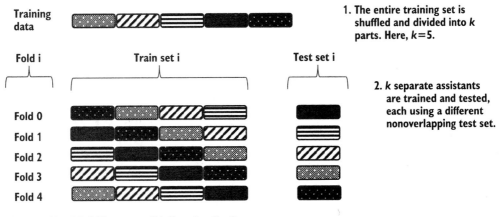

Figure 7.12 A k-folds cross-validation visualization

Why is it called k-folds?

The *k*-folds name comes from two concepts. The first part is *k*, and *k* is a number. I usually use *k*=3 or *k*=5 or *k*=10. The second part is *folds*, referring to an arrangement of data. When you apply *k*-folds to your training data, you are creating *k* arrangements of your training data.

If you're good at origami, maybe you could put your training data on paper and fold it *k* ways.

Let's explore a *k*-folds test with a small volume of data. Table 7.7 demonstrates a *k*=3 *k*-folds test with six utterances and two expected intents. In each fold, the assistant is trained on four utterances and tested on two utterances. The *k*-folds test shows many errors.

Table 7.7   *k*-folds test detailed results on a tiny training set

Data #	Utterance	Actual intent	Fold 0	Fold 1	Fold 2	Predicted intent
0	Locked out of my account	#reset_password	Test	Train	Train	No intent predicted
1	Can you help me reset my password	#reset_password	Test	Train	Train	#employment_inquiry
2	I need to log in and I can't	#reset_password	Train	Test	Train	#employment_inquiry
3	Help me apply for a job	#employment_inquiry	Train	Test	Train	#employment_inquiry
4	I need a job application	#employment_inquiry	Train	Train	Test	#employment_inquiry
5	Can I work for you	#employment_inquiry	Train	Train	Test	#reset_password

The total *k*-folds score in table 7.7 is 33.3%, with #reset_password scoring at 0. The specific errors have reasonable explanations:

- In Fold 0, #reset_password had only one example to #employment_inquiry's three.
- In Fold 2, #employment_inquiry had only one example to #reset_password's three.
- Data 0 has no overlap with any other word in the training data. When Data 0 is blind data, the assistant has no patterns to match against. This prediction is wrong; an intent should have been found but wasn't.

- Data 1 has overlapping words and phrases ("can," "you," "help me") in `#employment_inquiry`, and no overlap to `#reset_password`. Data 2 has the same problem with "**I need.**" These predictions are confused; an intent was selected, but it was **the wrong intent.**

- Data 5 has a similar **problem, but in reverse;** "can" and "you" are more indicative of `#reset_password` **in this small training set.** This prediction is also confused.

NOTE Critical thinking exercise: Can you explain why the *k*-folds test got Data 3 and Data 4 correct?

The *k*-folds results can also **be plotted in a confusion matrix, as shown in figure 7.13.

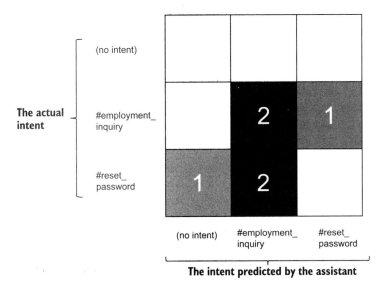

Figure 7.13 Confusion matrix **for a small *k*-folds test. The main diagonal is** almost empty, suggesting **that the assistant is highly confused.**

This *k*-folds test shows more **confusion between the intents than accurate predictions.** (Three predictions were **confused; two were correct.)** This poor performance is ultimately caused by the tiny volume of training data, but let's pretend for a minute we didn't know that. When there is such high confusion between intents, the intents and the training data should **be reviewed.**

Reasoning about individual *k*-folds results

One interesting challenge with *k*-folds is that many AI platforms perfectly remember their training data. In this case, if the training data includes "unlock my account" (as `#reset_password` intent), the assistant will not only predict that "unlock my account" has the intent `#reset_password`; it will also predict `#reset_password` with 100% confidence.

(continued)
In other words, your *k*-folds results may show the wrong intent predicted for "unlock my account." The synthetic assistant created by the fold won't have that example, but your real assistant will. The real assistant will not only predict "unlock my account" correctly, but also may predict variations of that phrase correctly ("unlock my online account," "help me unlock my account," "can my account be unlocked?"). Reasoning about *k*-folds results is tricky!

First, we should confirm that the intent definitions are not overlapping. If the intent definitions themselves overlap, the solution may be to revise the intent definitions themselves. In Fictitious Inc.'s case, there is no overlap between the concepts of resetting a password and applying for a job.

Second, the training data should be evaluated against the three Vs: variety, volume, and veracity. The six-example training data set is evaluated in table 7.8.

Table 7.8 Evaluating small training data set against the three Vs

V	`#reset_password`	`#employment_inquiry`
Variety	*Excellent*—Wide variety in the training samples, with little overlap in keywords	*Good*—Includes multiple verbs. Important words "job" and "apply" are repeated.
Volume	*Poor*—Well below the recommended 10 examples per intent	*Poor*—Well below the recommended 10 examples per intent
Veracity	*Excellent*—Each is a clear example of the intent.	*Excellent*—Each is a clear example of the intent.

This detailed evaluation of *k*-folds results is important. If we had looked only at the summary and seen the 0 score for #reset_password, we might have tried to fix that intent. In fact, we could get a much higher *k*-folds score by using all the synthetic and nonvarying examples. If every training utterance for #reset_password contained the words "reset" and/or "password," the *k*-folds test would not have made any mistakes on #reset_password. Removing the variety to improve a *k*-folds score could hurt the assistant.

> **NOTE** *k*-folds test scores can be artificially inflated by removing variety from your training data, but this approach will hurt your assistant when it's in production.

With this fundamental understanding of *k*-folds testing, Fictitious Inc. is ready to run a larger *k*-folds test on the same assistant it ran the blind test on, which has five intents and ten examples of each. The k=5 *k*-folds test will slice the data into five segments with 10 utterances in each segment. Five temporary models will be trained on four of those segments (40 utterances) and tested on the remaining holdout segment (10 utterances).

Fictitious Inc. wants to compare the results of this *k*-folds test with the result of the blind test. In both tests, the assistant had the same training set of 50 utterances. First, look at the overall test scores in table 7.9.

Table 7.9   Accuracy scores for data in *k*-folds and blind tests

Intent	*k*-folds score	Blind score
#appointments	0.86	0.78
#employment_inquiry	0.74	0.89
#reset_password	0.78	0.90
#store_hours	1.0	0.89
#store_location	0.6	0.7
Total	0.78	0.82

k-folds correctly predicted some patterns (#store_hours is the most accurate intent) but missed other patterns (#reset_password and #store_location are inaccurate). The tabular results show some interesting findings:

- Both tests suggest that #store_location is the least accurate intent.
- Both tests suggest that #store_hours is highly accurate.
- The *k*-folds test suggests that the #appointments intent is one of the most accurate intents, and the blind test suggests #appointments is nearly the least accurate.
- The tests also disagree about the relative accuracy of #reset_password and #employment_inquiry.

Despite these differences, the overall accuracy score is similar between the two tests (78% versus 82%). It's intriguing to get approximately the same answer for what appear to different reasons. Fictitious Inc. should use the confusion matrices in figure 7.14 to investigate the results completely.

The confusion matrix shows much more confusion between #employment_inquiry and #store_location, along with possible confusion between #reset_password and #appointments. The *k*-folds test shows four additional error patterns:

- Overprediction of #appointments
- Overprediction of #store_location
- Underprediction of #employment_inquiry
- Underprediction of #reset_password

The first three error patterns also appeared in the blind test. We can trust these insights. What if Fictitious Inc. had not run the blind test? Could it still trust the fourth

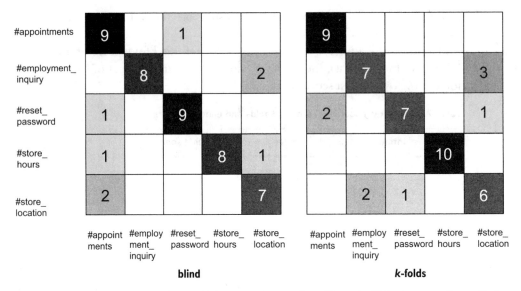

Figure 7.14   Comparing blind test and *k*-folds confusion matrices. The actual intents are on the vertical axis, and the predicted intents are on the horizontal axis.

insight? Does it really have a problem with the #reset_password intent? Explore the #reset_password errors in table 7.10.

Table 7.10   Exploration of the #reset_password underpredictions in the *k*-folds test

#	Utterance	Actual intent	Predicted intent
1	Wanna change my pass	#reset_password	#appointments
2	Locate pin	#reset_password	#store_location
3	I need to talk to customer service, but I've lost my password. Can you help me?	#reset_password	#appointments

The utterances in errors 1 and 2 are unambiguous. The utterance in error 3 is arguably a compound utterance with both #reset_password and #appointments intents. All three utterances add useful variety to the #reset_password training data. Except for the the compound utterance, the #reset_password training data looks better than the *k*-folds results might suggest. The *k*-folds score for #reset_password was lower than in the blind test precisely because that intent has lots of variety in its training examples (a good thing).

k-folds testing requires some interpretation and extrapolation. For any given misclassified utterance in the *k*-folds test, you can't be sure whether the classifier was wrong because of a real problem or because the classifier needed that utterance to learn a pattern. *k*-folds testing can find potential error patterns and sources of confusion but may not reflect the true accuracy of the assistant.

Run your own *k*-folds test

Plenty of software libraries can help you run *k*-folds cross-validation tests:

- You can build your own *k*-folds cross-validation test by using the scikit-learn library, documented at http://mng.bz/5WBZ.
- Botium has a general cross-validation framework with adapters for Watson Assistant, Google Dialogflow, Wit.ai, and Amazon Lex. Read more at http://mng.bz/6NdZ.
- Watson Assistant users can use the open source WA-Testing-Tool library at http://mng.bz/oGO2. This Python tool can run *k*-folds cross-validation and other tests, generating a variety of charts and diagrams. (The examples in this book were generated with WA-Testing-Tool.)

Note that you may get slightly different results each time you run *k*-folds because most tools fold the data randomly. The overall scores will differ between runs, but the error patterns should be stable. Look more closely at the overall patterns than at the specific predictions.

Given these caveats, it is important not to optimize for a *k*-folds score. Remember that a *k*-folds test is a synthetic test and cannot replace a blind test. When I review conversational AIs that do not have a blind test set, I am suspicious of *k*-folds scores greater than 0.9. Such a high *k*-folds can indicate that the training data has low variety. (If the production data also has low variety, that is fine, but production data usually has high variety.) I'm more comfortable with *k*-folds scores between 0.70 and 0.89. A score in that range suggests that the training data has some variety while still defining clear intents. A score lower than 0.70 may indicate that many intents are poorly defined or insufficiently trained.

> **NOTE** Do not optimize for a high *k*-folds score. Use *k*-folds only to find patterns of errors.

k-folds and blind tests are useful for assessing the accuracy of your AI. Both of these tests can provide summary and detailed metrics. I have generally referred to all of these metrics as accuracy. But we can use other metrics to assess AI accuracy.

7.3   *Selecting the right accuracy metric for the job*

Fictitious Inc. wants to use the results from blind tests to get a deep understanding of how well its conversational AI performs and to determine how best to improve the bottom line with the assistant. Some errors are more important than other errors, including these two:

- *Opt-outs being underdetected*—If a user gives any indication that they want to leave the AI assistant and speak to a human, they should be routed to a human immediately. Failure to detect this condition leads to angry users who are likely to stop being customers. The company does not want to miss #opt_out intents.

- *Fraud reports being overdetected*—Any conversation that touches on fraud is immediately transferred to a high-cost fraud specialist. The company does not want to incur an extra cost from conversations mistakenly routed due to an errant `#report_fraud` intent detection.

Fictitious Inc. considers all other errors to be equal. It wants a report on the assistant's accuracy that takes these errors into account. There's more than one way to measure accuracy. First, let's review the simplest possible definition:

accuracy = correct predictions / total predictions

For the blind and *k*-folds test examples in this chapter, the overall scores I provided for each test used this simple accuracy metric. The blind test score of 0.82 came from predicting 41 of 50 test utterances correctly, and the *k*-folds test score of 0.78 came from predicting 39 of 50 test utterances correctly.

But Fictitious Inc. doesn't want to know only how many predictions were right and wrong. It matters how the assistant was wrong. The company is worried about two types of errors: underselection of a correct intent and overselection of an incorrect intent. Examine these error types through the sample data shown in table 7.11. Data #0 shows an underselection of `#employment_inquiry` and an overselection of `#reset_ password`.

Table 7.11 Exemplary test results for exploring error types

#	Utterance	Actual intent	Predicted intent
0	Can I work for you	`#employment_inquiry`	`#reset_password`
1	I need a job application	`#employment_inquiry`	`#employment_inquiry`

If accuracy is our metric, Data #0 ("Can I work for you") is one error. But from a detailed point of view, Data #0 contains two errors:

- *Overselection of the* `#reset_password` *intent*—The predicted intent is a *false positive* of `#reset_password`. That intent was predicted but should not have been.
- *Underselection of the* `#employment_inquiry` *intent*—The predicted intent is a *false negative* of `#employment_inquiry`. That intent was not predicted but should have been.

Similarly, if accuracy is our metric, Data #1 ("I need a job application") is one correct prediction. But from a detailed point of view, Data #1 contains two correct predictions:

- *Positive prediction of the* `#employment_inquiry` *intent*—The predicted intent is a *true positive* of `#employment_inquiry`. That intent was predicted, and it should have been.
- *Negative prediction of the* `#reset_password` *intent*—The predicted intent is a *true negative* of `#reset_password`. That intent was not predicted, and it should have been predicted.

With these building blocks, we can build the precise metrics that Fictitious Inc. requires. When you are worried about overselection of an intent, you are most concerned about false positives for that intent. The metric that considers false positives is called *precision*. When you are worried about underselection of an intent, you are most concerned with false negatives for that intent. The metric that considers false negatives is called *recall*.

The equations for precision and recall are

$$\text{Precision: (True Positives)} / \text{(True Positives + False Positives)}$$

$$\text{Recall: (True Positives)} / \text{(True Positives + False Negatives)}$$

Two ways to be wrong but only one way to be right

It feels unfair that you don't get any credit for true negatives in the precision and recall equations. True negatives are not that useful in assessing performance.

Consider an assistant with 20 possible intents. When it makes a single prediction, it will have one true positive (the predicted intent was the actual intent) or one false positive with one false negative (the predicted intent and the actual intent). Every other intent will be a true negative, with 18 or 19 true negatives. The math is much simpler and useful when you omit the true negatives.

You can look at precision and recall on an intent-by-intent basis. If the different error types are not important, you can blend precision and recall into a single metric. That metric is called *F1*, and it is the harmonic mean of precision and recall. (F1 is a specific form of an F-score. There are other F-scores, including F0.5 and F2. Each F-score uses a different weighting for precision and recall. F1 gives equal weight to precision and recall, F0.5 gives more weight to precision, and F2 gives more weight to recall. I find it sufficient to look at only recall, precision, and F1.) The equation for F1 is

$$\text{F1: } (2 * \text{Precision} * \text{Recall}) / \text{(Precision + Recall)}$$

In the blind test earlier in this chapter, I used sleight of hand, giving each intent an accuracy score that was actually its F1 score. That blind test result is reproduced in table 7.12 with precision and recall included.

Table 7.12 Precision, recall, and F1 scores for blind test

Intent	Precision	Recall	F1
#appointments	0.90	0.69	0.78
#employment_inquiry	0.80	1.0	0.89
#reset_password	0.90	0.90	0.90
#store_hours	0.80	1.0	0.89
#store_location	0.70	0.70	0.70

Including precision and recall gives us more detailed information to fix the assistant, especially compared with the confusion matrix. We can see from table 7.12 that #store_location is overpredicted based on its lower precision score. By contrast, #appointment's low recall shows that it is underpredicted. (The low recall score for #store_location means that intent is also overpredicted. The training for this intent needs to be improved.)

Fictitious Inc. is concerned about underselection of #opt_out and overselection of #report_fraud. When the assistant is extended to include these intents, the company should focus on the recall of #opt_out and the precision of #report_fraud. For the other intents, we can look at the F1 scores.

> **NOTE**   An intent with low precision is overselected. An intent with low recall is underselected.

Precision and recall are naturally in tension. Adding training data to an intent usually improves its recall but may decrease its precision. Removing training data from an intent may improve its precision at the cost of decreasing recall. The first step in improving your assistant is understanding what kind of problem you have. Accuracy, precision, recall, and F1 are useful for making that assessment.

Fictitious Inc. should test its assistant's accuracy via an iterative approach, with steps for gathering data, training, testing, and improving, as shown in figure 7.15. The first iteration of this cycle will not be perfect, and that's fine. It's a safe assumption that multiple iterations will be required, and builders should plan to continue iterating after the first production release.

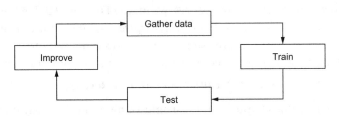

Figure 7.15   Testing and improving your classifier is a virtuous cycle. Assume that you will need multiple iterations of the cycle, and plan for some iterations after you go to production.

If you are unable or unwilling to find real user data from production, not only synthetic data from subject-matter experts, you should stop iterating after a couple of cycles. Each cycle has diminishing returns, and there is no reason to optimize an assistant on synthetic data when it is highly probable that you'll have to optimize again when you have production data. When you understand how accurate your assistant is, you'll be ready to test the rest of the solution.

Summary

- Blind testing with data from production users provides the most useful assessment of how accurate your assistant is.

- *k*-folds cross-validation testing can be used to identify potential accuracy problems in your assistant and is appropriate if you don't have production data to test with.

- Accuracy is a good general metric, but you can use precision and recall when you are concerned about overselection or underselection of a specific intent, respectively.

Testing your dialogue flows

Fictitious Inc. has designed a conversational AI to handle its most frequent customer service inquiries. The company formed a dream team to design and implement conversational flows for each of the major intents the assistant will handle. Now it needs to test the conversational assistant and make sure that it works as well as desired.

The first conversational flow to be tested is password resets (figure 8.1).

Fictitious Inc. has already evaluated how accurate the assistant is at identifying the intent in a user's question, including the ability to identify the #reset_password intent. A user who wants their password reset will start the conversation

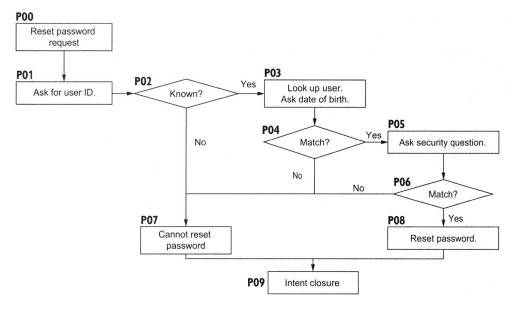

Figure 8.1 **Verifying the implementation of a reset password conversational flow**

with an utterance indicating their intent. The system will execute several additional steps in a process flow, including asking follow-up questions, before ultimately servicing the #reset_password intent.

In this chapter, we will learn how to test a dialogue process flow. We'll start by functionally testing dialogue responses for a single path in the process flow, using both manual and automated approaches. Then we will functionally test all paths through the process flow. When the process flow works functionally, we will test the process flow for both user experience and system performance.

8.1 Functionally testing a dialogue flow

Fictitious Inc.'s first goal in testing the password reset process flow is to make sure the user can get through all the steps in resetting their password. First, the company will test the *happy path*—the simplest case in which the user can get their password reset. This path has the following conversational elements:

1 The system acknowledges the #reset_password intent and asks for the user ID.
2 The system verifies that the user ID exists and asks for the user's date of birth.
3 The system verifies that the date of birth is accurate and asks a security question.
4 The system verifies the security-question response and resets the password.

In each step of this process, the assistant follows the steps in figure 8.2. The session starts with user input. The AI classifies that input, decides the appropriate response action, and responds to the input. The process repeats as long as the user keeps interacting with the system. For Fictitious Inc.'s password reset process, there will be four cycles.

Figure 8.2   Execution flow in an AI assistant

Figure 8.3 shows how the AI assistant components work together on the first cycle of the password reset process flow. When the user says, "I'm locked out of my account," the classifier assigns the intent #reset_password, the dialogue manager finds the action for the #reset_password condition, and the response "OK. What's your user ID?" is sent to the user.

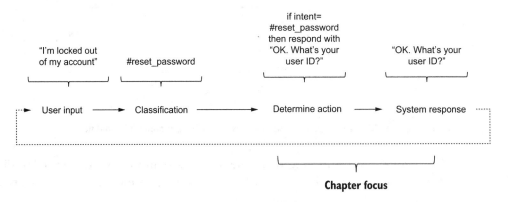

Figure 8.3   Execution flow in an AI assistant and the two major testing focuses

The system executes several steps internally before responding to the user. The user will see only the inputs and outputs. Process flow testing should use only these inputs and outputs, as shown in table 8.1. When debugging the solution, a builder can review the internal steps, but the process flow testing should verify only the outputs.

Table 8.1   Happy-path process flow for a password reset

Step #	Input	Output
1	I'm locked out of my account.	OK, I can help you reset your password. What's your User ID?
2	afreed123	I found your user ID. What's your date of birth?
3	12/25/1900	What's your favorite book?
4	Conversational AI	I reset your password. Can I help you with anything else?

8.1.1   *Manually testing a conversation flow*

The simplest way Fictitious Inc. can test its conversational AI is through the testing interface provided by the AI platform. Most platforms include some form of a graphical interface for the assistant. Some platforms include multiple interfaces:

- *Developer interface*—This interface is intended for developers to use as they build and unit-test the conversational AI. This interface provides debugging information, which may include the intents, entities, and specific dialogue nodes that were used in generating a system response. This debugging information is not shared with users in the deployed production assistant.
- *Sample user interface*—This graphical user interface is production-ready. It renders system responses exactly as they will be displayed to the user.

Either interface can be used to functionally test the dialogue in a process flow. Fictitious Inc.'s reset password flow is demonstrated in a developer interface in figure 8.4.

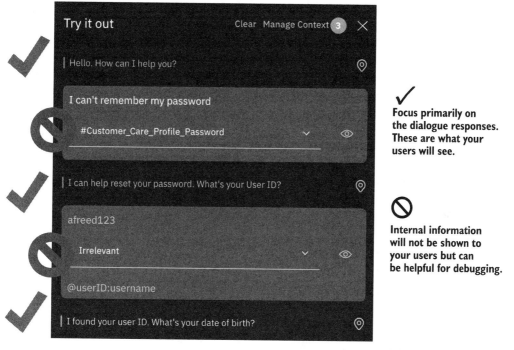

Figure 8.4 Use your platform's testing interface to test dialogue responses manually. The testing interface may give you more information than you need. Users do not know or care about the name of the intents or entities your system uses to understand their input.

Either interface can be used to test the password reset flow. The developers will probably prefer the development interface and the rich information it provides. The testers will probably prefer to use the same interface that the users will consume.

Regardless of the testing interface used, manual testing is simple to execute but does not scale well. Manually entering four inputs to reset a password is fine once, but Fictitious Inc. has multiple paths through its reset password process flow and is implementing 17 more intents. The more complex a conversational AI grows, the longer it will take to test all the process flows manually.

Fictitious Inc. won't test a process flow once; it will retest the assistant each time there are significant changes. Over the life of the assistant, there could be thousands of tests. The company will want to automate as many of these tests as possible. The following sections look at automating testing of the #reset_password process flow.

8.1.2   Automating a conversation flow test

Fictitious Inc. will want to create test scripts for each process flow and run these scripts at any time. To do so, it needs to write test scripts that use the API exposed by the conversational AI.

Every platform I surveyed for this book exposes an API for testing the assistant's dialogue flow. The API will require an utterance for input and will provide at least a dialogue response as output. Depending on your platform, you may need to provide additional configuration parameters, such as username, password, or version. The following listing demonstrates an exemplary API call.

Listing 8.1   Using an API to test the dialogue response to "I forgot my password"

```
curl -X POST -u "{your_username}:{your_password}" --header "Content-
    Type:application/json" --data "{\"input\": {\"text\": \"I forgot my
    password\"}}" "{your_url}/message?version=2020-04-01"
```

The input and output from this API call are shown in figure 8.5.

Your platform may provide an SDK that makes it easier to interact with their dialogue APIs. If the platform doesn't provide an SDK, you can write your own scripts to interact with these APIs. Having code that calls the dialogue API is the first step in automating dialogue tests. The second step is calling the API in a repeatable fashion. Fictitious Inc. created a shell script, dialogue.py, to test a single dialogue response.

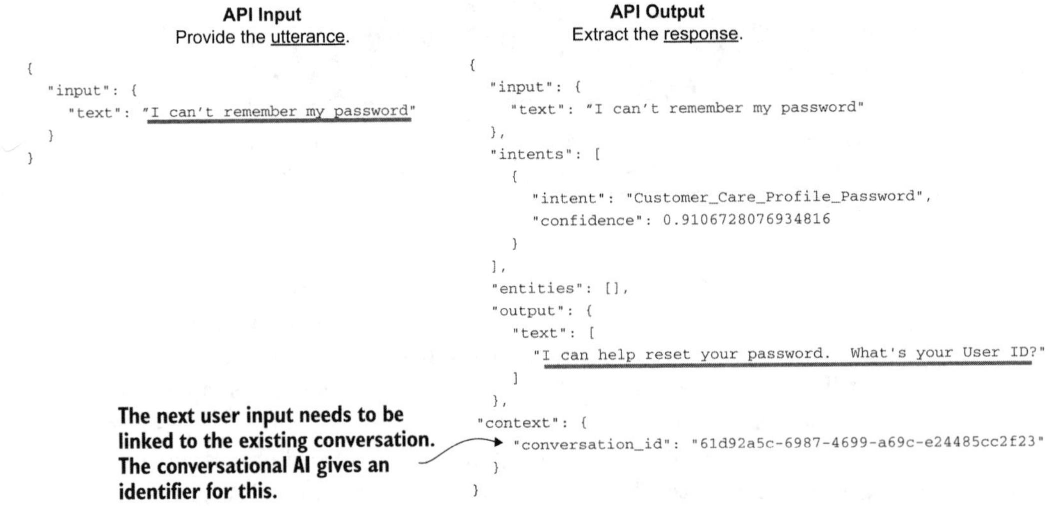

API Input
Provide the utterance.

```
{
  "input": {
    "text": "I can't remember my password"
  }
}
```

API Output
Extract the response.

```
{
  "input": {
    "text": "I can't remember my password"
  },
  "intents": [
    {
      "intent": "Customer_Care_Profile_Password",
      "confidence": 0.9106728076934816
    }
  ],
  "entities": [],
  "output": {
    "text": [
      "I can help reset your password.  What's your User ID?"
    ]
  },
  "context": {
    "conversation_id": "61d92a5c-6987-4699-a69c-e24485cc2f23"
  }
}
```

The next user input needs to be linked to the existing conversation. The conversational AI gives an identifier for this.

Figure 8.5   Using an API to test the assistant's dialogue response to the user's first utterance

The contents of this script are highly dependent on the AI platform, but the script should do the following:

1. Take two input parameters: an utterance and the expected response.
2. Initialize a connection to the AI assistant.
3. Call the assistant's dialogue API to get the system response.
4. Extract the dialogue response, and compare it with the expected response
5. Output four parameters: the utterance, the expected response, the actual response, and the correctness of the response.

The desired output from this script is shown in table 8.2. The four pieces of information form the basis for verifying all the conversational AI's dialogue responses.

Table 8.2 Example output format for an automated classification test

Utterance	Expected response	Actual response	Response assessment
I forgot my password	I can help reset your password. What's your User ID?	I can help reset your password. What's your User ID?	Correct

The reset password flow is implemented in a multistep conversation. After the assistant recognizes a `#reset_password` intent, the assistant asks the user for their user ID. The user's response to this question will be their second input in the conversation. When testing this dialogue flow via an API, this second input will be linked to the first input, so the assistant treats it as belonging to the same conversation.

The specific linkage mechanism varies by conversational platform. One common pattern is for conversations to be linked by a conversation ID. Figure 8.6 demonstrates

API Input
Provide the <u>utterance</u> linked to the existing conversation.

API Output
Extract the next conversational <u>response</u>.

```
{
  "input": {
    "text": "afreed123"
  },
  "context": {
    "conversation_id": "61d92a5c-6987-4699-
a69c-e24485cc2f23"
  }
}
```

```
{
  "input": {
    "text": "afreed123"
  },
  "intents": [],
  "entities": [
    {
      "entity": "userID",
      "location": [0, 9],
      "value": "username",
    }
  ],
  "output": {
    "text": [
      "I found your user ID. What's your date of birth?"
    ]
  },
  "context": {
    "conversation_id": "61d92a5c-6987-4699-a69c-e24485cc2f23"
  }
}
```

The second reset_password question is driven by finding an entity, not an intent.

Figure 8.6 Testing a password reset flow through an API, continuing the conversation with a user response to the question "What's your user ID?"

an API request and response for the second turn of a password reset conversation, linked by conversation ID.

The specific implementation for continuing a conversation via API varies by platform. One possible implementation is shown in listing 8.2, where each subsequent call to the conversational AI dialogue API uses the `conversation_id` from the previous call. (In this system, an API call that does not include a `conversation_id` is assumed to initiate a new conversation.)

Listing 8.2   Using an API to test "What's your User ID?"

```
curl -X POST -u "{your_username}:{your_password}" --header "Content-
    Type:application/json" --data "{\"input\": {\"text\":
    \"afreed123\"},\"context\":{\"conversation_id\":\"xxxxxxxx-xxxx-xxxx-
    xxxx-xxxxxxxxxxxx\"}}" "{your_url}/message?version=2020-04-01"
```

Fictitious Inc. wants to test multiple messages in a single conversation. Now that the company knows how to test a single message with their assistant's API, it can expand the `dialogue.py` script to test an entire conversation. The script is similar to testing a single message but has a `for` loop with an iteration for each message. The pseudocode of this script has the following steps:

1. Take one input: a comma-separated values (CSV) file with two columns, each row containing an utterance and its expected response (Other common formats include JSON or XML. These formats make it easier to expand the tests with additional input context or additional output verification parameters.)
2. Initialize a connection to the AI assistant.
3. For every row in the CSV file, call the assistant's dialogue API to get the dialogue response to the given input utterance; extract the actual dialogue response and compare it with the expected dialogue response; and output the utterance, the expected response, the actual response, and the correctness of the response.

A pseudocode version of `dialogue.py` is shown in listing 8.3. Note that this script uses exact string matching (`actual_response != expected_response`). This is the simplest type of test but is also the most brittle, since responses may frequently be updated.

Listing 8.3   Example dialogue.py contents

```
import json
import sys

# Script is called with a test data filename as parameter
all_test_data = json.load(open(sys.argv[1]))

# Pseudocode - this will vary per platform
assistant = new Assistant(your_username, your_password, your_url)
```

```
context = {}
assistant.message("")

for test_data in all_test_data:
    result = assistant.message(test_data['input'], context)
    expected_response = test_data['output']
    actual_response   = result['text']
    context = result['context']
    if(actual_response != expected_response):
        print("Expected {} but got {}".format(expected_response,
        ➥ actual_response))
        return -1

print("Passed the test")
return 0
```

The `dialogue.py` script can be invoked with a test case file such as `reset_password_happy_path.json`, shown in the next listing.

Listing 8.4 Example reset_password_happy_path.json contents

```
[
  {
    "input":"I'm locked out of my account",
    "output":"Ok, I can help you reset your password. What's your User ID?"
  },
  {
    "input":"afreed123",
    "output":"I found your user ID. What's your date of birth?"
  },
  {
    "input":"12/25/1900",
    "output":"What's your favorite book?"
  },
  {
    "input":"Conversational AI",
    "output":"I reset your password. Can I help you with anything else?"
  }
]
```

With this new script, Fictitious Inc. can execute any conversation test in seconds, creating a file for each conversation scenario it wants to test and automating the execution of all of them. These tests can be used to verify the functionality built into their assistant and used as a regression suite to run any time the assistant changes in the future.

An even faster path to automating your dialogue tests

This chapter shows you how to implement your own automated dialogue tests. You can tie these tests into testing frameworks such as JUnit and unittest. You can also use existing tools for even faster time to value:

Now that Fictitious Inc. can test any conversational flow, either manually or automatically, it is ready to test all its conversational flows. So far, the company has functionally tested only the happy path of its password reset process flow. The following sections look at testing the other paths.

8.1.3   Testing the dialogue flowchart

Fictitious Inc. drew a flow chart for each of the process flows its conversational AI supports. These process flows were useful during design and build time for showing every member of their dream team how the assistant would work. These process flows are also invaluable during the testing phase and can be used to build functional test cases. Fictitious Inc.'s password reset dialogue flowchart is displayed in figure 8.7.

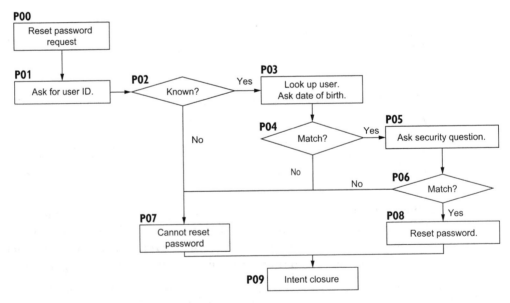

Figure 8.7   A dialogue tree for the reset password flow

This process flow includes several rule conditions. Each of these rule conditions affects the process flow and needs to be tested. The five rule conditions are shown in table 8.3.

Table 8.3 Dialogue rule conditions in the reset password process flow

Node	Rule condition	Response
P01	`if intent==#reset_password`	"I can help reset your password. What's your User ID?"
P03	`if user_id is not null`	"I found your user ID. What's your date of birth?"
P05	`if input_dob==user_id_dob`	Ask the user's specific security question.
P07	`if user_id is null or security_match==false`	"I'm sorry, I can't reset your password"
P08	`if security_match==true`	"I reset your password. Can I help you with anything else?"

Fictitious Inc. wants to test all the password reset flow paths, which means testing each of the conditional branches in the process flow. There are four paths through the reset password flowchart in figure 8.7:

- *Happy path*—The user's password is reset (P00, P01, P02, P03, P04, P05, P06, P08, and P09).
- *Unhappy path*—Security question incorrect (P00, P01, P02, P03, P04, P05, P06, P07, and P09).
- *Unhappy path*—User date of birth is incorrect (P00, P01, P02, P03, P04, P07, and P09).
- *Unhappy path*—The user ID is unknown (P00, P01, P02, P07, and P09).

There are five conditions but only four paths for the test case. The condition that does not get an individual dialogue test case is that the intent is truly #reset_password. The intent matching is tested in the accuracy tests (chapter 7). Two of Fictitious Inc.'s password reset conversation flows are shown in figure 8.8.

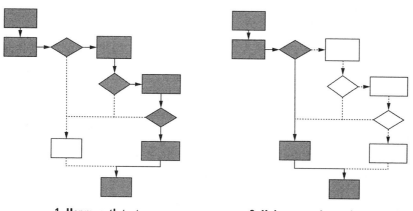

1. Happy path test   **2. Unhappy path test (one of several)**

Figure 8.8 Visual representation of individual test cases for the reset password flow. Each test case can test only a handful of dialogue nodes and conditions. The untested flows in each test case use dashed lines and unfilled boxes.

For the #reset_password process flow, the number of possible paths through the flow is finite. We can get complete functional test coverage of this process flow by enumerating the paths, creating test cases for each path. An example test case is shown in table 8.4. If automated, the test can verify each response produced by the system.

Table 8.4   Example test case for the reset password happy path

Step	Test action	Expected response
1	Enter "reset my password"	System responds, "I can help reset your password. What's your User ID?"
2	Enter "afreed123"	System responds, "I found your user ID. What's your date of birth?"
3	Enter "12/25/1900"	System responds, "What's your favorite book?"
4	Enter "Conversational AI"	System responds, "I reset your password. Can I help you with anything else?"
5	End test	

Testing a process flow for a conversational AI includes running many tests like these. The biggest challenge in testing dialogue flows is the sheer number of possible paths through your AI assistant. The number of test cases for a process flow can grow exponentially with the length of the flow, depending on how many paths there are through the flow and how intertwined those paths are.

Test cases can easily be written from a well-diagrammed process flow. In this diagram, each of the most common error conditions is captured, such as user ID or date of birth validation failures. These unhappy paths can be traced on the flow diagram. But what about the conditions that don't quite fit on the flow diagram?

8.1.4   *Testing the unexpected error paths*

Fictitious Inc. created dialogue flowcharts for each of its major intents and used them for testing. The flowcharts showed the most expected paths through each dialogue flow. But unexpected paths can be common across all process flows, and these paths were not included in the flowcharts. These paths are caused by errors that could occur on nearly any line of dialogue. They are often not included in dialogue flowcharts, but they still need to be tested. These unexpected paths include

- The assistant identified the wrong intent from the user's utterance.
- The user input was not understood.
- The user tried to opt out of the assistant.

The following sections explore how to test these paths.

WRONG INTENT

Fictitious Inc. has already tested how accurate their assistant is at identifying the user's intent. No matter how accurate the assistant is, there is still a chance that it will make mistakes. Any time the assistant interprets open-ended user input, there is a chance that the assistant will interpret that input incorrectly. In figure 8.9, the assistant selects the wrong intent for the user's problem by selecting the #reset_password intent instead of #employment_inquiry. Will the user be able to correct the assistant and get to the flow they need, or will the assistant stubbornly continue? We need to test the user experience to see how classification mistakes will affect the user.

In figure 8.9, the user's initial utterance is misclassified. The statement "I can't find the job application site" was classified as the #reset_password intent with 0.4 confidence, a fairly low value, instead of being classified as #employment_inquiry. The user gets frustrated by this misclassification.

"I can't find the job application site" "I can help you reset your password. What's your user ID?" "That's not what I want!" "I'm sorry, I could not find that user ID"

Make sure the user can get out of process flow if you are constraining the expected input. Or don't start a process flow without confirming it's what the user wants to do.

Figure 8.9 If your assistant selects the wrong intent, does the user have any way to bring the conversation back on track? Can the user escape when something goes wrong? It's good to test what will happen to a user when the wrong intent is selected. Users should be able to correct the assistant if it gets the intent wrong or should at least be able to escape a process flow.

We can reduce the number of process flows that start based on the wrong intent in multiple ways:

- Explicitly confirm the intent with the user before starting the process flow. Fictitious Inc. could start the #reset_password flow with the confirmation question "Would you like to reset your password?" This question lengthens the conversation but ensures that the system understands the user's input.
- The assistant can start a process flow automatically only if the confidence of the intent prediction is high. If the intent confidence is not high, the assistant can ask the user to confirm the predicted intent, or the assistant can offer a default response like "I'm sorry, I didn't understand that.".

These approaches are demonstrated for #reset_password flow in figure 8.10. Fictitious Inc. may decide to initiate the #reset_password flow automatically if that intent is detected with 0.75 confidence, to confirm the intent if the confidence is between 0.5 and 0.75 confidence, and to ask the user to restate their utterance if the intent is less than 0.5 confidence.

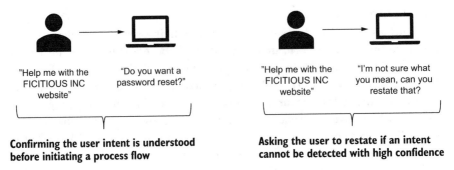

Confirming the user intent is understood
before initiating a process flow

Asking the user to restate if an intent
cannot be detected with high confidence

**Figure 8.10   Multiple ways to make sure that a process flow is started only with a
well-understood intent.**

Regardless of which design approach the company uses, it should test what happens when the assistant does not recognize the correct intent with high confidence.

> ## Mistakes happen
> User input can be misunderstood by the assistant, or users may say the wrong thing. Your assistant should be designed with the assumption that the classifier will make some mistakes, and there should be resolution mechanisms built into the assistant or the application that embeds the assistant. Your testing plan must include testing this functionality.

"I DIDN'T UNDERSTAND"

Fictitious Inc.'s `#reset_password` flow included four user inputs: the initial utterance, a user ID, a date of birth, and a security-question answer. The flowchart defined a success path and a failure path for each of these inputs. The user might provide a valid user ID (success) or an invalid ID (failure). But what happens if the input is not a user ID?

At any point in a conversation, a conversational AI may misunderstand the user. The user may say something completely unexpected. Text messages can be corrupted by bad autocorrect or by the user resting something on their keyboard. Voice messages can be corrupted by speech-to-text errors or by insidious background noise. An assistant should be adaptive in case user input does not match expectations.

Conversational AIs are generally coded with rules to handle input matching various conditions. The question "What is your User ID?", for example, may be coded to expect a single alphanumeric word in response, because user IDs don't contain spaces. If the input is anything else, the assistant may use a default or fallback condition to respond. This "anything else" response can be implemented generically so that it can be used on any dialogue node. Figure 8.11 illustrates a fallback condition that responds to unexpected input by first saying "I'm sorry, I didn't understand" and then repeating the question.

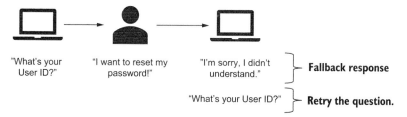

"What's your User ID?"   "I want to reset my password!"   "I'm sorry, I didn't understand."   } **Fallback response**

"What's your User ID?"   } **Retry the question.**

Figure 8.11   **If the user says something unexpected, they may get a fallback response like "I'm sorry, I didn't understand." The assistant can ask the original question again.**

In some AI platforms, this fallback condition can encapsulate additional logic by treating a misunderstood utterance as a digression or interruption. (Conversational AI platforms advertise digressions as a way for the user to switch topics in the middle of a conversation. Digressions are also convenient ways to implement a miniature dialogue flow that's initiated when a user is misunderstood. When a digression flow finishes, it returns the conversation to the place it was before the digression occurred.)

Fictitious Inc. can use this kind of digression to implement logic that retries any misunderstood question only once. The first time the user is misunderstood, the assistant replies, "I'm sorry, I didn't understand" and repeats the last question. The second time the user is misunderstood, the assistant replies, "I'm sorry, I still didn't understand" and directs the user to an alternative resolution, as shown in figure 8.12. The fallback condition needs to keep track of conversational context to determine whether it is being invoked for the first or second time in a conversation.

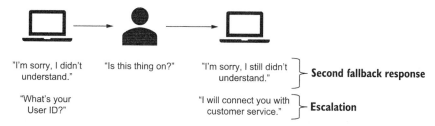

"I'm sorry, I didn't understand."   "Is this thing on?"   "I'm sorry, I still didn't understand."   } **Second fallback response**

"What's your User ID?"   "I will connect you with customer service."   } **Escalation**

Figure 8.12   **A fallback response can use context from earlier in the conversation. The assistant can be coded such that if the user is misunderstood twice, the assistant plays a different fallback message and escalates the user out of the conversation.**

When this kind of fallback logic is implemented in a global condition, how should it be tested? Should Fictitious Inc. update its flowcharts to show this conditional logic on every branch?

Most builders do not include this fallback logic on every single diagram, which adds a lot of clutter. Similarly, most builders do not write a test case of this fallback logic on every single dialogue condition. Fictitious Inc. is well served by testing this fallback logic in the dialogue branches where it is most likely to occur. For most of the process flows, including password resets, this includes the first two or three branches in the dialogue flow.

OPT OUT

Fictitious Inc. wants users to be able to opt out of the conversational AI. If the user ever says something like "Get me out of here" or "I want to speak to a human," the AI assistant will help the user get the human assistance they desire. (In another clever use of digressions, opt-out is frequently implemented as a digression that never returns. Using a digression is one way to make the opt-out logic globally available.) An exemplary opt-out dialogue flow is depicted in figure 8.13. Because Fictitious Inc. wants opt-out to always be an option, they've chosen not to include it in flowcharts.

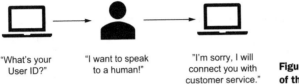

"What's your   "I want to speak   "I'm sorry, I will   **Figure 8.13   Allowing users to opt out**
  User ID?"   to a human!"   connect you with   **of the conversational AI at any time**
                                            customer service."

Because opt-out is possible on any dialogue node, should we write a test case opting out of every specific dialogue node? Probably not, because there is a point of diminishing returns in testing a global function like opt-out. The longer a user converses with the system, the less likely they are to opt out, so the most important dialogue nodes to test are the first few nodes. For password resets, we should especially verify that the user can opt out of the intent capture (the first message in the conversation) and the user ID capture (the first message in the reset password flow).

Letting the user opt out is good manners

Fictitious Inc. may be proud of its conversational AI, which may save them a lot of money compared with having human customer service representatives field inquiries. But it's a violation of a social contract with your users to ignore them if they explicitly tell you that they don't want to talk to a machine.

In practice, almost all user opt-out requests occur in the first two or three messages in the conversation. If a users make it to the fourth message, there's a good chance that they'll stick with the assistant.

Rather than preventing opt-outs, focus your energy on improving your assistant to the point where users don't want to opt out of it.

Fictitious Inc. has tested all functional aspects of the password reset process flow, verifying that the conversational AI faithfully implements the flowcharts, that the assistant can handle an unexpected utterance, and that the assistant lets users opt out. Now that the assistant works well functionally, the nonfunctional aspects should be tested as well.

8.2 Nonfunctionally testing a dialogue flow

It's important to make sure that your conversational AI works functionally. How well does it work for your users? You can't be sure until you've done some user experience testing.

8.2.1 User experience testing

Fictitious Inc. designed its assistant to satisfy users' most common needs. Dialogue flows were designed to help users get what they need as quickly as possible. But there's still a lot of time between the design, build, and test phases. There's a difference between whiteboarding a dialogue flow and experiencing it through a text or voice interface. When you test the design the way the user will actually use it, you'll find things that don't work as well as you thought they would on some diagram.

There's something even better than pretending to be a new user: finding some actual new users. There's no substitute for the fresh perspective of new users. Your subject-matter experts usually can't predict the full range of data users will send to the system, and they usually can't predict how the entire experience will work for users. Pretending to be a user is a cheap but inferior substitute; don't be afraid to get the real thing.

Fictitious Inc. can find some friendly faces to help in this phase. Developers can recruit people on nearby teams or even friends and family members. New users will not be biased by the thought processes used in the assistant's design. When these users test the assistant, they should be given only the amount of guidance that the company plans to give to production users; this approach prevents biasing these users in the areas where feedback and fresh perspective are most important.

Figure 8.14 contrasts two ways to introduce an assistant to new users. The way that an assistant is introduced significantly affects the way the users will consume the system.

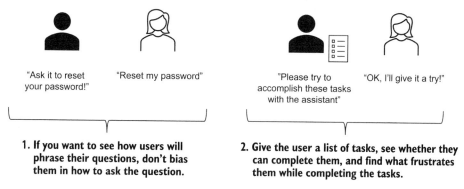

"Ask it to reset your password!" "Reset my password"

"Please try to accomplish these tasks with the assistant" "OK, I'll give it a try!"

1. If you want to see how users will phrase their questions, don't bias them in how to ask the question.

2. Give the user a list of tasks, see whether they can complete them, and find what frustrates them while completing the tasks.

Figure 8.14 The instructions you give your users will affect the experience they have and the feedback you give.

Design your user experience test so that you get the feedback you need most. I never want to pass up an opportunity to find out how users ask their initial questions, so I prefer not to give too much advice on what to ask. Users may spend a little time playing around (asking the assistant to tell them a joke, for example), but they will quickly discover what's in bounds for the assistant.

> **Don't forget to observe how users react to the dialogue**
> In every conversational assistant I've built, I have found some dialogue that seemed OK during the design phase but felt wrong when I acted like a user, especially in voice conversational systems, where some seemingly important caveat turned a system response from useful into an interminable bore. With a careful eye (or ear), you can often find some rough edges that you can smooth to improve the user experience.

Most builders will want to test whether users can get into a process flow and execute it to completion. You can give the user specific instructions, which may include the initial question you want them to ask. This approach will take less time and give you feedback on the process flow itself, but you won't find out how well the intents are designed. Instead, you can give the user a set of open-ended tasks. This approach will help you test how well you can identify intents and how well the process flows for these intents work. Table 8.5 has sample instructions that Fictitious Inc. can give new users, based on what part of the user experience the testing will focus on.

Table 8.5   Specific and open-ended instructions for specific user experience tests

Process flow	Specific instructions	Open-ended task
store hours and store location	Ask the assistant where they are located and when they are open.	Plan a trip to Fictitious Inc. with the assistant.
reset password	Ask the assistant to reset your password.	The Fictitious Inc. website gave you an error "Incorrect username or password." Resolve this by using the assistant.
employment inquiry	Ask the assistant for a job application.	You're looking to earn some extra cash in your spare time. Apply to Fictitious Inc.

The differences between the approaches in table 8.5 are stark. Giving specific instructions to users heavily biases their experience but ensures that you will test the process flow you intend. For the "store hours and store location" tests, the specific instructions will certainly execute the #store_hours and #store_locations process flows. The open-ended version of this test asks a user to "plan a trip," but may not specifically ask for both hours or locations and may not ask for either. Depending on the feedback needed, the instructions can be adjusted to be more specific or more open-ended. The instructions might instead say "Plan a trip to Fictitious Inc. with the assistant, including the when and where."

> **User experience testing takes time, but it's worthwhile**
> Allow some time to review the feedback from this user experience testing. The feedback from this test is the closest you will get to postproduction feedback. This feedback can be worth its weight in gold. Incorporate the most significant feedback into your assistant before going into production, which can ensure a much smoother rollout.

8.2.2 Load testing

After Fictitious Inc. has tested the functionality and user experience of each intent for a single user, it needs to make sure that the assistant works at scale, responding quickly and correctly when multiple consumers use it at the same time. *Load testing* occurs when a software system is tested with many simultaneous users. (The strain on the system from serving multiple users at the same time is called the *load*—hence, the name *load testing.*)

Fictitious Inc. should have a plan for how many concurrent users it expects to serve in production and can estimate this number from existing support channels. If 500 unique users visit the company's website in an hour, we could assume that half of the users will use the chat feature. If each chat takes 2 minutes to complete, we assume an average load of approximately 10 simultaneous users. (If we have 250 users, 250 users times 2 minutes per user chat divided by 60 minutes is slightly fewer than 10 simultaneous users, assuming a random distribution.) Then we would load-test the system with 10 concurrent tests.

We may be able to have 10 different humans testing the system. Perhaps we can throw a pizza party while the team works on manual simultaneous tests of the assistant. This approach will not scale well, however. The more concurrent users we need to test, the harder it is to test manually and the more valuable automated tests become. Ideally, we have already automated functional testing and can use these automated functional tests to do the load testing as well.

Load testing can be an expensive proposition. If Fictitious Inc.'s conversational AI is hosted on a cloud provider, the company could run up a hefty cloud bill because the test traffic looks real to the provider. The company should check its cloud plan details to see whether or how they will be charged. Still, it may provide good peace of mind to verify that a cloud provider can handle a projected production level.

If Fictitious Inc. is self-hosting its assistant, it should certainly stress-test the assistant with some concurrent testing to ensure that the AI assistant has been allocated the right infrastructure and that the infrastructure has been configured properly to handle production loads.

The first thing we should do in a load test is verify that each individual test runs as expected. Fictitious Inc. verified the functionality of its reset password flow by making sure that it identified the intent, asked for and verified the user ID, asked for and verified the date of birth, asked for and verified a security question, and reset the password. This flow should work the same way whether there is one user using the assistant or many. Figure 8.15 depicts what could happen in an unsuccessful load test.

"What's your
User ID?"   "afreed123"   "I'm sorry, I didn't   Huh? This worked when
                                                    understand. What's   I was the only one
                                                    your user ID?"   testing the assistant.

Figure 8.15   Process flows should work the same way regardless of the number of users. Load testing verifies that the system performs correctly under concurrent use.

As long as the system is performing correctly for simultaneous users, Fictitious Inc. should also verify how quickly the system responds to the user. The time between the user's message and the system's response is called *response time*. Users expect responses in a few seconds at most. If the system takes longer to respond, they will get frustrated and possibly leave the assistant. Figure 8.16 shows the user's perspective when response time is high.

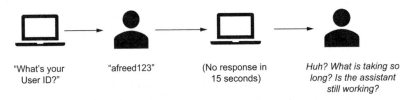

"What's your
User ID?"   "afreed123"   (No response in   Huh? What is taking so
                                                    15 seconds)   long? Is the assistant
                                                                               still working?

Figure 8.16   If the assistant responds slowly, users will wonder what is going on. Load testing ensures that the assistant is responsive enough to provide a good user experience.

Ways to mitigate slow responses from your assistant

Ideally, your AI assistant will always respond to the user in a few seconds or less. This may not always be possible. The assistant may slow down under heavy use or interaction with slow external systems. A password reset service might always take 30 seconds to execute.

A good user experience can be preserved if the assistant indicates to the user that progress is being made and that the assistant has not failed. Assistants should always announce when they are starting a process that will take more than a few seconds ("Please wait up to 30 seconds while I reset your password").

Depending on the specific type of assistant, there are additional ways to let the user know the assistant is still active. For a text-based conversational assistant, the user interface can display a temporary thinking icon or message, like the ones that chat programs show when a user is typing. For a voice-based assistant, the assistant can play music during a waiting period instead of staying silent.

Fictitious Inc. should include all the intents in the load test. Ideally, the load test will simulate the distribution of requests expected during production. If password resets are the most common intent, using 30% of expected call volume, 30% of the tests in the load test should test the password reset flow. Using a representative variety of tests is important. Load-testing only the simplest intents will not properly stress-test the system.

NOTE Loadrunner and JMeter are two popular load-testing tools. Either tool can test your AI assistant by exercising its APIs.

When you've successfully verified your assistant's functionality, user experience, and performance under multiple users, it's time to deploy your assistant to some real users.

Summary

- Each dialogue flow should be tested thoroughly to ensure that it works as designed. The flows can be tested manually or via automation.
- The assistant should be resilient if the user does something unexpected or if the assistant makes a mistake.
- Feedback from users who didn't design or build the assistant is invaluable and should be collected carefully.
- The assistant should be tested to ensure that it responds correctly and quickly with multiple simultaneous users.

Part 4

Maintenance

Congratulations! You've built and tested your AI assistant, and now you're ready to deploy it. This section of the book helps you keep your assistant in good working order as it matures. It's exciting to build a new assistant. But your assistant will spend much more time in production than you spent in that initial build phase. It's important to have good maintenance hygiene and processes to keep your assistant working well.

Chapter 9 shows you how to keep track of the software assets that make up your assistant. It introduces source code management and shows how to manage multiple versions of your assistant at the same time. You will have different needs for your development, test, and production environments. This chapter shows you how to balance all those needs.

Chapter 10 teaches you how to analyze and improve your assistant. No assistant will be perfect, especially not on the first release. This chapter shows you how to find the problem spots in your assistant that have the biggest impact on your success metric. It introduces several methodologies that you can use not only to find these problems, but to fix them as well.

After reading this part, you'll be able to keep your assistant running smoothly in production. Getting to production is not the end; it's only the beginning.

Deployment and management

9

This chapter covers

- Tracking changes to your AI assistant over time
- Managing multiple versions of your assistant
- Safely deploying code to production

The day Fictitious Inc. decided to build a conversational AI assistant was the happiest day of John Doe's life. John, a developer at Fictitious Inc., could not wait to get started building. He raced ahead of the rest of his project team, spending nights and weekends developing the assistant. John's project team was happy about his enthusiasm, but nobody on the team was exactly sure what John was up to all the time.

Communication with John was a struggle. He was slow to respond to instant messages and emails. Occasionally a team member would walk to John's desk find him furiously typing new code on his workstation. They would ask John how the latest feature was going, and John would give a lengthy soliloquy. By the time the team member got back to their own desk, they had forgotten what John told them.

Early in the development phase, this eccentricity did not bother the rest of the Fictitious Inc. project team. John Doe was pumping out code, he seemed generally happy, and the team had a vague sense he was making progress. But as Fictitious

Inc. readied to functionally test the conversational assistant, this lack of transparency was causing strife for the project team. Nobody knew exactly what features were done and which features were working. The assistant changed multiple times per day, but nobody was sure how or why.

This chapter is the story of how Fictitious Inc. escaped this Wild West scenario and how they established transparent development and change control procedures. In this chapter, you will learn how to manage changes to your AI assistant in a transparent way, and how to track which version of your assistant each member of your team is using.

9.1 *Where to store your code*

Fictitious Inc.'s development team currently consists of one developer: John Doe. Let's track their evolution of source code management.

9.1.1 *Taking the Wild West approach*

As the first developer on the Fictitious Inc. AI assistant project, John has not worried about sharing his code with anybody. John is only worried that the hard drive on his laptop may die someday. Thus, John tries to remember to save a copy of the assistant code to a shared drive about once a day or whenever he remembers. (Many AI platforms store code online rather than on physical workstations. The source code management problems in this section still apply. When I use a hosted AI platform, I still download a copy of the code to my workstation to review it.)

John does not have any hard and fast rules about how he backs up the code. He usually changes filenames to indicate the date of the backup or to add a note about the state of the code. Sometimes he makes a mistake when he backs up the code, overwriting a previous version of the assistant. John feels a little guilty when this happens, but not too bad. He knows in his head what state the code is in . . . mostly. His backup strategy can be seen in figure 9.1.

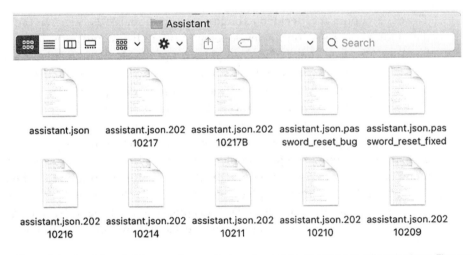

Figure 9.1 A quick and dirty way of managing versions of an AI assistant. What do these filenames mean? Which one is the latest version, and which versions are obsolete? Does the file assistant.json work?

This backup strategy makes it hard to work with John. John's team can find his files on the shared drive. But when someone wants to test the assistant, which version should they use? They can guess by choosing a file based on the filename or date, but they have no assurances of what is actually in that file. They don't know what's in the file, if it works well, or if it contains features and functions they are interested in.

Fictitious Inc.'s team could just go ask John, but we can see that John is a bit unreliable and hard to get a hold of. And what if John is out sick? How can anyone know which version of the code to use?

Fictitious Inc. has a handful of problems:

- They don't know which files represent the latest versions of the code.
- They don't know what's in any particular version of the code.
- They don't know which files represent stable versions of the code.

Let's see how Fictitious Inc. can address these problems with source control.

9.1.2 Using source control for code

Source control is the practice of tracking and managing changes to a series of files, particularly source code files. John Doe's ad hoc process barely meets this definition. There are many software solutions that offer robust source control management capabilities. At a minimum, a source control solution should be able to provide a complete list of all the files it is tracking, the file contents, all the changes made to those files, who made the changes, and why. This information is stored in a source code *repository*.

There are many possible source control platforms. At the time of this book's writing, the most popular source control platform is Git (https://git-scm.com). Git has a powerful command-line client, and there are many third-party user interfaces as well as hosting platforms. GitHub (https://github.com) is a popular hosting platform for using Git. The source code used in this book is stored in a GitHub repository (http://mng.bz/PaB8). The home page in GitHub for that source code is shown in figure 9.2.

1. Every file tracked in source control
2. Reason for last update
3. Last update date for each file

Figure 9.2 Summary view of the source code for this book in its GitHub repository

Anyone who connects to a GitHub repository gets all of this information. They can browse the repository and view each of the files. They can immediately see when each file was last updated. They can even download all of the files to their own computer using Git's *clone* command.

This solves Fictitious Inc.'s first problem: identifying the latest version of the code. Git goes above and beyond this requirement by tracking all versions of the code. Git also supports viewing and downloading any version of code stored in its repository. No more walking down the hall and asking John which version is which. Fictitious Inc. can easily find the version they want in Git. Now let's look at how Fictitious Inc. can use source control to solve their second problem: what's in a given version of code.

By default, source control systems will show you the most recent version of every file in the repository. It's often useful to see what changed in a file and why. Figure 9.3 shows a history of the source code I used for the demo in chapter 2.

In figure 9.3, several pieces of information are immediately available:

- The latest copy of `skill-Customer-Service-Skill-Ch2.json` was saved on October 1, 2020 by Andrew Freed.
- The reason that `skill-Customer-Service-Skill-Ch2.json` was updated was to capitalize the Elm and Maple entities.
- The contents of `skill-Customer-Service-Skill-Ch2.json` after the change are stored in version 016854e. (Git calls these commit hashes. For technical reasons beyond the scope of this book, versions are referred to by hash rather than by a number. Using numbers for versions is much harder than you might expect. You'll need to take my word on this one.) The contents of this file before the change are stored in version d7e3619. Each version of the file belongs to a different commit.

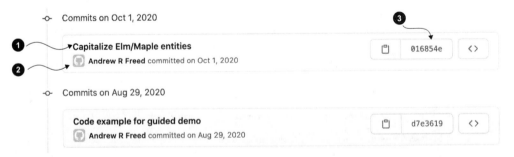

History for **CreatingVirtualAssistants** / code / **skill-Customer-Service-Skill-Ch2.json**

Commits on Oct 1, 2020

1 ➔ ▾**Capitalize Elm/Maple entities**

2 ➔ Andrew R Freed committed on Oct 1, 2020

3 → 016854e < >

Commits on Aug 29, 2020

Code example for guided demo
Andrew R Freed committed on Aug 29, 2020

d7e3619 < >

1. What was updated
2. Who updated and when
3. View the file contents at that specific version.

Figure 9.3   Using a source control management application lets you see what changed, when, and why. On October 1, I updated the source code for chapter 2 to include the capitalization of the Elm and Maple entities.

This solves part of Fictitious Inc.'s second problem: what each version of the code means. The descriptive summaries attached to Git commits describe the evolution of code. The commit histories in a source repository can be combined into a single stream called a *commit log*. If John was using Git, Fictitious Inc. could review the commit log to find out what was in the code. They wouldn't have to walk down the hall to ask John. Figure 9.4 shows an exemplary commit log for a single file in this book's GitHub repository.

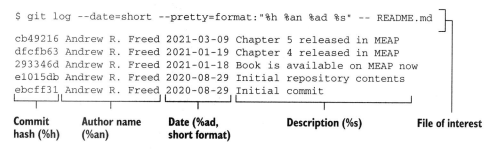

Figure 9.4 Commit log for one file in this book's GitHub repository

> ### Use descriptive commit messages
>
> A commit log is much more useful if it contains a detailed description of the changes. The message "Capitalize Elm/Maple entities" is much more useful than a message that says "fixed bug."
>
> Commit messages are a good way to share what was done and why. Developers, take the time to write descriptive commit messages. It helps the whole team. (And it will help future you too.)

A commit log may not be enough information, so source control also provides an additional level of detail. Figure 9.5 demonstrates a Git view that compares two versions of the same file. This viewer can be used to drill down into a specific change to see how it was done. Reviewing changes at this detailed level serves two purposes. First, a reviewer can determine if the change summary matches the actual changes. Second, a reviewer can provide feedback on the changes through a process called code review.

Drilling down into this level of detail fully solves Fictitious Inc.'s second problem. The line-level detail shows them exactly what each version of the code means. Before using source control, members at Fictitious Inc. had to walk down to John's office and ask, "What's new in `assistant.json` today?" Now they just review the commit log.

Fictitious Inc.'s final challenge was identifying a stable version of the code. By convention, the latest stable code in a Git repository should be found in the `main` branch. (A branch represents a line of development. Every source code repository has at least

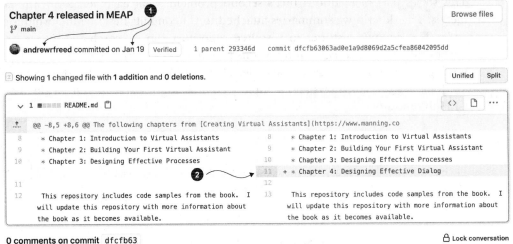

1. Summary of changes
2. Line-for-line comparison showing the exact changes

Figure 9.5 Differences between two versions of the same file in a Git repository. This view shows the before and after versions side by side and annotates the differences between them. In this case, the change was to add one line of text as denoted by the + sign. (Lines that are removed are marked with the - sign.)

one branch, and in Git the default branch is called main. A full explanation of Git branching is beyond the scope of this book.) Fictitious Inc. has multiple ways they can establish this convention. The first and simplest path is shown in figure 9.6.

This simple development process ensures that the main branch always has stable code. The steps in the process are

1 John gets the latest stable code from the Git repository.
2 John makes one or more changes to the code, then tests the code to ensure it works well and is stable.
3 John commits the updated code to the Git repository.

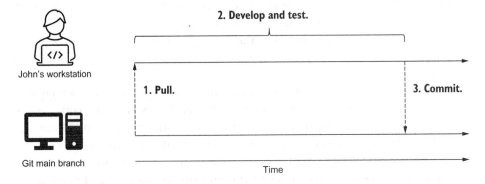

Figure 9.6 Simplest possible Git development model. John pulls the latest code from the Git repository, makes some changes, and when the changes are stable, he commits them back to the repository.

The best part of this development process is its simplicity. There are only three steps, and the `main` branch always has stable code. However, there are a handful of drawbacks to this approach as well:

- Nobody can see the code John is working on until he commits it. Since John can't commit code until he's sure it is stable, significant time may elapse before anyone else can test or review it.
- This puts a significant burden on John. It's difficult for him to share any work unless he shares files another way.
- Interim versions of John's code are not stored in the Git repository.

These shortcomings can be addressed by modifying the development process. When John starts new development work, he can create a new branch in the repository for the specific feature he is working on. John can safely commit interim updates to this branch, and only commit code to the `main` branch when he's sure it is stable. This updated process is depicted in figure 9.7.

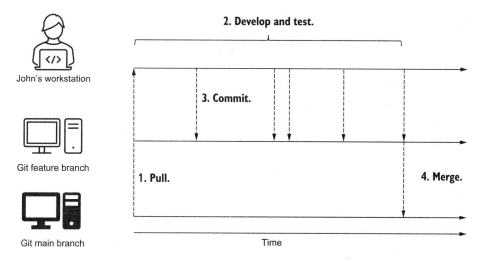

Figure 9.7 Enhanced development process. John's interim updates are stored in Git in a working space called a feature branch. (A feature branch is a temporary or short-lived line of development used to isolate changes from the main branch until those changes are stable.) Other team members can access his code through this branch. Only stable changes are moved to the main branch.

Now the steps in this new process are

1. John gets the latest stable code from the Git repository (same as before).
2. John makes one or more changes to the code and tests them.
3. At any time, John can commit code to his feature branch. This allows other team members to access it through the Git repository.
4. When his new code is stable, John merges his code into the `main` branch.

Fictitious Inc. can use this process to elegantly answer two of their biggest questions:

- *What's the latest version of John's code?* John's feature branch contains his latest code.
- *What's the latest stable version of the team's code?* The `main` branch contains the latest stable code for the entire team.

> **Choose the right size process and workflow for your team**
>
> The processes demonstrated in this book work well for teams with a small number of developers. Git workflows can be simple if the number of developers is one. As your team increases in size, additional rules or coordination processes will be required. Git is a powerful and highly configurable system and can support a variety of complex processes. These processes are out of the scope of this book. There are many good Git books available on the market.

With Git, Fictitious Inc. can fully track the lineage and status of their AI assistant source code. They can find any version of the code and understand what it means. Now they need a process for testing and sharing this code.

9.2 *Where to run your code*

Fictitious Inc.'s development process evolved as they moved John's code from John's laptop to a shared network drive, and then to a Git repository. This made it easy to track the code as it was developed. Fictitious Inc. doesn't just want to store code, they want to run it. In this section, we'll see how Fictitious Inc. evolves the runtime environment for their conversational AI code.

9.2.1 *Development environment*

At the beginning of the process, John Doe is working by himself. John writes code and tests the conversational AI in the same place. Figure 9.8 shows John's working process. As John writes code, it runs in a development environment.

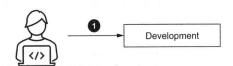

1. John writes code. He commits interim updates to his personal feature branch.

Figure 9.8 The simplest runtime environment. There is one version of the code, and it is used by one developer.

Depending on Fictitious Inc.'s AI platform, the development environment may run on his workstation, on a Fictitious Inc. server, or on a cloud. Regardless of platform, a development environment is where new features and functionality are first built. The development process often requires exploration and may have a "two steps forward, one step back" ethos. Because of this, the development environment should be expected to have the latest code but not necessarily stable code.

> ## Latest code vs stable code
> When new code is written, it often does not function correctly the first time. This latest code may take experimentation or effort to repair a piece of code. The development environment is the place where code repair happens. Once the code is repaired, it is declared stable and ready for sharing with others.

John can store his unstable code on his workstation or in a personal feature branch on the Git repository. Eventually, John will stabilize his code and it will be ready to share with his team for them to test. John knows to move his stable code into the `main` branch and his team knows to look in that branch for stable code. But where will they run this new code? If they use John's development environment, John is not able to do any further development work. Similarly, John's team cannot test code on the development server while he is using it.

9.2.2 Test environment

Fictitious Inc. has two different environmental needs. John needs a space with potentially unstable code to do his development. John's broader team needs a space with stable code for testing the assistant. Fictitious Inc.'s new *test* environment is shown in figure 9.9.

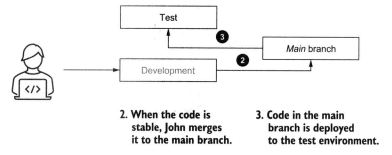

2. When the code is stable, John merges it to the main branch.

3. Code in the main branch is deployed to the test environment.

Figure 9.9 Development process with separate environments for development and test

Development and test environments should at minimum be logically separated. Table 9.1 includes other common isolation requirements based on AI assistant type.

Table 9.1 Comparing development and test environment isolation requirements

Requirement	Cloud-based AI assistant	On-premises AI assistant
Isolation between development and test is achieved by	Using a separate service or instance (depending on the platform's terminology)	Using separate hardware
Access control is achieved by	Using different access control lists per service or instance	Using different access control lists per machine

The test environment is called a higher environment. (In figure 9.9, the test environment is intentionally drawn above—higher than—the development environment.) In higher environments, processes are more strict. In this development process, every code change is first built and tested in a development environment. John never writes code directly on the test environment. John only works in a development environment, committing interim code to his feature branch and stable code to the `main` branch. The only code source for the test environment is the `main` branch. Code may be *developed* in the development environment, but it may only be *deployed* in the test environment.

The code deployment process varies by platform. In some platforms, an AI assistant is deployed by importing a single file through the platform's user interface or API. In other platforms, several source code files may need to be compiled and built into one or more packages that are deployed to a server. There is significant variation between the major AI platforms in the deployment process.

Automating deployment

Regardless of the platform, it is best if the deployment process can be automated. (Automated deployments are referred to as Continuous Integration/Continuous Deployment, or CI/CD.) An automated continuous integration process for AI assistants could look like this:

1 Wait for code to be merged into the `main` branch.
2 Extract the latest code from the `main` branch.
3 Build and/or package the code into a deployable bundle.
4 Deploy the bundle to the test environment.

The development process will repeat many times over the life of the AI assistant. John will develop code in the development environment, and it will be tested (when ready) in the test environment. Any time someone proposes a change, like fixing a defect, it will first go through the development environment and then to the test environment. Eventually, Fictitious Inc. will build enough features with sufficient quality that they are ready to deploy the assistant to production. How will Fictitious Inc. do that?

9.2.3 *Production environment*

You may have guessed already that Fictitious Inc. can't repurpose their development or test environments. They need a third environment: a *production* environment. This environment is shown in figure 9.10.

Fictitious Inc.'s production environment is an even higher environment than the test environment. The production environment must be logically separated from development and test environments, and physical separation is a good idea if Fictitious Inc. can afford it.

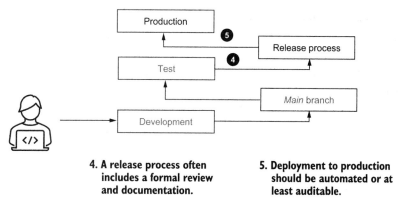

4. A release process often includes a formal review and documentation.

5. Deployment to production should be automated or at least auditable.

Figure 9.10 Fictitious Inc. adds a production environment.

Production needs additional separation from development and test

Logical separation of production from other environments is a must and physical separation is an extra safeguard. Many companies go even further and enforce a separation of duties. In a separation of duties approach, a person who has access to a development environment cannot have access to a production environment, and vice versa.

Most builders have some release process they go through before deploying to production. (This chapter describes a basic development and release process. I have seen many processes much more complex than the ones I describe here. The important thing is to establish *some* process and make sure it is understood and followed by the entire team.) At a minimum, the release process should include some quality assurance, such as the assistant passing a series of manual or automated tests. Additionally, the process should include logging the specific version of the code that is deployed to production. (Perhaps the simplest way to record the code deployed to production is to note the Git commit hash of main and store it in a document. A better way is to use Git's tag feature to mark the specific commit with an easily found identifier like release-1.0.)

Fictitious Inc. should deploy to their production environment with the same tools they use to deploy to the test environment. Ideally, the deployment process should be automated. If it is not automated, it should at least be carefully monitored. It's one thing to make a mistake when deploying to the test environment; it's inconvenient for your testers. It's another thing to break the production environment; now nobody can use your AI assistant.

Fictitious Inc. has achieved a wonderful milestone the first time they deploy to production. AI assistants are never done the first time they are deployed to production. Fictitious Inc. will be making many updates to production over the life of their solution. How can they manage this process?

9.2.4 *After the first production deployment*

Fictitious Inc. followed a relatively lightweight development process for their first production release. They only had one stream of development by definition since they did not have a AI assistant in production. The development stream only included new feature work. After Fictitious Inc. takes their assistant to production, they have a second stream of changes for improving the existing functionality. These two views are shown in figure 9.11.

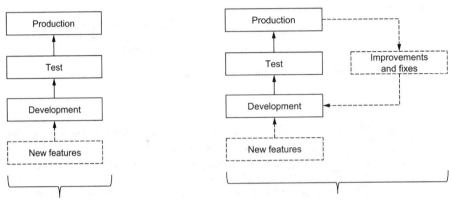

1. With nothing in production, all work is new.

2. After the first production deployment, there will be changes to add new features and improve existing features.

Figure 9.11   Once an assistant is in production, the nature of development changes. New feature development needs to be balanced with improving existing features.

Fictitious Inc. has several release planning options for how to handle these two different modes of input.

"ONE THING AT A TIME" RELEASE PLANNING

The first way Fictitious Inc. can treat the two competing streams of improvement and feature development is to make the streams take turns. For every new release of their AI assistant, they can focus on either adding features or improving existing features. One version of this approach is shown in figure 9.12.

Figure 9.12   "One thing at a time" release planning. Each release includes only new features or only improvement of existing features.

The virtue of this approach is its simplicity. Fictitious Inc. can use their existing development, test, and production environments as is. The entire team can focus entirely on improving the assistant, or entirely on new features, without worrying if one of those efforts is impacting the other. Fictitious Inc. can even vary the length of the iterations, perhaps following each two-week cycle of improvement with a four-week cycle of new feature development.

The downside of this approach is its rigidity. If Fictitious Inc. wants to do an improvement in the middle of a new feature iteration, they have to wait for the next improvement cycle. Fictitious Inc. could instead consider a less rigid release planning approach.

"TWO THINGS AT A TIME" RELEASE PLANNING

Rather than isolating improvement and feature development into separate releases, Fictitious Inc. can do them both at the same time. Each release of their assistant can contain a mixture of new features and improvements to existing functionality. This release model is shown in figure 9.13.

Figure 9.13 Improving the assistant while adding new features. Each release iteration contains some improvements and some new features.

Like the "one thing at a time" approach, Fictitious Inc. can use this approach with their existing development, test, and production environments. The team can vary the blend in each release iteration—some may be heavier on improvements, some on new features.

The best part of this approach is that it is very flexible. Fictitious Inc. can incorporate an improvement into any release iteration. If we assume four-week iterations, then any particular improvement or bug fix is only four weeks or less from being deployed to production. I favor short iterations. Short iterations limit the number of changes going into a single deployment and thus reduce risk.

However, even this flexible approach may not be enough for Fictitious Inc.. Fictitious Inc.'s assistant is probably not production-ready in the middle of an iteration. If a critical bug is found, waiting several weeks for it to be production-ready so that a hotfix can be deployed may not be an option. (My definition of a hotfix: a critical fix that must be deployed as soon as possible, or sooner. For instance, if your legal department says "Fix this or we'll get sued.") Fortunately, there's one more release planning approach Fictitious Inc. can consider.

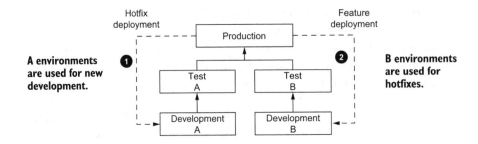

1. When hotfixes are deployed to production, they are merged back into the A environments.

2. When new features are deployed to production, the B environments are overwritten with the new production code.

Figure 9.14   Complete separation of development and hotfix environments

SEPARATE DEVELOPMENT AND HOTFIX ENVIRONMENTS

Fictitious Inc. can adjust either of the two previous approaches to release planning and still be ready to quickly deploy hotfixes. The only cost is that they will need additional development and test environments, with the new development and test environments solely dedicated to hotfixes. These environments and the associated workflow are shown in figure 9.14.

Development follows the same path as before for feature and improvement work. Changes are propagated from development to test to production. The hotfix environments are generally idle and are only actively used when a hotfix is being developed and tested. When a hotfix is deployed to production, it must be merged back into the main development branch. When a regular release is deployed to production, the hotfix environments must be refreshed with the latest production code.

> ## Caveats for the multiple workstreams and environments approach
>
> The separate development and hotfix environments approach is very doable in Git, but a bit beyond the scope of this book. Research the Gitflow workflow to find out how to set up the Git branching for this approach. The other two approaches can be achieved with the minimalist branching scheme described in this chapter.
>
> The multiple workstreams approach can be more difficult to do in low-code platforms. If your AI assistant code is stored in a JSON file, it can be hard to merge changes from one branch to another, and you may instead need to duplicate the changes in multiple branches. This difficulty can be mitigated by keeping hotfixes as small as possible.

There are many possible variations of these release planning approaches. You can always start with a simple approach and evolve into a more sophisticated approach when you need it. The release planning approaches are summarized in table 9.2.

Table 9.2 Comparison of release planning approaches

	One thing at a time	Two things at a time	Separate streams
Release contents	Features or improvements	Features and improvements	Development stream is mostly features. Hotfix stream is only fixes.
Number of environments	Three (one development, one test, one production)	Three (one development, one test, one production)	Five (two development, two test, one production)
Resource use	High: all environments are in frequent use.	High: all environments are in frequent use.	Hotfix stream is mostly idle.
Hotfix delivery timing	Deliver at the end of the current iteration.	Deliver at the end of the current iteration.	Delivery as soon as the fix can be built and tested.
Analysis and improvement	Improvements are isolated iterations; the analysis is performed against a stable base.	Improvements are made while new features are being added. Iterative analysis may be skewed by the new features.	Improvements can be isolated if they are done on the hotfix stream.

9.3 *Using source control for other assets*

Source control is not just a good idea for source code, it's a good idea for any asset related to an AI assistant. You can use the same source control repository for all of your AI assistant artifacts.

For instance, both the training data and test data for your assistant should be tracked in source control.

The training data for your assistant will evolve as you add new intents and improve existing intents. Changes to your assistant's training data can have a big impact, positively or negatively, on your assistant, and it's important to be able to trace a variation in the assistant's accuracy back to the change(s) that caused it. Training data is commonly stored in comma-separated value (CSV) files which are easily tracked in Git.

The longer an assistant is in production, the more opportunities you have to collect test data. It's important to add more test data in the early days of your assistant, especially if you had a small amount of test data to start with. You will likely run many different accuracy tests against your assistant over its lifetime. When the accuracy changes, you'll want to be able to track it back to the training and test data used in the experiment.

Figure 9.15 demonstrates how Fictitious Inc. tracks the accuracy of their assistant over time, and how they know exactly which version of their training and test data they used for each test. By tracking these data sources so closely, they can extrapolate why the assistant's accuracy went up (or down) based on how the data changed.

The revision history in Git can be a great reminder to keep your test data fresh. If your Git repository shows your test data was last updated 11 months ago, it's probably time to refresh your test data.

Training and test data are probably the most important non-code assets to store in source control, but it's also a good idea to store any scripts you use to test or deploy your assistant in the source control repository as well.

	①	②	③	④	⑤
Assistant overall accuracy	80%	77%	87%	85%	88%
Training data version	1	2	3	3	4
Test data version	1	1	1	2	2

1. The initial accuracy assessment is stored as a baseline.
2. New training data made the assistant less accurate.
3. New training data improved the assistant's accuracy.
4. New test data showed the assistant was less accurate than expected.
5. The training data is improved to increase the assistant's accuracy.

Figure 9.15 Evolution of Fictitious Inc.'s assistant accuracy, associated with the version of training and test data used

Summary

- Source control helps you manage changes to your AI assistant. It can show you the who, what, and why behind every change.
- Use separate development, test, and production environments. Each environment has a specific purpose.
- Source control is not just for code. Use it to version your training data, test data, deployment scripts, and more.

Improving your assistant 10

This chapter covers

- Examining and deciphering where your AI assistant needs improvement
- Finding where your assistant is failing and rectifying these failures
- Improving the assistant where it has the highest inaccuracy
- Motivating AI owners for continuous improvement

Fictitious Inc. has deployed their conversational AI assistant to production, but they are not achieving the success metrics they outlined for the solution. The assistant was supposed to reduce the burden on other customer service channels, but these channels have not seen a significant reduction in user activity. Fictitious Inc. knows how to troubleshoot their traditional applications but does not know where to start troubleshooting their conversational AI assistant.

Fictitious Inc. needs to quickly drill down into why their assistant is not performing well. They need to find out if their conversational flow does not work for users, if the intent mapping they have done does not work, or if there is some other core problem with their assistant.

Fictitious Inc. is in good company. Deploying a conversational AI to production is not the end; it is only the beginning. Figure 10.1 demonstrates the continuous improvement in an assistant's life cycle. Continuous improvement is broadly applicable in software projects, and it is especially applicable for AI assistants.

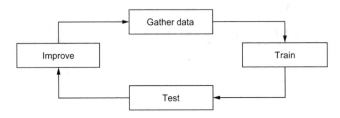

Figure 10.1 **Improvement is part of a continuous cycle in the life of an AI assistant. This cycle continues even after an assistant is deployed to production.**

This cycle does not stop for Fictitious Inc. when they deploy their assistant. The first improvement cycle after deploying to production is the most informative. This is where Fictitious Inc. will learn which of their assumptions were correct and which ones need to be revisited.

In this chapter, we will learn how Fictitious Inc. can identify where their assistant needs the most improvement. Fictitious Inc. has chosen successful containment as their key success metric, and we will use that to drive our investigation. *Containment* for conversational AIs is the percentage of conversations handled entirely by the assistant. (A conversation that is not escalated to a human is *contained*.) Fictitious Inc.'s successful containment modifies this definition: only conversations that finish at least process flow are successfully contained.

With successful containment in mind, we will use a data-driven approach to evaluate their conversational AI, including the dialogue flows and intent identification. We will conduct a single evaluation of Fictitious Inc.'s assistant. Fictitious Inc. will need to evaluate their assistant many times over its lifetime. Let's start by looking for the first improvement Fictitious Inc. needs to make.

Change is the only constant in life.

—Heraclitus

10.1 *Using a success metric to determine where to start improvements*

Analyzing a conversational AI can feel like a daunting process. There are many different types of analyses. Where should Fictitious Inc. begin their analysis? Analysis should be centered on a success metric. This success metric forms a guiding principle for all analysis and improvement. Any potential analysis or improvement work should be prioritized based on how it impacts a success metric.

Fictitious Inc.'s chosen success metric is successful containment. Successful containment is better aligned with their users' needs than containment. If a user quits a conversation before getting an answer, that conversation is contained, but Fictitious Inc. does not consider the conversation a success. Table 10.1 contrasts containment and successful containment. Fictitious Inc. will use successful containment.

Table 10.1 Sample scenarios and how they are measured

Interaction ends with	Containment	Successful containment
The assistant suggests escalating the conversation to a human agent.	Not contained	Not contained
The user demands a human agent before a process flow completes.	Not contained	Not contained
The user quits the chat in the middle of a process flow.	Contained	Not contained
The user starts and finishes a process flow successfully.	Contained	Contained

Fictitious Inc. will use three data points to start the analysis of their assistant: overall successful containment, volume by intent, and successful containment by intent. These data points enable analysis of each intent. From these data points we can find which intents are having the largest impact on the overall successful containment.

To simplify the analysis, we will only consider five of Fictitious Inc.'s intents. These intents and their associated metrics are shown in table 10.2. Based on this table, which intent would you explore first?

Table 10.2 Metrics for conversation volume and successful containment, broken down per intent

Intent	Volume	Contained	Uncontained	Volume	Containment
#appointments	50	15	35	10%	30%
#employment_inquiry	50	40	10	10%	80%
#reset_password	200	80	120	40%	40%
#store_hours	100	95	5	20%	95%
#store_location	100	90	10	20%	90%
Total	500	320	180	100%	64%

#appointments has the lowest overall containment at 30%, but it is a low-volume intent. And #reset_password is the largest source of uncontained conversations, comprising two-thirds of the total uncontained conversations. If Fictitious Inc. can fix what's wrong in those two intents, their conversational AI will have much higher containment and thus be more successful. Since #reset_password has the biggest problem, Fictitious Inc. should start there.

10.1.1 Improving the first flow to fix containment problems

Solving problems is easier when you know what the specific problems actually are. Fictitious Inc. has identified the #reset_password flow as the biggest source of non-contained conversations. This is the most complex of Fictitious Inc.'s process flows, and that's probably not a coincidence. Let's reacquaint ourselves with Fictitious Inc.'s #reset_password flow in figure 10.2.

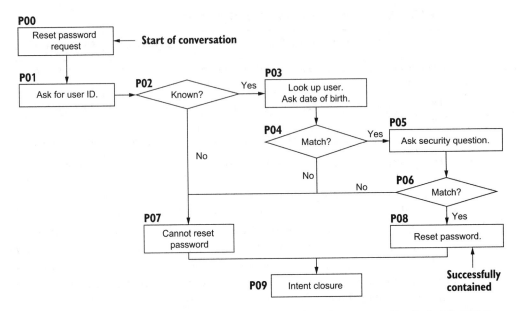

Figure 10.2   Fictitious Inc.'s reset password conversational flow. Any conversation that visits P00 is counted as a password reset conversation. Only conversations that include P08 are successfully contained.

A password reset conversation always starts with dialogue P00 and P01. After that, the password reset flow has only one path to success. The successful path includes dialogue nodes P00, P01, P03, P05, and P08. These nodes form a conversion funnel, which is shown in figure 10.3. Every conversation that includes P03 must necessarily include P01, but some conversations that include P01 will not include P03. A conversation that includes P01 but not P03 will have drop-off at P01. By measuring the drop-off between P01, P03, P05, and P08, Fictitious Inc. can narrow in on why password reset conversations fail to complete.

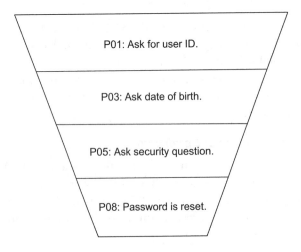

Figure 10.3   A successful password reset flow, visualized as a funnel. A conversation that completes each step in this funnel is successfully contained.

Fictitious Inc. can analyze their password reset process flow via a conversion funnel by analyzing their assistant logs and counting how many times each dialogue node is invoked. Then, they can compute the drop-off in each step of the funnel. This high-level analysis will illuminate what parts of the process flow require further analysis. The parts causing the most drop-off should be improved first.

How can you run log analysis in your specific platform?

There are multiple ways to perform the analysis done in this section. The specific steps vary by platform. For instance, your platform may make it easy to find conversations that include one dialogue node but not another.

The techniques in this chapter are purposely generic, even if somewhat inefficient. If your platform does not include analytic capabilities, you will likely want to build the analyses described in this section.

Fictitious Inc.'s password reset conversion funnel metrics can be found in table 10.3. This analysis shows a steep drop-off after asking for the user ID and the security question.

Table 10.3 Conversion funnel for password reset dialogue flow

Dialogue node	Conversations including this dialogue node	Conversations that don't include this dialogue node	Drop-off from previous node
P01: What's your user ID?	200	0	0%
P03: What's your date of birth?	135	65	33%
P05: What's your security question?	130	5	4%
P08: Password reset complete	80	50	38%

The conversion funnel tells Fictitious Inc. that one-third of password reset flow conversations included the question "What's your user ID?" but do not include the question "What's your date of birth?" The "What's your user ID?" question has a 33% drop-off rate. It's also the largest source of drop-offs, causing containment failure on 65 total conversations. The entire conversion funnel can be visualized as in figure 10.4.

The severe drop-offs between P01 and P03, as well as P05 and P08, are both detrimental to Fictitious Inc.'s successful containment metric. The P05 to P08 drop-off is more severe from a relativistic perspective (38% versus 33%), but the P01 to P03 drop-off affects more conversations in total. Fictitious Inc. should first focus on the P01 to P03 drop-off.

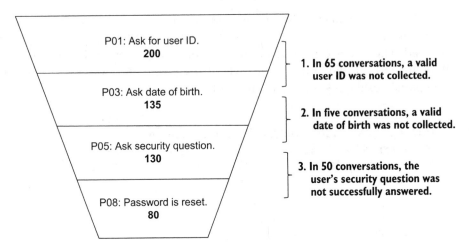

Figure 10.4   Password reset flow conversion funnel annotated with the number of conversations containing each step of the dialogue. P01 and P05 cause most of the total drop-off.

ANALYZING THE FIRST SOURCE OF DROP-OFF IN THE FIRST INTENT

The first detailed analysis for the P01 to P03 drop-off is to find out what users are saying to the assistant between P01 and P03. Depending on their AI platform, Fictitious Inc. can query for

- What users say immediately after P01
- What users say immediately before P03

This query will tell Fictitious Inc. what users are saying in response to the "What is your User ID?" question. Fictitious Inc. can inspect a small sample of these responses, perhaps 10 or 20, in their initial investigation. The query results are shown in the following list. All valid Fictitious Inc. user IDs follow the same format: four to twelve alphabetic characters followed by one to three numeric characters. Any other user ID string is invalid. Before reading ahead, see if you can classify the response patterns:

- afreed1
- don't know, that's why i called
- ebrown5
- fjones8
- hgarcia3
- I don't know it
- I'm not sure
- jdoe3
- mhill14
- nmiller
- no idea
- pjohnson4

- pdavis18
- tsmith
- vwilliams4

The analysis of these responses is shown in figure 10.5. The analysis surfaces several patterns in the response utterances. The expected response to P01 is a valid user ID consisting of 4–12 letters followed by one to three numbers. But that is not what users always provide.

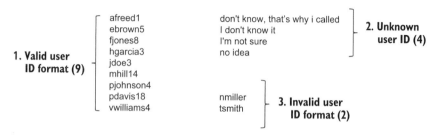

Figure 10.5 Patterns in user utterances given in response to Fictitious Inc.'s question P01, "What is your User ID?"

Fictitious Inc. can transform these patterns into actionable insights that will improve successful containment:

- *Insight 1: Many users don't know their user ID.* Fictitious Inc. could build an intent for #i_dont_know. When a user is asked for their ID and responds with #i_dont_know, the assistant could provide the user with instructions on how to find their user ID. Or the assistant could be programmed to validate the user another way.
- *Insight 2: Many users provide their user ID incorrectly.* This may be because they don't actually know their user ID, or they may have entered it incorrectly. (In the case of voice assistants, the assistant may not have heard the user correctly. One possible resolution is to improve the assistant's voice training on user IDs.) These users could be given another chance to enter their ID or guidance on what a valid user ID looks like.

NOTE Couldn't these insights have been found during the design phase? The design phase will never be perfect. Improving an assistant based on real-world feedback can be better than building an overengineered assistant with features that nobody actually needs.

There may be additional problems occurring at this point in the dialogue, but with this quick analysis, Fictitious Inc. has already found two unique error patterns causing password reset conversations to fail. These two patterns will address most of the 65 drop-offs caused between P01 and P03. Fictitious Inc. can assign resolution of these patterns to their design and development teams and move on to further analysis. Let's continue Fictitious Inc.'s password reset analysis at the other major source of drop-offs.

ANALYZING THE SECOND SOURCE OF DROP-OFF IN THE FIRST INTENT

Fifty of Fictitious Inc.'s 120 drop-offs in password reset occurred immediately after P05: asking the user's security question. The user has gotten tantalizingly close to P08 which actually resets the password—they are only one step away. Fictitious Inc. can modify their trusty query depending on their AI platform to find:

- What users say immediately after P05
- What users say immediately before P08

As with the prior analysis, a sample of query results should suffice to identify patterns. This analysis is somewhat more difficult if the user's specific security question is not known; however, in a quick analysis the questions are not necessarily needed. The alphabetized query results are shown next. As in the preceding exercise, try to find the patterns before reading ahead:

- 02/04/2018
- Anderson
- FLUFFY
- Jones
- Lopez
- new york
- null
- null
- null
- orange
- PEnnsylvania
- purple
- skiing
- trains
- Volleyball

An analysis of these utterances is shown in figure 10.6. Similar to the previous analysis, three patterns are present in the data.

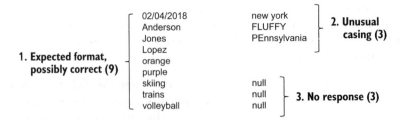

Figure 10.6   Patterns in user utterances given in response to Fictitious Inc.'s question P05: Answer your security question.

Two insights jump out from this data:

- *Insight 3: Several responses are* `null`. (The specific value will vary by conversational platform. You may also see "conversationEnd," "hangup" or even the empty string "".) This indicates that the user ended the conversation without answering the question—closing the chat window or hanging up the phone. This could happen because the user didn't know the answer or because the user was frustrated with a process that took longer than expected. Fictitious Inc. could alter the dialogue for this question to indicate that it's the final step. Or Fictitious Inc. could investigate an alternative verification option for these users.

- *Insight 4: Responses include unusual casing.* The responses "FLUFFY," "new york," and "PEnnsylvania" seem like possible correct answers, but with questionable upper- and lowercasing. Fictitious Inc. should investigate if the response to this question needs to be case-sensitive.

ANALYZING THE THIRD SOURCE OF DROP-OFF IN THE FIRST INTENT

Fictitious Inc.'s password reset flow has a third place where drop-offs occur. Out of the total 120 drop-offs, 5 happen between P03 and P05, when the user is asked for their date of birth. What analysis should Fictitious Inc. do about these drop-offs in their initial assessment of their assistant?

Fictitious Inc. probably does not need to do anything for now. There are several good reasons for this:

- *Data-driven approach*—The five drop-offs are a small fraction of the 120 total in the password reset flow. Fictitious Inc. already has four solid leads to solve the other 115 drop-offs. (Existing leads: unknown user IDs, invalid user IDs, no security question response, and unusual casing of security question response.)

- *Intuitive sense*—There are three questions in the password reset flow, and it makes intuitive sense that the date of birth question would have the least number of problems. We expect less people to forget their date of birth than their user ID or the answer to their security question. The low number of drop-offs at date of birth confirms this.

- *Opportunity cost*—The time and energy Fictitious Inc. focuses on this small problem is time and energy they can't spend on another problem.

- *Prioritize bigger problems first*—Fictitious Inc.'s biggest containment problem came from 120 uncontained password reset conversations. Their second biggest containment problem was appointments with 35 uncontained conversations. The appointments flow should be analyzed before the date of birth issue.

- *Alignment with success metrics and business value*—There is more business value from focusing on the appointments flow first. Fictitious Inc. doesn't get any credit for analyzing 100% of a process flow. Their success comes from improving successful containment.

- *The Golden Rule of prioritization*—Not now doesn't mean not ever.

Always keep the business success metric in mind when analyzing and improving on your assistant. Depending on the size of Fictitious Inc.'s development team, the analysis done so far may already be enough to keep them busy improving their assistant. But if they have the capacity, they can continue analysis. Fictitious Inc.'s success metric of successful containment dictates that they should analyze the appointments containment issue next.

> **NOTE** Keep your business success metric in mind when analyzing and improving on your AI assistant.

10.1.2 Inspecting other process flows for containment problems

Fictitious Inc.'s second major source of uncontained conversations was in the `#appointments` flow. Users wanting an appointment with Fictitious Inc. will need to provide a store location, a date, and a time. They can provide this information all at once or the assistant can prompt them for the information one piece at a time. The `#appointments` flow is depicted in figure 10.7.

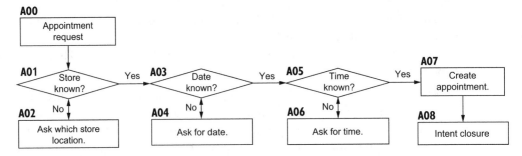

Figure 10.7   Fictitious Inc.'s appointment process flow. An appointment requires a store location, date, and time. The user may provide these all at once or one at a time.

This process flow presents an interesting analysis challenge due to the inclusion of the optional nodes. Every successful `#appointments` conversation must include A00 and A07, but it's unclear how many should include the optional nodes A02, A04, and A06. Thus, counting conversations including the optional nodes does not have immediate value. Fictitious Inc. should start with the simple conversion funnel in figure 10.8.

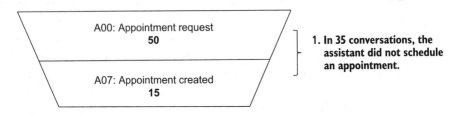

Figure 10.8   Conversion funnel for the appointment process flow. Because A02, A04, and A06 are all optional steps, they are not included.

With only two guaranteed steps in the process, the analysis options are limited. The optional questions throw a wrinkle into a purely funnel-based analysis. Based on our familiar analysis method Fictitious Inc. can look for either

- What users say immediately after A00
- What users say immediately before A07

Fictitious Inc. will start by analyzing utterances immediately after A00. A sampling of those utterances is shown next. Before reading past the list, what conclusions can you make for Fictitious Inc.? What is causing the containment problem for #appointments?

- at Maple
- elm
- Elm please
- no i don't want an appointment
- not what I want
- today
- tuesday at 9pm
- what time are you open?
- what??
- why do i need an appointment for this?

These utterances are analyzed in figure 10.9, which shows two clear patterns in the data.

Figure 10.9   Sample utterances received by Fictitious Inc. after dialogue A00, where the user is asked to provide details on the location, date, and/or time for an appointment

The utterances fall into two patterns:

- *Happy path*—Five of the utterances are clearly responding to A02 (where do you need the appointment) or A04 (what day would you like the appointment). There is no immediately obvious reason why these conversations would fail to complete successfully.
- *Unhappy path*—Four of the utterances are clearly not enthusiastic about setting up an appointment.

(The final utterance "what time are you open" could fit into either pattern. Without additional context, it's too hard to tell.)

The key insight from this analysis is

- *Insight 5: Users are surprised when the assistant creates an appointment.* Users appear to enter the #appointments flow when that is not their actual intent.

Fictitious Inc.'s primary problem with password resets was that users didn't know how to answer the questions in the process flow. But Fictitious Inc.'s primary problem with appointments looks like users are getting a process flow they didn't want. Fictitious Inc. can confirm this hypothesis by exploring the user utterances received immediately before A00. These utterances are

- Can I make an appointment at Maple?
- Can you ship to my house?
- Consults available at 9pm today?
- Do I need an appointment for login problem?
- Help me set up a consultation
- I need to talk to someone at Elm on Friday.
- Schedule appointment
- What's the schedule for the sales promotion?
- When can I make a return at Maple?
- When can I shop in-person at your store?

The utterances are analyzed in figure 10.10.

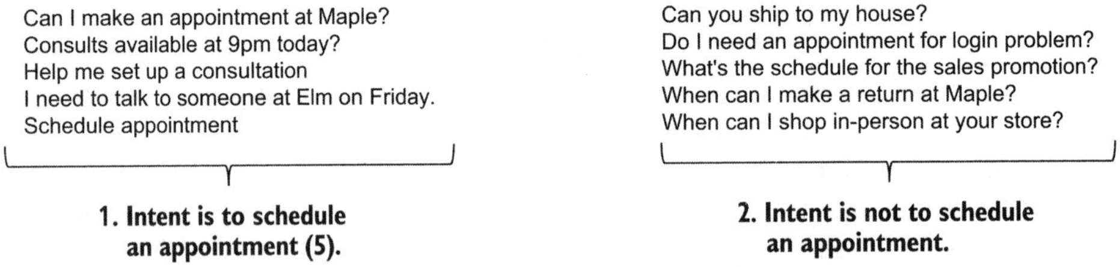

Can I make an appointment at Maple?
Consults available at 9pm today?
Help me set up a consultation
I need to talk to someone at Elm on Friday.
Schedule appointment

1. Intent is to schedule an appointment (5).

Can you ship to my house?
Do I need an appointment for login problem?
What's the schedule for the sales promotion?
When can I make a return at Maple?
When can I shop in-person at your store?

2. Intent is not to schedule an appointment.

Figure 10.10   Sample utterances received by Fictitious Inc. before dialogue A00. The conversational AI is currently initiating the #appointments flow after each one of these utterances.

The hypothesis holds. Several of these utterances are not asking to set up an appointment. Fictitious Inc.'s #appointments intent is capturing too many utterances that are not related to appointments. This analysis makes some intuitive sense; we would not expect users to have chronic problems with the location, date, or time questions. While you cannot yet rule out that some conversations fail at these questions, the over-selection of the #appointments intent is the primary problem in the appointments flow. Fictitious Inc.'s assistant is inaccurate when it comes to identifying the #appointments intent.

Fictitious Inc.'s five analysis insights and suggested next steps are summarized in table 10.4. Each of these insights directly affects the successful containment success metric.

Fictitious Inc. has three more intents we have not analyzed for containment problems. Each of #employment_inquiry, #store_hours, and #store_location had high containment in the very first analysis. These intents each use a single question-and-answer response, so it is difficult for a conversation that starts one of those intents not

Table 10.4 Summarized analysis and next steps

Insight	Next steps
Many users don't know their user ID.	Design a response that helps users find their user ID.
Many users provide their user ID incorrectly.	Design a response that gives users a second chance, possibly with additional advice.
Several users don't attempt to answer the security question.	Investigate an alternate method of validating the user.
Security question responses include unusual casing.	Consider a case-insensitive evaluation of the answer.
Users are surprised when the assistant creates an appointment.	Improve the assistant's training around the #appointments intent.

to finish it. (If there is just a single response, the user would have to close the assistant while the assistant was generating the response for the conversation to not be contained.) Users are reaching the end of the conversations for these intents, which is enough to declare the conversations contained. But is the assistant recognizing these intents correctly?

10.2 Analyzing the classifier to predict future containment problems

If Fictitious Inc.'s assistant identifies the wrong intent, it may still "contain" the conversation, yet not satisfy the user. (This is why it is difficult to evaluate an assistant using only one success metric.) Users who get responses based on the wrong intent may be "contained" today but are unlikely to return to the assistant in the future. Therefore, an inaccurate assistant can reduce the total volume of contained conversations. This harms Fictitious Inc.'s bottom line. The user may select a more expensive resolution option (calling a human agent) or may stop being a Fictitious Inc. customer altogether.

Fictitious Inc. should analyze the assistant's classifications to see how often it predicts the wrong intent. There are two different analyses Fictitious Inc. can run:

- *Representative baseline*—Take a random sampling of utterances and see how they are classified. The variation in this sample will ensure an accurate evaluation of the assistant.
- *Find gaps in the training data*—Any utterance for which the assistant predicts an incorrect intent is a potential candidate for improving the assistant, especially if the prediction was made with high confidence. Similarly, any utterance correctly predicted but with low confidence sits in a similar gap. Fictitious Inc. should collect some of both types of utterances for use in improving the system.

10.2.1 Representative baseline

Before making any changes to the classifier, Fictitious Inc. should understand how well it already works. Now that their assistant is in production, they have the perfect data set to test their assistant's accuracy. Before they were in production, they may have run a blind test on data they expected to see in production, but now they have the real thing. Fictitious Inc. needs to gather some production data for a blind test. This test will give a baseline for how accurate the assistant was before changes were made.

The baseline needs to include a representative variety of data. The easiest way to accomplish this is to take a random sampling of all utterances that were used to start a conversation. (A random sampling of first user utterances is good enough. This sampling will not include any retries, or any intents attempted after the first. The analytic query to get first user utterances is easy to write and jump-starts analysis. Don't let the perfect be the enemy of the good.) Fictitious Inc. can take this data and build a blind test set. A sampling of conversation-starting utterances for Fictitious Inc.'s assistant is shown in table 10.5. The predictions in the table look mostly correct, but Fictitious Inc. shouldn't eyeball this. They should create a *blind test set*. A blind test set is a spreadsheet with two columns: user utterances and the *actual* intent for those utterances. Table 10.5 includes the utterances with their *predicted* intent. We've seen multiple times that the assistant makes some mistakes. Some predicted intents do not match the actual intent.

Table 10.5 Sample conversation-opening utterances received by the assistant

User utterance	Assistant's prediction	Assistant's confidence
Can you ship to my house?	#appointments	70%
I want to apply for a job	#employment_inquiry	81%
I forgot my password	#reset_password	100%
Reset my password	#reset_password	100%
Need my password reset	#reset_password	93%
I can't log in	#reset_password	82%
What are your hours on Wednesday?	#store_hours	99%
How late are you open tonight?	#store_hours	98%
Where is the nearest store to me?	#store_location	99%
I need driving directions to Maple	#store_location	72%

Fictitious Inc. can take multiple approaches to convert table 10.5 to a blind set: fully unassisted, partly assisted, or fully assisted. Let's explore these approaches.

FULLY UNASSISTED

In this approach, Fictitious Inc. takes the utterances from table 10.5 and copies them into a new spreadsheet with one column. They have an SME fill in a second column, containing the actual intent for each utterance. Ideally the SME should have the list of Fictitious Inc.'s intents and the definition of those intents, but no other guidance. This approach is demonstrated in figure 10.11.

User utterance	Intent
Can you ship to my house?	
I want to apply for a job	
I forgot my password	
Reset my password	
Need my password reset	
I can't log in	
What are your hours on Wednesday?	
How late are you open tonight?	
Where is the nearest store to me?	
I need driving directions to Maple	

The person filling in the intent column needs to do all the work.

Figure 10.11 Fully unassisted labeling of production user utterances for a blind test set. This table does not include any prediction data from the assistant. The person providing the intent has a completely unbiased view, but they have a lot of work to do.

The biggest argument in favor of the fully assisted approach is that the person providing the intents is not biased by the assistant's predictions. This should ensure high-quality intent labeling, but it comes at a cost. This is the slowest of the three approaches. If Fictitious Inc. uses this approach, they are likely to build a smaller blind test set due to time considerations alone. Let's examine the partly assisted option.

PARTLY ASSISTED

In this approach, Fictitious Inc. transforms table 10.5. First, all predictions below a certain confidence threshold are removed. Then, the confidence column is removed. A subject matter expert only needs to fill in the remaining blanks in the intent column. This approach is demonstrated in figure 10.12.

The best part of this approach is that it is faster. There's no need to have utterances reviewed if the assistant handled them with 100% confidence. A variation on this approach is to trust the assistant's predictions if they are above some non-100% confidence threshold. The farther this threshold is lowered, the less work for an SME,

User utterance	Intent
Can you ship to my house?	
I want to apply for a job	
I forgot my password	#reset_password
Reset my password	#reset_password
Need my password reset	
I can't log in	
What are your hours on Wednesday?	#store_hours
How late are you open tonight?	
Where is the nearest store to me?	
I need driving directions to Maple	

Predictions above the confidence threshold are assumed correct.

The subject-matter expert fills in all remaining blanks.

Figure 10.12 Partially assisted option for building Fictitious Inc.'s blind test data set. In this example, the original predictions from the assistant with 99% or higher confidence are assumed to be correct.

but there's a higher chance of mistakes slipping by. Since Fictitious Inc. is doing this exercise for the first time, I'd recommend using at least 99% as the threshold. Once they are more in tune with their assistant's performance, they can consider a lower threshold.

A partly assisted approach is my preferred method of adding production utterances for a blind test set. There's one more approach Fictitious Inc. can consider, and it's even faster.

FULLY ASSISTED

In the fully assisted approach, the subject matter expert is given table 10.5 as is and is told to correct any mistakes in the prediction column. If the assistant's prediction is correct, there is no work for the expert. This is demonstrated in figure 10.13.

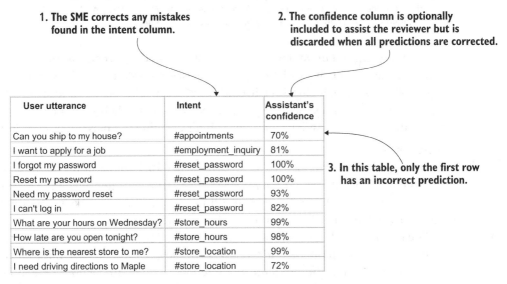

1. The SME corrects any mistakes found in the intent column.

2. The confidence column is optionally included to assist the reviewer but is discarded when all predictions are corrected.

User utterance	Intent	Assistant's confidence
Can you ship to my house?	#appointments	70%
I want to apply for a job	#employment_inquiry	81%
I forgot my password	#reset_password	100%
Reset my password	#reset_password	100%
Need my password reset	#reset_password	93%
I can't log in	#reset_password	82%
What are your hours on Wednesday?	#store_hours	99%
How late are you open tonight?	#store_hours	98%
Where is the nearest store to me?	#store_location	99%
I need driving directions to Maple	#store_location	72%

3. In this table, only the first row has an incorrect prediction.

Figure 10.13 Fully assisted approach. The subject matter expert is shown all of the assistant's predictions and only updates the incorrect predictions. This is the fastest approach but biases the expert with the assistant's opinion.

This is the fastest way to produce a blind test set from production logs. For the SME, correcting mistakes is easier than producing new answers. However, this approach has the highest risk of introducing bias into the test data. For a given utterance, the assistant may make a good prediction even though a better prediction is possible. By showing the expert the good prediction, they may be biased to accept it. If the expert has to generate their own prediction, they choose the better prediction.

Fictitious Inc. can use any of these approaches to generate their blind test data set: a fully unassisted approach, partly assisted, or fully assisted. The trade-offs are shown in figure 10.14. For Fictitious Inc.'s first improvement cycle, I recommend the partly assisted approach.

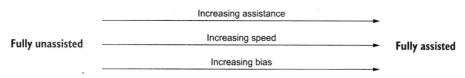

Figure 10.14   The trade-offs in the approaches used to generate test data from production logs

No matter which approach **Fictitious Inc.** uses to create a blind test set, they are ready to start looking at where the **assistant can be more accurate at identifying intents. One great source they can use is low-confidence** predictions.

10.2.2   Finding gaps in the training data

Fictitious Inc. has now gathered a blind test set which they can use to understand how accurate their assistant is. They need to know how accurate the assistant is before they start making changes to improve it. They know the assistant misclassifies some utterances. They need to gather some misclassified utterances to help improve their assistant. They first need to find these utterances and then can work on testing and improving the classification of these utterances.

There are three ways Fictitious Inc. can find training gaps:

- *Find utterances with low-confidence intent predictions.* The assistant assigns a confidence value to each prediction it makes. We can define low confidence as a confidence value below a threshold, for example below 0.5. Predictions with low confidence are generally of lower quality than those with higher confidence. (The assistant can still be wrong with high confidence. Because a human is required to tell if the assistant is right or wrong, we use a low-confidence filter to reduce the number of utterances a human has to review.) This set of utterances is likely to identify problem spots in the assistant's training.
- *Work backward from containment problems.* When Fictitious Inc. analyzed the #appointments process flow, they found several conversations that were not contained because the wrong intent was identified.
- *Find incorrect predictions that had high confidence.* Where the assistant is both confident and wrong, there is a significant training gap. These gaps are the rarest and hardest to find.

FIND LOW-CONFIDENCE INTENT PREDICTIONS

Low-confidence predictions are a great place to find gaps in training. A low-confidence prediction means the assistant was not very sure which intent to select. Because many low-confidence predictions will be wrong, assistants are often configured not to select an intent with if the confidence is low and will instead ask the user to restate their question. An assistant that does not take action on intents with low confidence will prevent false positives (responding with a wrong intent) but will also suffer from false negatives (not responding, when it could have).

A sampling of low-confidence predictions from Fictitious Inc.'s assistant is listed in table 10.6. Some predictions are correct: "when and where can I schedule time with an expert" is indeed an #appointments intent. Some predictions are incorrect: "I need help finding you from my house" is #store_location, not #appointments. For each of these utterances, the user was prompted to restate their question. The system does not use any intent predicted with less than 0.5 confidence.

Table 10.6 Low-confidence predictions made by the assistant

Utterance	Intent	Confidence
where and when can i schedule time with an expert	#appointments	0.43
i need help finding you from my house	#appointments	0.37
time to talk in person	#appointments	0.33
what roles do you have available?	#employment_inquiry	0.27
log in problem	#reset_password	0.44
Open on Valentine's day?	#store_hours	0.42
Valentine's day hours	#store_hours	0.31
gps directions to you	#store_location	0.3
where do you deliver?	#store_location	0.3
do you ship to store or my house	#store_location	0.23

Low-confidence predictions are also a great place to find new intents. Table 10.6 includes two utterances where the user is asking about delivery options. Currently, Fictitious Inc.'s #store_location intent is matching to these utterances. Fictitious Inc. can consider adding a #delivery_options intent if it turns out to be a common user need. Figure 10.15 annotates the sample of Fictitious Inc. low-confidence predictions.

Figure 10.15 Sample of Fictitious Inc. low-confidence predictions.

Based on these findings, Fictitious Inc. should start by improving the `#store_location` training data. They have unambiguous false-negative utterances like "GPS directions to you" that could be added to the training for `#store_location`. They also have unambiguous false-positive utterances like "where do you deliver" that should go to a different intent (creating `#delivery_options`) or should be negative examples for `#store_location`. (Most training data is a list of positive examples: "Directions to your store" means `#store_location`. Some AI platforms let you create negative examples, or counterexamples, like "Where do you deliver," which does *not* mean `#store_location`.) The assistant also is slightly weak at identifying `#store_hours` requests specific to holidays. This could be fixed by updating the `#store_hours` training examples.

Not every low-confidence prediction indicates a gap in training. The utterance "tell me a joke" does not match any intent in Fictitious Inc.'s assistant. For this utterance, the system responds with a message like "I'm sorry, I did not understand." That is a perfectly fine response. Fictitious Inc. is trying to improve their containment, not to make their assistant sentient. A set of low-confidence predictions will contain some useful patterns as well as some noise.

Evaluating low-confidence predictions is a good analysis because it is fast. These predictions can be found with a generic query and are likely to illuminate training gaps. Fictitious Inc. can also search for possible training gaps by looking at uncontained calls.

WORK BACKWARD FROM CONTAINMENT PROBLEMS

Process flows with poor containment can also be mined for training data gaps. In Fictitious Inc.'s analysis of the `#appointments` flow, they found that many conversations started the appointments process flow when that's not what the user wanted. An example is shown in figure 10.16.

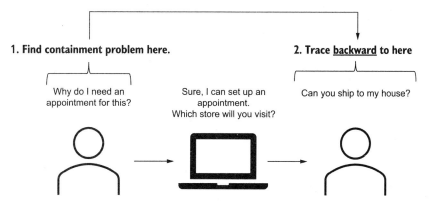

1. Find containment problem here.

Why do I need an appointment for this?

Sure, I can set up an appointment. Which store will you visit?

2. Trace <u>backward</u> to here

Can you ship to my house?

Figure 10.16 Fictitious Inc. can find conversations that were not contained, then walk backward to find utterances with poor classification.

In figure 10.16, Fictitious Inc. found an uncontained appointments conversation that ended with "Why do I need an appointment for this?" They could walk backward in that conversation to find what the user initially said: "Can you ship to my house?" That utterance was misclassified as #appointments.

Fictitious Inc. previously analyzed the #appointments process flow and found the uncontained conversations. They can walk backward in each of these conversations to find utterances that were misclassified as #appointments, and these utterances will also help identify error patterns and gaps in the Fictitious Inc. assistant's training.

Uncontained conversations are a good candidate source for finding problems in training. Not every uncontained conversation will start with a classification error, but many will. Since the definition of successful containment may vary by intent, it can be more work to query and walk back through uncontained conversations instead of querying for low-confidence predictions. Still, looking at uncontained conversations is a nice complement to the data found in low-confidence predictions. Fictitious Inc. can save time in this first analysis by first focusing on process flows with poor containment. They can review the other process flows in future analysis cycles if needed.

There's one more source of potential training gaps: high-confidence, but incorrect, predictions.

FIND HIGH-CONFIDENCE INCORRECT PREDICTIONS

Fictitious Inc. would like to find all of the times their assistant made the wrong prediction, but with high confidence. These errors are particularly hard for the assistant to deal with. It makes sense to ask the user to restate an utterance if the assistant isn't sure what the intent is. That mechanism acts like self-correction and keeps the assistant from going down the wrong path too often. But if the assistant identifies the wrong intent with high confidence, it has no mechanism to address that at runtime. When the wrong intent is predicted with high confidence, there may be a serious gap in the training.

Figure 10.17 shows Fictitious Inc.'s analysis of the assistant's high-confidence but incorrect predictions.

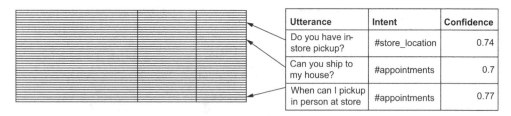

Utterance	Intent	Confidence
Do you have in-store pickup?	#store_location	0.74
Can you ship to my house?	#appointments	0.7
When can I pickup in person at store	#appointments	0.77

Figure 10.17   Finding high-confidence but incorrect predictions in Fictitious Inc.'s assistant can be like finding a needle in a haystack. Only three utterances out of five hundred matched these criteria.

Unfortunately, there is no simple way to find these utterances. Fictitious Inc.'s assistant handled hundreds of conversations. Most of these conversations started with a high-confidence prediction, and most of those predictions were correct. Only a painstaking review of the conversation-opening utterances could surface these problematic utterances. High-confidence predictions are easy to find; narrowing down those predictions to the incorrect ones takes time.

Fortunately, these utterances and the patterns they represent can be found in the other analytic methods. Figure 10.18 surfaces two error patterns:

- There's a need for a `#delivery_options` intent.
- The `#appointments` intent is prone to false positives.

Fictitious Inc. was able to find both of these insights in other analyses. This shows that there are multiple ways to find the same insights. This also demonstrates a diminishing return to analysis. The first analyses were relatively quick to perform. This last analysis took much longer to execute but did not turn up anything that wasn't found in a simpler analysis.

Fictitious Inc.'s analysis process started with them building a baseline of their accuracy by building a blind test set and testing their assistant against it. Next, they identified specific areas for improvement. They can now use this new data to do additional training and testing of their classifier using the same process they learned earlier in this book.

In God we trust, all others must bring data.

—W. Edwards Deming

10.3 *When and why to improve your assistant*

This chapter followed Fictitious Inc.'s first analysis of their assistant after it went to production. Through this analysis, they found several surprising shortcomings of their assistant and formed an action plan to improve the assistant. The analysis was done quickly with the intent of identifying the most severe problems first. Implicit in this analysis was that there would be multiple cycles of analysis and improvement.

Fictitious Inc. can fairly ask: How many improvement cycles will be needed? How long will those improvement cycles take? There's no set answer. The important thing is that AI assistants are not one-and-done; they need frequent improvement. Consider giving your assistant a thoughtful analysis every three months. A more frequent analysis is good early in an assistant's life, and stable assistants may need less analysis and revision. There are several good reasons why continual analysis and improvement of your assistant is a good idea:

- You can't fix everything at once.
- Users will not always react the way you expect them to.
- User needs will change.

10.3.1 *You can't fix everything at once*

Fictitious Inc.'s first analysis of their assistant surfaced several insights that could improve the assistant. Their multifaceted analysis found the most severe problems in their assistant but there's no reason to believe it found all of the problems. Though

Fictitious Inc. could continue their analysis and find even more problems, the analysis will have diminishing returns.

Fictitious Inc.'s goal is to increase successful containment, and their analysis has found the biggest sources of uncontained conversations. Fixing the most severe containment problems directly aligns with Fictitious Inc.'s success metrics. Further, time and energy are limited. Every hour spent on analysis is an hour not spent on improvement.

Additionally, some of the containment problems have interdependencies. When Fictitious Inc. updates their intent training to fix some intents, it may adversely affect other intents. Fictitious Inc. is best served making small, incremental changes and verifying that they help drive successful containment. Smaller changes are easier to make, to observe, and to roll back if they don't work. Figure 10.18 demonstrates that shorter improvement cycles accelerate your ability to learn and improve the assistant.

1. Big-bang iteration gives you only one chance to get it right.

2. Smaller iterations are easier to manage and give more chances to adjust.

Figure 10.18   The smaller the set of improvements, the more improvement cycles you can run. Shorter cycles are less risky and offer more chances for learning.

10.3.2   *You can't always predict how users will react*

Fictitious Inc. carefully designed their assistant with the needs of their users in mind. However, as their analysis showed, users did not react as expected. In the password reset flow, users frequently did not know their user ID and often answered their security question with insensitivity to case. Fictitious Inc. will need to adjust that process flow based on this user behavior if they want to increase the successful containment of password resets.

> *The best-laid plans of mice and men oft go awry.*
>
> —Robert Burns

The more an assistant's design process is centered on user needs, the better the assistant will serve users. But no matter how good the design process is, there will be some unexpected user behavior that's not accounted for in the design. These differences are the "unknown unknowns." It's impossible to predict what they are, but it's a certainty that they exist.

There's no shame in an imperfect Version 1 design that misses some user needs. Additional versions will inevitably be needed. There's only shame in never improving the design.

10.3.3 *User needs will change*

Fictitious Inc. discovered a new user need in their first analysis: users requesting different delivery options. Other user needs will likely emerge over time.

> *In theory, there's no difference between theory and practice. In practice, there is.*
>
> —Benjamin Brewster

No matter how well you designed your assistant, users will eventually make new requests. In 2020, COVID-19 rocked the world with a bevy of new request types:

- Healthcare companies saw new requests for COVID symptom checking and processes on testing.
- Employers were bombarded with questions on new work-at-home policies.
- Food-service companies saw the new phrase *contactless delivery.*
- Governments fielded questions about new COVID-19-related policies.

Even outside of a global pandemic, user needs will change. New intents will arise, and some existing intents may wane. You may be able to predict the rise of new intents, but as alluded to earlier, your ability to predict rising trends is probably not as good as you think it is. A periodic review of your assistant logs will help you discover new intents requested by users and also the way they phrase them. This periodic review can also quantify how frequently the new intents are used. Figure 10.19 demonstrates how development looks when you do frequent adjustments.

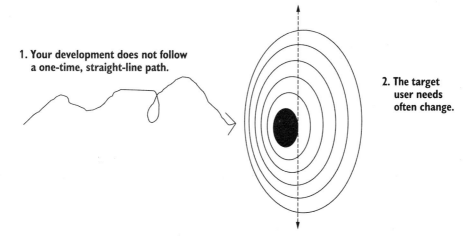

1. Your development does not follow a one-time, straight-line path.

2. The target user needs often change.

Figure 10.19 Improving your assistant must be done iteratively because user needs will change. You can't use a straight line to hit a moving target; you must be able to course-correct.

Periodic analysis and improvement of your assistant keeps it up to date with how users interact with it. The improvement process should be done as often as needed, but a reasonable cadence is to do it every three months.

10.3.4 *Not every problem is technical*

The preceding sections outlined a number of technical techniques for analysis and improvement of a conversational AI. The technical solutions in this chapter assumed that user behavior cannot be changed. I enjoy a good technical solution, but that assumption about user behavior is not always valid. Sometimes user behavior can be influenced or changed in a way that makes both the users and the assistant more successful.

Users who are not expecting to interact with an assistant may try to immediately opt out of the assistant. This involves trying to find a way to escape the assistant and get to a human. This desire is understandable; these users may have had bad experiences with other automated solutions, or they may think a human will get them what they need faster. Or these users may have tried your AI assistant once before, not known what to do, and decided to never give it a chance again.

Fictitious Inc. had problems with successfully containing calls about password resets and appointment scheduling. Fictitious Inc. could proactively reach out to users and give them tips on how to achieve their needs quickly with the conversational AI. This communication could take many different forms: email, instructions on a website, or a physical form. Figure 10.20 is a business-card-size cheat sheet Fictitious Inc. can send to their users which addresses two of the key challenges in the assistant.

FICTITIOUS INC

Our automated assistant can help you with common problems like **password resets** in less than one minute! Be sure you have this information when you chat:
- User ID
- Date of birth
- Answer to security question

You can also **schedule an appointment** with our assistant. You'll be asked for:
- Location (Elm or Maple)
- Date
- Time

Figure 10.20   Fictitious Inc. can create a business card-sized cheat sheet for their users telling them what they can do with the assistant and what information will be expected from them. This will make users more successful in using the assistant.

This postcard has several benefits:

- *Speaks directly to user value*—You can get your password reset in *one minute* using the assistant. (It might take 15 minutes to get connected to a human agent to do the same.)
- *Sets expectations*—Users know exactly what the assistant needs. Rather than being surprised during the conversation, the user can prepare ahead of time what they need to finish their transaction.

- *Small and concise*—The business card form factor easily fits inside a wallet or can be taped onto a user's landline or computer monitor or placed somewhere else that is easily accessible.
- *Biases user language toward what your assistant already understands*—The users are primed to use the utterances "password reset" or "schedule an appointment." Your assistant will have no problem identifying the intent in these utterances.

Behavior is easier to change in some user groups than others. Fictitious Inc.'s easiest possible user population would be other Fictitious Inc. employees. Fictitious Inc. would have many ways to reach and influence those users. There's usually a way to reach your users, even if it requires some creativity. Influencing user behavior can be cheaper and easier than making purely technical changes.

Summary

- Analysis and improvement should be tied to the business success metrics.
- Analyze the most serious process flow failures to find the most significant areas for improvement.
- Assistants need frequent improvement because user needs change in unpredictable ways.

Part 5

Advanced/optional topics

The first four parts of this book applied to every type of AI assistant. This final part applies only to some types. However, even if you don't need these topics directly, understanding them will make you a stronger AI assistant developer.

Chapter 11 demonstrates building a new classifier from scratch in Python code. Most AI platforms come with good classifiers that only require training, no coding required. Nonetheless, understanding how classifiers are built will give you a better appreciation for how and why training and testing work the way they do. This chapter builds a naive "bag of words" classifier to demonstrate the general concepts. I mastered classification concepts by building my own classifier. I hope this chapter helps you as well.

Chapter 12 teaches you how to train and test speech recognition for voice assistants. Voice assistants are a popular type of conversational AI as companies integrate automated solutions into their telephony systems. Voice assistants often require custom speech training. This chapter shows you how to gather speech data, as well as three different methodologies for training a custom speech recognition model.

11
Building your own classifier

In previous chapters, we learned about how to design and construct an AI assistant, and how to make sure it responds appropriately to the user. AI assistants use classifiers to extract meaning (as an intent) from a user's natural language input, as shown in figure 11.1. (Some AI platforms refer to the classifier as the natural language understanding [NLU] component.) The intent detected by the classifier is used by the assistant to determine the best response. Thus, getting the right intent from user input is a key part of a well-functioning AI assistant.

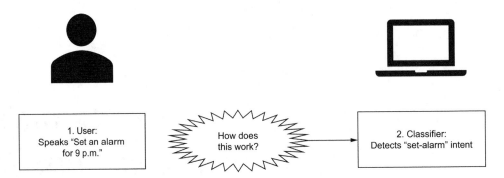

Figure 11.1   Orientation for this chapter. How does the classifier work? How can you make it better?

We have briefly discussed that AI assistants are trained, but we have not discussed how that training works. In this chapter, you will learn how to train your own classifier. We will build a simple text classifier for Fictitious Inc.'s conversational AI assistant.

If you are not interested in building your own classifier, you can safely skip this chapter. However, if you understand how a classifier is built, you will be much more successful at training and improving your AI assistant. Building a custom classifier is most important for classification and routing assistants. Most conversational AI developers use the classifier provided by their AI platform.

In chapter 6, I talked about how the training data for a classifier requires volume, variety, and veracity. The mathematical examples in this chapter drove home why each of those is required. Specifically, you saw how volume and variety drive the classifier's quality of learning.

Having a good working knowledge of how a classifier works will help you make better decisions while training, testing, and improving your classifier. You do not need to work out the calculations by hand or implement these patterns in code. Having a fundamental understanding of the mathematical underpinnings in the calculation moves you from beginner mode to expert mode.

In this chapter, I will demonstrate the simplest possible text classifier. I will start with a classifier that detects one intent (#reset_password). It will take an utterance and decide if it is a reset password intent or not a reset password intent.

After testing a single intent, I will expand to multiple intents. There are two ways to detect multiple intents: with an array of binary classifiers (each detecting one intent only) or a single all-in-one classifier that can detect all intents. I will compare and contrast those two methods with a set of three intents. For every classifier example, I will show the internal calculations used by the classifier to determine the intent behind a user utterance.

By the end of this chapter, you will be able to assess a set of training data as having enough volume and variety to make good predictions. You will be able to differentiate between the binary classifier and all-in-one approaches and determine which one your chosen AI platform uses. You will also be ready to train a classifier and have high confidence in its predictive capability.

11.1 Why build your own classifier?

There is a classic build-versus-buy decision when it comes to classifiers. The classifier is one of the most important pieces of the system, but it can also be the most cryptic. Many AI providers expose their classifier only through low-code or no-code interfaces to shield users from the internal complexity. This makes it easier and faster to start building virtual assistants.

AI providers are good at text classification. They usually have teams of data scientists and machine learning experts dedicated to providing accurate text classifiers that are easy to use. They constantly tune algorithms to work for a variety of use cases and try to minimize the volume of training data required. Because of these algorithms, you can focus on providing good training data instead of having to provide both training data and an algorithm.

Further, for most conversational assistants, you are unlikely to build a better classification algorithm than what is provided by AI platforms. I'm reminded of the adage "Never build your own database." Even though it does not quite apply here, caution is warranted. But there are still good reasons to build your own classifier.

11.1.1 Classification is a differentiator

The first and perhaps most compelling reason to build your own classifier is if having a better classifier is a differentiating feature of your solution. This is primarily the case if you are not building a conversational assistant. Most AI providers optimize for the conversational assistant use case and provide good general-purpose classifiers, and consumers can use intents and entities to drive conversations, as shown in figure 11.2.

Utterance ⟶ Intent + Entities

Figure 11.2 Conversational assistant classification is fairly simple. An utterance generally has one intent and zero or more entities.

If you are building a classification and routing assistant, the user's input is probably not a single utterance, but rather contains several parts. Let's look at a couple of typical use cases:

- *Email*—An email has several fields useful in classification: a sender, a recipient list, a subject line, and a message body. Each may be treated differently. An email may be less interesting if the sender's address is from a certain domain. An email can be more interesting if certain words appear (or do not appear) in the body.
- *Support requests*—A support request usually has a title and a body. Within the body, you may specifically look for a product or operating-system names to route the request to the appropriate party.
- *Documents*—Documents can be classified according to their filename, file type, file size, and overall contents.

When you have data that does not easily fit into a general text classifier, you have three options. First, you could choose a single field to classify against, and use a general text classifier on that field. Second, you could concatenate several fields into a single field and use a general text classifier on that field. Last, you could build a custom classifier. Figure 11.3 demonstrates the options.

**1. Classify a single field   2. Concatenate and classify a single   3. Build a custom classifier
   with a general classifier.   field with a general classifier.   that uses many fields.**

Figure 11.3   Classification options for email. The first two options can use a general-purpose classifier; the third option requires custom work.

Simple classification options can provide quick value, but you may need a custom classifier depending on how accurate you need to be and how much time you are willing to spend.

11.1.2 Classification is a core competency

If you have a team full of data scientists, you can build a strong classifier that favorably compares with other classifiers on the market. Your data scientists will appreciate the challenge.

Conversely, if data science is not a strong skill for you or your organization, you may not want to build your own classifier. If you are new to data science, you will need to invest time and energy in learning at least the basics.

11.1.3 Traceability

If you need full traceability that a closed-source or black-box algorithm can't provide, you may choose to build your own classifier. There are plenty of open source options for text classification, including Scikit-learn, Natural Language Toolkit (NLTK), SpaCy, TensorFlow, PyTorch, and Keras.

When you have access to the source code of your classifier, you know what it is doing every step of the way, and you can see all code changes. Closed-source or Software as a Service (SaaS) solutions can change any code detail at any time, and you will not be aware of what has changed. Without access to the source code, your only ability to control changes is to select a specific version of the classification software.

Source code level traceability is especially important for people working in highly regulated environments and industries.

11.1.4 To learn

Building a classifier for the sheer sake of learning how to do it is a fine motivation. I salute any hobbyists or lifelong learners who want to attempt to build a classifier. It's a rewarding experience and helps you appreciate what machine learning can and can't do.

Additionally, while building your own classifier you will get a strong sense of how the training process affects the classifier. This will help you as you train and test other classifiers. You will gain an intuitive sense for what will work well, or not work at all, in other classifiers you encounter.

11.1.5 Build or buy?

There are good reasons for building your own classifier or using an existing classifier. These reasons are summarized in table 11.1.

Table 11.1 Decision matrix for whether to build your own classifier

If you are . . .	You should favor . . .
Building a conversational AI	Existing classifier
Building a classification and routing assistant	Building a classifier
Not skilled at data science	Existing classifier
Skilled at data science	Building a classifier
Requiring source code control of all components	Building a classifier
Low on free time	Existing classifier
Learning for the sake of learning	Building a classifier

For the rest of the chapter, we assume that you are interested in building a classifier.

11.2 Build a simple classifier from first principles

Fictitious Inc.'s chief technical officer is uncomfortable with using a closed-source classifier and wants to build a new classifier for their retail conversational assistant. In the following sections, we will explore how to build a classifier suitable for use in the conversational assistant.

Recall that Fictitious Inc.'s assistant handled more than one dozen intents. Their classifier must therefore be able to classify utterances to over one dozen classifications. We will start by first learning how to classify into two classifications: `#reset_password` and "not `#reset_password`." After that, we will expand into three classifications: `#reset_password`, `#store_hours`, and `#store_location`. Then we will discuss how to expand to as many additional classifications as Fictitious Inc. needs.

Let's look inside our classifier. Let's take the utterance "Help me reset my password," which has the intent `#reset_password`. How does the classifier know that's a `#reset_password` utterance rather than any other type of utterance?

The first secret to reveal is that machine learning does not operate directly on text. Under the covers, all machine learning algorithms ultimately work on numbers, not text. We don't mean this in a pedantic view (that everything reduces to zeros and ones), but the mathematical functions and algorithms have a numerical basis. Figure 11.4 shows how one might think about a classifier.

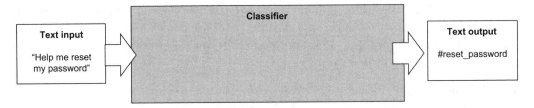

Figure 11.4   Simplistic mental model of how a text classifier works

We could consider the classifier as a function *f*. It would then be appropriate to think of classification as the following equation:

f(input) = prediction

A potential numerical view of function *f* is shown in figure 11.5.

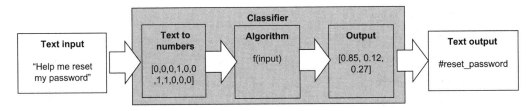

Figure 11.5   A text classifier uses numbers under the covers. This chapter discusses how those numbers are used.

The conversion from text to numbers is not immediately intuitive. There are multiple methods for converting text to numbers. Let's walk through an example based on a common classification technique. We will build a simple text classification algorithm and demonstrate how it converts text to numbers and numbers to text.

11.2.1 The simplest text classifier

The simplest way to convert text to numbers is through a technique called *bag of words*. As the name implies, any text string fed into a bag of words classifier is treated as a mere collection of words. There is no meaning attached to any of the words; the order of the words does not matter. The words are simply counted. A simple bag of words algorithm may lowercase input, and remove common words ("a," "the," and so on), but that's about it.

Let's train a bag of words classifier with two text statements: "Reset my password" and "When does the store open." This is the simplest possible classifier we can train: two input examples. In fact, we will train it to recognize only one intent (#reset_ password) by including positive and negative examples.

Table 11.2 shows how a bag of words algorithm breaks down some sample text statements. The resulting bag of words now has some numeric representation of the text statements. The bag still has some words in it; our text statements are not fully converted to numbers. The order of the words doesn't matter; the classifier may alphabetize the bag of words for convenience. For each bag, we count the number of words in the bag.

Table 11.2　Example conversion of text to a bag of words for a classifier that will detect `#reset_password`

Text statement	Bag of words	Class label
Reset my password	my:1, password:1, reset:1	Positive
When does the store open	does:1, open:1, store:1, when:1	Negative

Table 11.3 shows how the classifier references each bag of words by an array index. Our bag of words algorithm indexes the words alphabetically.

Table 11.3　Indexing of words to numbers

Word	does	my	open	password	reset	store	when
Index	0	1	2	3	4	5	6

With this numeric reference, we can now get rid of the words entirely. The statement "Reset my password" contains three words: "reset" (index: 4), "my" (index: 1), and "password" (index: 3). Thus, we can numerically represent "reset my password" as an array, setting 1 in the index positions for the words found in the statement and 0 for the other index positions. Figure 11.6 shows the journey "reset my password" takes in becoming the numeric array [0, 1, 0, 1, 1, 0, 0].

Now we know how the bag of words classifier converts any text statement into a numerical array. This array covers the input to the classifier; we still need to show the output from the classifier. Our simple classifier has two output states: Positive (the input is `#reset_password`) and Negative (the input is not `#reset_password`).

Table 11.4 shows how several example utterances are mapped to numerical arrays by our simple bag of words classifier and what output is assigned to each input.

Table 11.4　Numeric representation of some text statements

Textual input	Bag of words as a numeric array	Classification output
Reset my password	[0, 1, 0, 1, 1, 0, 0]	Positive
Password reset	[0, 0, 0, 1, 1, 0, 0]	Positive
When does the store open	[1, 0, 1, 0, 0, 1, 1]	Negative
When does my password reset	[1, 1, 0, 1, 1, 0, 1]	Negative

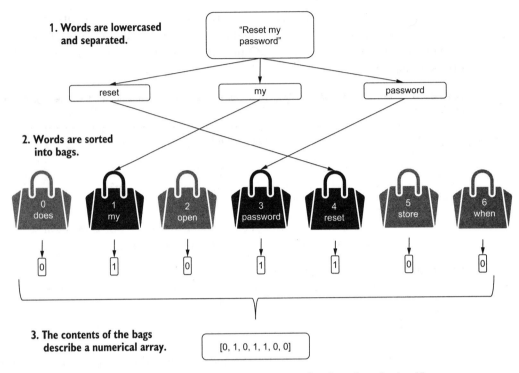

Figure 11.6   The journey from text statement to numeric array in a bag of words classifier

11.2.2   *The mathematics behind a simple classifier*

In the previous section, we saw how an input text phrase is converted to a numeric expression. This is only half the battle; we do not have a fully functional equation yet. We have described the input but not the output.

Let's continue with our small example. By representing positive examples as 1 and negative examples as 0, we can build a fully numeric representation of our textual training data (table 11.5).

Table 11.5   Numeric representation of input and output

Text statement	As Input	As Output
Reset my password	[0, 1, 0, 1, 1, 0, 0]	1
When does the store open	[1, 0, 1, 0, 0, 1, 1]	0

We can describe this training data via two equations:

$$f([0,1,0,1,1,0,0]) = 1$$

$$f([1,0,1,0,0,1,1]) = 0$$

All we have to do now is discover the function *f*. The function *f* will be discovered through a regression technique. Regression is a way of looking backward at a set of data to discover a function that best fits that data. Regression techniques iterate over a range of candidate functions, testing each one against the training data and selecting the function that makes the fewest total errors.

The function selected by the regression process is only an estimate. (A perfect function would never have any errors.) We want the function to learn patterns from the training data and extrapolate those patterns to data it has not seen.

For classification, we will use a logistic regression algorithm. Logistic regression is a technique similar to linear regression, except that the target is a discrete classification. In our example, that classification is binary (0 or 1). The central equation in logistic regression is a linear function where every parameter is multiplied by a weight and then summed. There is also a constant added called the bias; we will refer to it as `weight_0`. For a logistic regression with two parameters, the function would be as follows:

$$f = weight\_0 + weight\_1 \times parameter\_1 + weight\_2 \times parameter\_2$$

The amazing part of machine learning is that given enough examples, it will infer (learn) the parameter weights. The detailed math behind this learning is beyond the scope of this book, but we will describe the math at a high level.

Recall that our training data has two output values: 1 and 0, based on whether the input is a positive (1) or negative (0) example of the class we are trying to detect. The values between 0 and 1 should represent the probability that an input belongs to the positive class. Thus, the machine learning algorithm should be constrained to returning values in the range [0,1]. The logistic function is shown in figure 11.7.

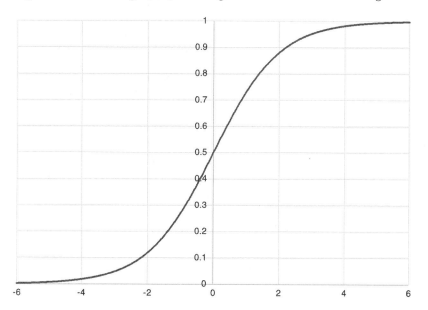

Figure 11.7 The logistic function

The horizontal axis represents all the possible values of the function f (shown earlier). The vertical axis is the probability that the value of f represents a positive example. This axis is bounded between the values of 0 and 1:

$$\text{Probability of positive example} = e^f / (1 + e^f)$$

Let's find out what our regression function really looks like. First, because our bag of words contains seven words, we know our regression function should have seven parameters (one for each word). We will also expect a constant value in the function (sometimes called the bias), as is typical in regression algorithms. We can find the exact parameter values learned by the classifier by training it on our two example statements ("reset my password" and "when does the store open").

Listing 11.1   Training a simple classifier

```
training_data = read_data_from_csv_file("training_2class_small.csv")
vec, clf, pipe = train_binary_classifier_pipeline("reset_password",
➥ training_data)
display(eli5.show_weights(clf, vec=vec, top=20, target_names=pipe.classes_))
```

I trained a logistic regression classifier on this example (code available via http://mng.bz/JvWz) and inspected the weights learned by the classifier. These weights are shown in figure 11.8.

The weights in the figure may be surprising. There is almost no variation in the weights. This is because we have only provided two examples ("reset my password" and "when does the store open"), and the classifier does not have much to learn from. As the number of training examples increases, the weights assigned to each feature will change.

y=reset_password top features

Weight[?]	Feature
+0.378	reset
+0.378	password
+0.378	my
+0.189	<BIAS>
-0.378	does
-0.378	open
-0.378	store
-0.378	when

Figure 11.8   Learned weights in the simple bag of words classifier

The fact that "password" and "my" have the same weight is a strong signal that we have undertrained (and that our classifier is not very clever).

Now that we have learned the feature weights, we can use the logistic equation to classify any example we like. Let's first test "reset my password." Each of the words "reset," "my," and "password" contributes a 1 (feature value) times 0.378 (feature weight). And we must always include the bias parameter (0.189) when using the classifier. When the classifier sees "reset my password," it classifies it as #reset_password with 0.79 confidence:

$$f = 0.189 + 0.378 \times 1 + 0.378 \times 1 + 0.378 \times 1 = 1.323$$

$$e^f = e^{1.323} = 3.755$$

$$\text{probability} = e^f / (1 + e^f) = (3.755/4.755) = 0.790$$

The system has fairly high confidence that this utterance should be classified as #reset_password. That's good—the utterance really has the intent #reset_password. The closer to 1 the confidence is, the more likely the utterance belongs to that intent.

Similarly, we can build the equation for "when does the store open." The equation starts with the bias parameter. The classifier removes common words, so "the" is removed; we'll show it in the equation with a 0. The other four words have a negative weight, as shown in figure 11.8, so our equation includes four sets of the feature value 1 times the feature weight -0.378:

$$f = 0.189 + 0 - 0.378 \times 1 - 0.378 \times 1 - 0.378 \times 1 - 0.378 \times 1 = -1.323$$

$$e^f = e^{-1.323} = 0.266$$

$$probability = e^f / (1 + e^f) = (0.266 / 1.266) = 0.210$$

The system has fairly low confidence (0.21) that this utterance is a #reset_password example. That's also good; this utterance does not have the #reset_password intent. The closer to 0 the confidence is, the more likely the utterance does not belong to that intent.

The classifier only knows how to score words that are in the training set. Any words it has not trained on will be ignored. Consider the phrase "where are you located." None of the words "where," "are," "you," and "located" exists in the training set, so the equation includes only the bias parameter. "Where are you located" is classified as #reset_password with 0.547 confidence:

$$f = 0.189$$

$$e^f = e^{0.189} = 1.201$$

$$probability = e^f / (1 + e^f) = (1.201 / 2.201) = 0.547$$

Wait a minute—is "Where are you located" more likely to be #reset_password than not? That's what the 54.7% probability means. This may be a surprising result, but recall that this classifier is severely undertrained. With only two training examples, it should be no wonder that this classifier makes some questionable predictions. A classifier must be trained with a larger volume and variety of training data if it is going to make good predictions.

Try it yourself
Try to classify some utterances with this classifier. Note that if your utterances do not contain any of the words "reset," "my," "password," "where," "are," "you," and "located," it will be classified as #reset_password with 0.547 confidence.

Let's visualize the previous three classifications. In figure 11.9, each example is plotted on the logistic regression curve. Try a few examples of your own and predict how the classifier will treat them. What happens if you repeat words ("password help please I

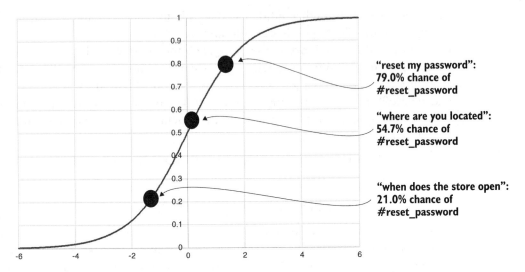

Figure 11.9   Logistic regression results for a classifier trained on two examples

need my password reset")? What happens if you have a short statement ("password reset")? What happens if you mix words from the two training examples ("when does the password reset")? Explore via the Jupyter notebook in this chapter's source code repository.

Why don't we see 100% confidence anywhere?

You may be surprised that the classifier does not make predictions with 100% confidence (or, in fact, 0% confidence). The examples we tested the classifier on came straight from the training data, so we might reasonably expect the classifier to remember that.

Different classifiers have different training methodologies. Some classifiers do, in fact, remember their training data and will return 100% confidence when you test them with an example seen in training. Other classifiers make inferences during training and then forget the rest of the training data. Our simplistic bag of words classifier is in this latter group.

A classifier with such light training is hardly trustworthy and is only used for illustrative purposes. When more training data is added, with both volume and variety, the results from the classifier will be more accurate.

11.3   *Expanding the simple classifier*

In the previous section, our classifier could only predict one class (one intent). Either an utterance was #reset_password or it was not. You may call this a prediction of two classes (#reset_password and everything else), but this is still far short of useful. A typical AI assistant will support dozens of classes. Fictitious Inc. needs to support at least a dozen intents in their conversational AI.

11.3.1 Predicting more than one class

Can we extend this simplistic model to identify more than one class? Yes, we can. Let's make a small extension to our previous classifier. Instead of predicting one class, let's predict three classes. We will provide training data as in table 11.6. This table has three intents, each with one example utterance.

Table 11.6   The smallest possible training set for three output classes

Input (utterance)	Output (intent)
Reset my password	#reset_password
When does the store open	#store_hours
Where is my nearest store	#store_location

In the one-class example, we had seven bags of words: "reset," "my," "password," "when," "does," "store," and "open." The new third utterance in table 11.6 adds three new bags for the words "where," "is," and "nearest." (We already have bags for "my" and "store" from the previous utterances.) We will now have ten bags of words, and we should expect that the weights will be different in the new model.

Before we train the model, we have to figure out how to assign a numeric value to the output. You may consider giving each class an arbitrary number, say 0 for #reset_password, 1 for #store_hours, and 2 for #store_location. This presents a numeric problem. How can we design a function whose minimum value is #reset_password, and what does it mean for #store_hours to be in the middle? (And what would happen if we changed the order of the intents?)

The answer is to use multiple classifiers. Each classifier can focus on detecting a single class, and we can use the aggregated results to determine which class is the most likely. The classifier that returns the highest positive confidence will give us the output class. Table 11.7 shows how each classifier uses a sort of tunnel vision so that it only worries about one class at a time.

Table 11.7   Each classifier has a binary view of the training data.

Input (utterance)	Classifier 1	Classifier 2	Classifier 3
Reset my password	#reset_password	#not_store_hours	#not_store_location
When does the store open	#not_reset_password	#store_hours	#not_store_location
Where is my nearest store	#not_reset_password	#not_store_hours	#store_location

I used a code snippet like the following to train three classifiers. This code is available in the book's GitHub repository. The training data from table 11.6 was stored in the file training_3class_small.csv.

Listing 11.2 Training three classifiers

```
training_data = read_data_from_csv_file("training_3class_small.csv")

#Train the three classifiers
reset_password_vec, reset_password_clf, reset_password_pipe = \
 train_binary_classifier_pipeline("reset_password", training_data)
store_hours_vec, store_hours_clf, store_hours_pipe = \
 train_binary_classifier_pipeline("store_hours", training_data)
store_location_vec, store_location_clf, store_location_pipe = \
 train_binary_classifier_pipeline("store_location", training_data)

#Inspect the weights for each classifier
display(eli5.show_weights(reset_password_clf, vec=reset_password_vec, top=20,
➥ target_names=reset_password_pipe.classes_))
display(eli5.show_weights(store_hours_clf, vec=store_hours_vec, top=20,
➥ target_names=store_hours_pipe.classes_))
display(eli5.show_weights(store_location_clf, vec=store_location_vec, top=20,
➥ target_names=store_location_pipe.classes_))
```

When we train the three classifiers, we now get three sets of weights, as shown in figure 11.10.

y=reset_password top features

Weight?	Feature
+0.542	reset
+0.542	password
+0.254	my
-0.254	does
-0.254	open
-0.254	when
-0.288	is
-0.288	nearest
-0.288	where
-0.500	\<BIAS\>
-0.542	store

y=store_hours top features

Weight?	Feature
+0.502	when
+0.502	open
+0.502	does
+0.251	store
-0.251	is
-0.251	nearest
-0.251	where
-0.251	password
-0.251	reset
-0.502	my
-0.812	\<BIAS\>

y=store_location top features

Weight?	Feature
+0.542	where
+0.542	nearest
+0.542	is
+0.288	store
+0.254	my
-0.254	does
-0.254	open
-0.254	when
-0.288	password
-0.288	reset
-1.331	\<BIAS\>

Figure 11.10 Three binary classifiers, each with their own independent weights. Our only training data was "reset my password" for #reset_password, "when does the store open" for #store_hours, and "where is my nearest store" for #store_location.

We can make a couple of observations from the weights:

- For the #reset_password classifier, the word "my" has a lower weight than "reset" and "password." This is because "my" also shows up in the #store_location example. The classifier only associates "reset" and "password" with one intent, while it associates "my" with two intents. (For the same reason, the word "store" has reduced weight in #store_hours.)

- The `#reset_password` classifier has a strong negative weight on the word "store," which has appeared in every single utterance that is not `#reset_password`.
- Each classifier has a negative bias. This is because each classifier has seen more negative than positive examples. This is an implicit signal that each class is somewhat rare.
- Several of the weights are larger within each classifier as compared with figure 11.8, which had a maximum weight of 0.378 (and minimum weight of -0.378). Having more examples per classifier (three examples versus two) is allowing stronger inferences to be made.

To test a single utterance, we now need to run through a series of three equations. Let's evaluate "reset my password":

$$\text{f\_reset\_password} = -0.430 + 0.531 + 0.234 + 0.531 = 0.866$$

$$e^{f\_reset\_password} = e^{0.866} = 2.377$$

$$\text{probability} = e^{f\_reset\_password} / (1 + e^{f\_reset\_password}) = (2.377/3.377) = 0.704$$

$$\text{f\_store\_hours} = -1 - 0.230 - 0.460 - 0.230 = -1.920$$

$$e^{f\_store\_hours} = e^{-1.920} = 0.147$$

$$\text{probability} = e^{f\_store\_hours} / (1 + e^{f\_store\_hours}) = (0.147/1.147) = 0.128$$

$$\text{f\_store\_location} = -1.258 - 0.297 + 0.234 - 0.297 = -1.618$$

$$e^{f\_store\_location} = e^{-1.618} = 0.198$$

$$\text{probability} = e^{f\_store\_location} / (1 + e^{f\_store\_location}) = (0.198/1.198) = 0.165$$

The predictions can be summed up in the probability table shown in table 11.8. In this table, we also add a negative prediction probability, which is one minus the positive prediction probability. This negative prediction probability is how likely it is that an utterance does not belong to the intent. `#reset_password` has the highest positive prediction confidence, so it is chosen as the output.

Table 11.8 Probabilities from three binary classifiers on input "reset my password"

Classifier	Positive prediction probability	Negative prediction probability
`#reset_password`	0.704	0.296
`#store_hours`	0.128	0.872
`#store_location`	0.165	0.834

Table 11.8 has the promising result that utterances completely unrelated to an intent are not predicted to belong to that intent. The system has 0.872 confidence that "reset

my password" is not a `#store_hours` utterance. The more we train the classifier, the more confident it can be.

> ### Why don't the probabilities add up to one across classifiers?
>
> Within a classifier the probabilities do add up to one: every input is either a positive or negative example of that class. The probability for positive and the probability for negative must sum up to one.
>
> The three classifiers are completely independent. There is no reason why their positive probabilities need to be related.
>
> If your AI provider returns probabilities that add up to one, there are two likely possibilities:
>
> - They are scaling the probabilities so that they add to one.
> - They are using a different algorithm, like an all-in-one classifier, which we will explore later in this section.

We can also see a promising trend when we test a brand new, off-the-wall utterance that does not have any overlap in our training data. The utterance "tell me a joke" contains no words that overlap with the training data. The predictions for "tell me a joke" are summed up in the probability table shown in table 11.9. The negative predictions have higher confidence since this example has no overlap with any intent class.

Table 11.9 Probabilities from each of the three binary classifiers on the input text "tell me a joke"

Classifier	Positive prediction probability	Negative prediction probability
`#reset_password`	0.394	0.601
`#store_hours`	0.269	0.731
`#store_location`	0.221	0.779

None of the classifiers returns a probability greater than 50% on this utterance. This means that "tell me a joke" is not predicted to belong to any of our three intents. This is good news. We can infer that any utterance that has no overlap with our training data will not belong to any of the three intents. Our three classifiers can identify out-of-scope utterances by default.

What classification should the system give to "tell me a joke"? `#reset_password` is the highest-scoring intent, but the confidence of 0.394 is low. Consider that if you picked a random intent, you would have 0.333, or 1 in 3, confidence. Your platform may return `#reset_password`, or no intent found (try it out). AI assistants generally apply thresholds to intent confidence, so that low-confidence intents are not chosen.

The more training examples we add to the training data, the better predictions we will get. In a reasonably balanced training set, the bias parameter will naturally trend downward. This will help the classifier recognize that for any given intent, most utterances do not belong to that intent. Let's pretend you have 10 intents, each with five examples; each intent will be trained with five positive examples and 45 negative examples. Because each intent has nine times as many negative examples as positive, each classifier will naturally learn that most utterances aren't positive examples.

11.3.2 An all-in-one classifier

Your AI platform may use a single classifier rather than an array of binary classifiers. A single classifier has a similar mathematical structure but slightly different equations. I will demonstrate the classifier here and provide code in my GitHub repository (http://mng.bz/JvWz) for you to explore.

Figure 11.11 shows a set of weights for a single classifier trained on our three input classes. Compared with figure 11.10, the weights are overall smaller in this single classifier, and the bias parameter is not always negative. This is because every input is assumed to belong to this classifier; there is no concept of an out-of-scope utterance in this classifier. (If we wanted to detect out-of-scope, we'd have to add a new intent specifically for it.) Thus, it is harder for the weights to get large; all the probabilities have to add up to one.

y=reset_password top features		y=store_hours top features		y=store_location top features	
Weight[?]	Feature	Weight[?]	Feature	Weight[?]	Feature
+0.122	reset	+0.119	when	+0.122	where
+0.122	password	+0.119	open	+0.122	nearest
+0.086	<BIAS>	+0.119	does	+0.122	is
+0.059	my	+0.059	store	+0.063	store
-0.059	does	+0.014	<BIAS>	+0.059	my
-0.059	open	-0.059	password	-0.059	does
-0.059	when	-0.059	reset	-0.059	open
-0.063	is	-0.059	is	-0.059	when
-0.063	nearest	-0.059	nearest	-0.063	password
-0.063	where	-0.059	where	-0.063	reset
-0.122	store	-0.119	my	-0.100	<BIAS>

Figure 11.11 Feature weights in the all-in-one classifier

Figure 11.12 shows predictions for the same two utterances we tested on the binary classifiers: "reset my password" and "tell me a joke." The classifier will pick the classification with the highest probability. We can see that the classifier got it right on "reset my password," while giving that prediction a 47.3% probability of being correct. "tell me a joke" is also classified as #reset_password with a lower probability of 36.8%.

We can once again compare these predictions with randomly picking an intent. The 47.3% confidence for "reset my password" is significantly higher than random selection (33.3%). The 36.8% confidence for "tell me a joke" is almost indistinguishable from random selection.

```
In [17]: display(eli5.show_prediction(clf, "reset my password", vec=vec, show_feature_values=True))
```

y=reset_password (probability 0.473, score 0.390) top features			y=store_hours (probability 0.256, score -0.224) top features			y=store_location (probability 0.271, score -0.166) top features		
Contribution[?]	Feature	Value	Contribution[?]	Feature	Value	Contribution[?]	Feature	Value
+0.122	reset	1.000	+0.014	<BIAS>	1.000	+0.059	my	1.000
+0.122	password	1.000	-0.059	password	1.000	-0.063	reset	1.000
+0.086	<BIAS>	1.000	-0.059	reset	1.000	-0.063	password	1.000
+0.059	my	1.000	-0.119	my	1.000	-0.100	<BIAS>	1.000

```
In [18]: display(eli5.show_prediction(clf, "tell me a joke", vec=vec, show_feature_values=True))
```

y=reset_password (probability 0.362, score 0.086) top features			y=store_hours (probability 0.337, score 0.014) top features			y=store_location (probability 0.301, score -0.100) top features		
Contribution[?]	Feature	Value	Contribution[?]	Feature	Value	Contribution[?]	Feature	Value
+0.086	<BIAS>	1.000	+0.014	<BIAS>	1.000	-0.100	<BIAS>	1.000

Figure 11.12   Output from two predictions with the all-in-one classifier. In the first example, each classifier has learned how the words in "reset my password" contribute to an intent, and the utterance is easily classified as #reset_password. In the second example, the prediction is ambiguous because the classifier has not seen any of the words in "tell me a joke."

11.3.3 *Comparing binary classifiers to all-in-one classifiers*

An all-in-one classifier may consume fewer system resources than an array of several classifiers, but I find the confidence math confusing. Is 47.3% a good probability? Is 36.8% bad? When the training volume is small, it's tough to say what a good probability level is. Fortunately, when the classifier is trained on higher volumes of data, the classifier will make stronger predictions.

Our previous test was not quite fair to the all-in-one classifier. It must be trained with an additional class that you could call "other" or "everything else." This class would represent all of the statements that do not belong to any of the intents you are specifically training. In practice, training this other class can be difficult and time-consuming due to the sheer number of possibilities that could be loaded into that class.

Regardless of which classifier type you use, every positive example for one intent is necessarily a negative example for every other class. The binary classifiers thus automatically get lots of negative examples and start to implicitly handle an other class through their bias parameter. The all-in-one classifier must be explicitly trained with other examples.

Binary classifiers can be trained with an other class if you choose. AI platforms expose this in a variety of ways. Some let you create counterexamples or negative examples, inputs that should be treated as negative examples for every intent. In other platforms, you must define other as a positive class; some developers call it #out_of_scope.

Do commercial vendors use the bag of words algorithm?

No. The bag of words technique is a quick way to train a text classifier, but it has numerous shortcomings. Your commercial provider uses an algorithm much smarter than the simplistic bag of words counter used in this example.

Here is a summary of failings in bag of words that stronger algorithms solve for:

- "Open" and "opening" are different words with the same lemma, which means they should be treated the same. Lemmatization helps make that happen. Lemmatization also ensures that plurals are treated the same as singulars ("store" and "stores").
- Bag of words does not know that "sotre" means "store."
- *Order matters.* Word sequences have more meaning than individual words.
- *Synonyms and similar words are treated independently.* "Help" and "assist" should have the same meaning.

All words are not created equal. Rare words generally are more important than common words and should be given more weight. The term frequency-inverse document frequency (TF-IDF) algorithm solves for this.

11.4 Extending even further

We started the chapter predicting a single intent using a tiny amount of data. In the previous section, we expanded by predicting multiple intents, but still with a small amount of data. You should start seeing the patterns of how we expand the assistant with more training data and more intents.

11.4.1 What happens when you add more training data?

As you expand your training data with increased volume and variety, you will improve the performance of the classifiers. In my original test, I used three total utterances, one for each intent. Let's see what happens when we increase the training volume with 500% more examples. We also enhance the variety by using different words and phrases. Table 11.10 shows the new training data. This has 500% more examples than the first training data set.

Table 11.10   New training data for our classifier

#reset_password	#store_hours	#store_location
Reset my password	Are you open on Thanksgiving	Where are you located
I can't log in	How late are you open today	Are you downtown
I forgot my password	Give me your hours please	Are you near the mall
I have a pw issue	When does the store open	Where is my nearest store
Stuck at the home screen	What time do you close	How do I find you
Can't remember my login info	What are your hours	I need a map to your location

The increased training data has a significant effect on the classifier. In figure 11.13, I show the weights learned by this classifier after training on the new data. You can see the stronger inferences the classifier is learning through the wider variation between the weights. The first classifier in this chapter assigned equal weights (0.378) to every word, suggesting that each of the words was equally important. The updated classifier

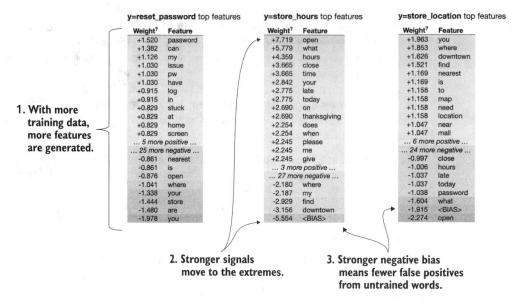

1. With more training data, more features are generated.

2. Stronger signals move to the extremes.

3. Stronger negative bias means fewer false positives from untrained words.

Figure 11.13 This classifier was trained with six times as much data variation as the original classifier and produces more features and stronger signals. We will show that this also leads to predictions with higher confidence.

set, with its different weights, knows that some words are more important than others for identifying intent.

This variation of weights is important; it starts to capture the subtlety in natural language. The original classifier felt that the words "reset," "my," and "password" were equally important. The improved classifier group has learned variation: "password" is the most important word of that set for the #reset_password intent. Similarly, the word "open" is much more important for #store_hours than "store."

The feature weights still seem questionable; what gives?

In figure 11.13, words like "you," "your," and "in" are providing more signal than makes sense intuitively.

The classifiers in this chapter are all still naive; they treat all words the same way. You can treat words differently with features like stopword removal, term frequency weighting, stemming and lemmatization, or other features you can imagine. More sophisticated features like these can make your classifier smarter.

Most commercial vendors do not expose the algorithms that they use, but they do use more sophisticated algorithms than bag of words. This helps them produce stronger results with less training data.

The classifiers in figure 11.13 also make better predictions. The phrase "reset my password" is now predicted as #reset_password with 0.849 probability (it was 0.704 before we added more training data); the phrase "tell me a joke" is predicted as not #reset_password with 0.623 probability (previously 0.601). As we can see in table 11.11, the performance of our classifiers improved as we added a greater volume and variety of training data.

Table 11.11 Summary of classifiers and performance in this chapter

Reference	Number of intents	Number of training examples	"reset my password" prediction	"tell me a joke" prediction
Figure 8	1	2	#reset_password: 0.790	#reset_password: 0.547
Figure 10	3	3	#reset_password: 0.704	Not #reset_password: 0.601
Figure 13	3	18	#reset_password: 0.849	Not #reset_password: 0.623

11.4.2 Exercise: Experiment on your own

The code used to generate all of the figures and tables in this section is available in the book's Git repository at http://mng.bz/JvWz. The code consists of a Jupyter Notebook (https://jupyter.org) and some sample data. Download the notebook and explore.

Experiment by adding more training data or more intent classes and see how the predictions change. Change one thing at a time so that you can assess its impact. Add a single new intent before adding a second new intent; this way you can understand the impact from each intent you've added.

If you are feeling adventurous, try changing the classification algorithm itself. Can you come up with better features than just counting the words? Stronger features will help you train a classifier with less input data. Even though commercial vendors use strong classification algorithms, you may find it instructive to experiment with your own algorithms.

Summary

- Classifiers convert text to numeric values to build predictive regression models.
- The predictions of a classifier are strongly influenced by the volume and variety of the training data used.
- AI assistants may use a single classifier or an array of binary classifiers. This implementation choice affects how you interpret the prediction and the associated probability behind that prediction.

Additional training
for voice assistants

This chapter covers

- Collecting data to test and train a speech-to-text model
- Evaluating the impact of a speech-to-text model on the AI assistant's success metric
- Identifying the most appropriate speech training option for a conversational AI assistant
- Training custom speech recognition models for open-ended and constrained inputs

Fictitious Inc. created its first conversational AI assistant through a text chat channel. That assistant has been so successful that Fictitious Inc. is now planning to expand to a telephone-based assistant as well. This assistant will cover the same customer care intents as the original assistant, but will take voice input rather than text input.

Speech-to-text models transcribe audio into text. In a voice assistant, the user speaks, and the transcription of that audio is passed to the assistant for intent

252

detection and dialogue routing. In previous chapters, we have seen how assistants use text: data must be collected, and the assistant needs to be trained and tested.

Fictitious Inc. will add speech recognition technology to their existing assistant to transcribe audio input into text. They have experimented with speech recognition technology in the past with mixed results. Fictitious Inc.'s transcriptions have been accurate on generic language like "reset my password," "what time are you open," or "I need to apply for a job." Figure 12.1 shows how an untrained speech-to-text model integrates with a conversational assistant. The model may make small mistakes (confusing "a" and "the") but captures the essence of the user's statement.

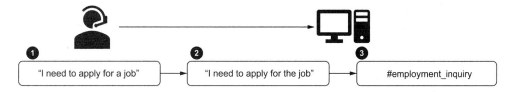

1. User speaks into a microphone.
2. Speech-to-text engine transcribes audio into text.
3. The assistant infers an intent from the textual transcription (not from the audio).

Figure 12.1   Speech-to-text integration into a conversational assistant. An out of the box speech-to-text model works well on common language.

However, the speech-to-text technology has struggled with some of Fictitious Inc.'s jargon. (Fictitious Inc.'s loyalty program is called Fiction Bucks, for example.) An untrained speech-to-text model is unlikely to have come across that language before, as seen in figure 12.2. Fictitious Inc. needs a speech-to-text solution that can handle both generic language and jargon.

In this chapter, you will learn how to use speech recognition technology. You will learn how to collect audio data for testing and training speech recognition technology. Then you will learn how to train a custom speech-to-text model and use it in your AI assistant.

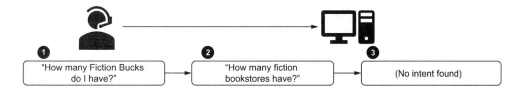

1. User asks how many loyalty points they have.
2. Speech-to-text engine fails to transcribe the key phrase "Fiction Bucks."
3. The assistant cannot find an intent in the transcribed text.

Figure 12.2   An untrained speech-to-text model will struggle on jargon. The model has never seen "Fiction Bucks" before and does not understand it well.

12.1   Collecting data to test a speech-to-text model

Fictitious Inc. needs data to test its speech-to-text model. With this data, they can find out how accurate a speech-to-text model will be in the assistant and where they will have to train the model to get more accurate transcriptions. They can use many of the same data sources they used when training their text-based AI assistant. As with the textual data, the speech data they collect can be used for both training and testing the assistant.

Speech data is a pairing of an audio file and the textual transcription of that audio file. Table 12.1 shows some sample speech data. Every audio file is associated with the text spoken in that file. When we play the audio file `Password.wav` we will hear someone saying "reset my password." Training and testing a speech-to-text model requires this paired data format: audio and text.

Table 12.1   Sample speech data

Audio file	Text
Password.wav	"reset my password"
EmploymentInquiry.wav	"I need to apply for a job"
LoyaltyPoints.wav	"how many Fiction Bucks do I have?"

This format is required because we want the speech-to-text model to know what words sound like. As seen before, the words "Fiction Bucks" sound a lot like the words "Fiction books." Because Fictitious Inc. wants their speech-to-text model to recognize the phrase "Fiction Bucks," they need to have examples of what that phrase sounds like.

Transcription works using phonetics behind the scenes

Words are a sequence of phonetic sequences. Each segment of the sequence is called a phoneme.

Speech-to-text engines extract potential phonemes from an audio signal and attempt to combine them into legitimate words or word phrases.

The International Phonetic Alphabet (IPA) pronunciation for "Fiction Bucks" and "Fiction Books" is similar:

.ˈfɪk.ʃɨn .ˈbʌks = Fiction Bucks

.ˈfɪk.ʃɨn .ˈbʊks = Fiction Books

The only difference in these two phrases is in the third phoneme (ˈbʌks versus ˈbʊks).

The three Vs of data apply to speech data too. Speech data must have variety, volume, and veracity to evaluate and train a speech-to-text model:

- *Variety*—Representative variety in data includes both what people will say and how they will say it. There should be audio data for each of the intents (what people will say), as well as demographic diversity in the speakers (how they will say it).
- *Volume*—Depending on the use case, it can take between 5 and 25 hours of audio data to train a speech-to-text model. Less data is required if the model is only going to be tested.
- *Veracity*—The audio files must be accurately transcribed for both evaluating and training a speech-to-text mode ("garbage in, garbage out").

> **Bias alert**
>
> A common pitfall in artificial intelligence projects is when data does not come from a diverse set of users. Beware the temptation to gather audio data only from your development team. It is highly unlikely that the demographics in your team match the demographic diversity of your user population. Without diverse data, you may be biasing your solution against some groups of users.

An expert takes six to ten hours to transcribe one hour of audio into text. The most common transcription practice is to feed audio into a speech-to-text engine to get an initial transcription. Then the human transcriber listens to the audio and corrects any mistakes in the initial transcription. Transcription takes longer than you might expect.

The three Vs of data are useful for understanding what Fictitious Inc.'s data needs are. Let's now look at potential sources for this data. The two primary sources of data are call transcripts and synthetic data. Let's start with call transcripts.

12.1.1 Call recordings as speech training data

Fictitious Inc. is like many companies with human-staffed customer service call centers. They record customer service calls for quality and training purposes. These recorded calls help train their AI assistant. Fictitious Inc. has already reviewed these calls to extract textual utterances; now they can extract audio segments as well.

Call center recordings need some work done on them before they can be used for speech training and evaluation. As shown in figure 12.3, a call center recording includes more audio than is needed, because it contains two speakers. The audio segments where the call center agent is speaking are not useful for the assistant. Only the segment where the user is speaking is useful, and this part needs to be extracted from the recording.

Figure 12.3 shows the first eight seconds of audio in a call recording. In this call, the agent speaks for the first five seconds, there's a one-second break, and then the user speaks for the last two. Fictitious Inc. needs to cut these two seconds out of the recording and save them into a new file, such as can_you_reset_my_password.wav, and also make sure the transcription is stored with the file. (Putting the transcription in the filename is a potential shortcut.)

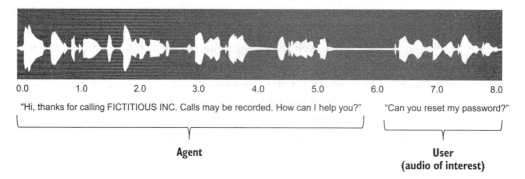

"Hi, thanks for calling FICTITIOUS INC. Calls may be recorded. How can I help you?"   "Can you reset my password?"

Agent   User
(audio of interest)

Figure 12.3   Sample call recording including agent greeting and user intent statement. Only the user's statement is useful for training and testing the AI assistant.

Extracting the audio of interest from an audio file

If the audio file contains separate channels for each speaker, the channel from the caller can be automatically extracted for use in speech training. If the audio file does not separate the channels, the caller's audio needs to be extracted manually.

Figure 12.3's phone call was direct and to the point. Figure 12.4 depicts a contrasting call. In this call, the user is verbose. The user seems grateful to connect with another human being and engages indirectly. This is not how users interact with AI assistants. This recording should not be segmented only on the user speech. Instead, only the audio segment including the intent statements should be extracted. The recording arguably includes three intent statements, each of which could be extracted to an isolated file.

Figure 12.4   Users can be verbose when talking with agents. They are unlikely to greet a conversational AI in the same way. Only part of the user's statement is relevant to the AI assistant.

After Fictitious Inc. has processed these two call recordings, they will have four pieces of audio data, as shown in table 12.2.

Table 12.2 Audio data collected after reviewing two call recordings

File	Transcription
File 1	Can you reset my password?
File 2	I've been trying all morning to get to my account.
File 3	I'm getting an error message about my account being locked.
File 4	I don't know how to unlock it, I don't know if I need to do something, or reset my password, or what.

Call recordings are a wonderful source of speech data because they are real data. Fictitious Inc.'s call recordings will include a variety of callers with demographic diversity. These recordings include the way users pronounce Fictitious Inc. jargon in a variety of accents. Fictitious Inc. employees may enunciate "Fiction Bucks," but their callers may slur the two words together. This distinction is important for the speech engine. Last, Fictitious Inc. has already been reviewing call recordings to gather intent training data. Using the recordings for speech training is a second benefit from the same data source.

Call recordings also have downsides. Processing call recordings is a lengthy process because the audio of interest must first be isolated and then transcribed. Call recordings contain more data than is useful for training an assistant: everything the agent says can be omitted, as well as any greetings or off-topic banter from the caller. Because humans talk differently to each other than they do to automated solutions, there may be large segments of each recording that are unusable.

Call recordings can take a lot of disk space. Many call centers re-encode and compress their recordings to save disk space. This process can reduce disk space needs by an order of magnitude, but also lowers the quality of the call recordings. (A WAV file may be ten times larger than an MP3 version of the same call.) If the call recording quality is too low, it may be unusable for speech training or it may skew speech training results. Speech engines are more accurate when using lossless formats (like WAV and FLAC) rather than lossy (like MP3, MULAW, and OGG).

The benefits and downsides of using call recordings are summarized in table 12.3.

Table 12.3 Summary of the benefits and downsides of using call recordings as speech data

Benefits of call recordings	Downsides of call recordings
▪ Recordings contain a representative variety of caller demographics, accents, and pronunciations of domain-specific words and phrases. ▪ Recordings contain a representative variety of topics. ▪ Recordings can be used for identifying intents and training speech-to-text models—multiple benefits from the same source.	▪ Extra time is required to process a recording to extract the segments of interest. ▪ Recordings require a lengthy transcription process. ▪ Humans talk differently to humans than automated assistants. ▪ Recordings are sometimes saved in a lossy format. The audio quality of the recording can be worse than the actual call.

Call recordings can be a good source of speech data, but they also have challenges. Let's look at another source of speech data.

12.1.2   *Generating synthetic speech data*

Instead of extracting real speech data from call recordings, Fictitious Inc. can generate their own speech data. Because this data will not come from real users, we will call this synthetic data. The data collection process is outlined in figure 12.5.

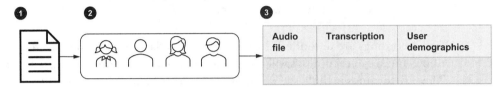

1. **Build a script of utterances. Each scripted line is an intent or entity training example.**
2. **A diverse set of users reads the script. An audio file is created for each line in the script.**
3. **Audio data is stored with the textual transcription and demographic summary.**

Figure 12.5   Synthetic data collection process. Multiple people record multiple audio segments to create speech data.

Fictitious Inc. can take some or all of the textual utterances they were going to train their intent classifier on and add them into a script for users to read. Then they will get a variety of users to record these utterances. The recorded utterances will be stored in individual audio files, accompanied by their textual transcription and summary demographic information. A sampling of Fictitious Inc.'s synthetic speech data is shown in table 12.4. Demographics of the speaker are collected for assuring a diversity of voices.

Table 12.4   Sample speech data from synthetic data collection

Audio file	Transcription	Demographics
reset_my_password_1.wav	"reset my password"	Male, U.S. Southern English accent
reset_my_password_2.wav	"reset my password"	Female, Hispanic accent
how_many_fiction_bucks_do_i_have_1.wav	"how many Fiction Bucks do I have"	Female, U.S. Northeastern English accent

Synthetic data collection is a popular option because of control and speed. Fictitious Inc. can dictate exactly what data they want to request. They can specify an exact distribution of data collected for each intent or domain-specific phrase. The uniformity in the data collection process helps them be aware of any skew in speaker demographics, and they can apply targeted efforts to close those gaps.

Fictitious Inc. can request synthetic data in a crowdsourced manner, with individuals contributing as little as five minutes each to record audio. The transcription process for synthetic data takes less time than for call recordings because the transcriber knows what the speakers are expected to say.

> **Why is transcription needed in synthetic data collection?**
> Speakers are expected to follow a script and speak a handful of known phrases. But speakers are human and make mistakes. In synthetic data collection, the role of the transcriber is to verify that each audio file contains the expected text. Speakers make enough mistakes that this extra effort is worth it.

Synthetic data collection has drawbacks as well. The usefulness of synthetic data is directly related to the quality of the script read by the speakers. If the script is filled with phrases that real users don't say, the audio data will not be useful. Additionally, synthetic data is often collected from people who are pretending to be real users, not the real users themselves. They may speak and intonate differently from real users. (Do they say "can you reset my password" with a sense of urgency or nonchalance?)

Last, the demographic distribution of users in the synthetic data collection may be completely different than the distribution of the real user population. If the difference between these distributions is too large, the data will be biased and will likely bias the AI assistant. User demographic groups that are underrepresented may find that the assistant does not understand them. The benefits and downsides of using call recordings are summarized in table 12.5.

Table 12.5 Summary of the benefits and downsides of synthetic recordings as speech data

Benefits of synthetic recordings	Downsides of synthetic recordings
■ Collect exactly what phrases you want. ■ Data uniformity helps identify gaps in speaker demographics. ■ Transcription takes less time. ■ Recordings can be crowdsourced.	■ Data collected is only valuable if the script is representative of what callers will say. ■ Does not come from real users but from simulated users. ■ It can be difficult to match the demographic distribution of the real user population.

Once Fictitious Inc. has gathered some audio data, they can test a speech-to-text model.

12.2 *Testing the speech-to-text model*

Most AI platforms integrate with one or more speech-to-text engines. These engines often come with default, pre-trained models. These default models are generally trained on generic text. Most of Fictitious Inc.'s terminology is generic; lots of call centers deal with password resets, appointments, and employment inquiries. A default model may suffice for Fictitious Inc.. Even if a generic model is not good enough,

Fictitious Inc. should test against a generic model before training their own custom model. The generic model is a baseline to compare any custom model against.

> **Test data volume**
>
> In theory, you may want to test your model against the largest possible data set. In practice, it's good to use 20% of your audio data for testing your model and use the other 80% for training a model (if training is needed).

Fictitious Inc. will build a test set from their audio data. Each piece of test data is a pair of an audio file and the correct transcription of that audio file. Each piece of test data will be tested with the process depicted in figure 12.6.

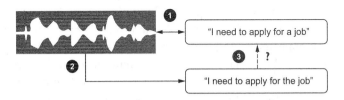

1. **The audio file and correct transcription are collected.**
2. **The speech model transcribes the audio file.**
3. **The model's transcription is tested by comparing it**
   with the correct transcription.

Figure 12.6   Testing a speech-to-text model on a single audio file

For each piece of test data, the speech-to-text model will transcribe the audio. Each test data pair becomes a triple, with the addition of the model's transcription. An exemplary output from a speech-to-text model test is shown in table 12.6.

Table 12.6   Comparing the model's transcription with the correct transcription of the audio file

Audio file	Expected (correct) transcription	Actual model transcription
Password.wav	reset my password	reset my password
EmploymentInquiry.wav	I need to apply for a job	I need to apply for the job
LoyaltyPoints.wav	how many Fiction Bucks do I have?	how many fiction bookstores have?

Table 12.6 is raw data. The output can be manually inspected, but it's not clear what the data tells us. Does this speech model work well or not? How much will the speech model contribute to (or detract from) Fictitious Inc.'s success metrics? This is difficult to determine when manually inspecting transcriptions for accuracy. An automated analysis of speech accuracy is both more valuable and easier to tie to success metrics.

There are three metrics commonly used to evaluate speech models:

- *Word error rate (WER)*—Evaluates number of words with a transcription error
- *Intent error rate (IER)*—Evaluates number of intent detection errors caused by a transcription error
- *Sentence error rate (SER)*—Evaluates number of sentences containing a transcription error

Let's start with WER.

12.2.1 Word error rate

The simplest way to measure speech transcription accuracy is by evaluating the *WER*. The WER is a ratio of the number of incorrect words in the model's transcript divided by the number of words in the correct transcript. Fictitious Inc.'s speech data is evaluated for WER in table 12.7. Each word error is boldfaced.

Table 12.7 Word errors in Fictitious Inc.'s test data

Expected (correct) transcription	Actual model transcription	WER
"reset my password"	"reset my password"	0% (0 of 3)
"I need to apply for **a** job"	"I need to apply for **the** job"	14.3% (1 of 7)
"how many Fiction **Bucks do I** have?"	"how many fiction **bookstores** have?	42.9% (3 of 7)
		Total: 23.5% (4 of 17)

There are three types of word errors:

- *Substitution*—The model's transcription replaces a correct word with a different word.
- *Insertion*—The model's transcription adds a word that was not in the correct transcript.
- *Deletion*—The model's transcription removes a word that was in the correct transcript.

The phrase "I need to apply for a job" had one substitution error ("the" for "a"). The phrase "how many Fiction Bucks do I have" had one substitution error ("bookstore" for "Bucks") and two deletion errors ("do" and "I").

Speech model providers often make it easy to compute WER because it can be computed generically by counting errors. For Fictitious Inc., the WER is missing important context. There's no clear way to tie the 23.5% WER to containment. (*Containment* is the percentage of conversations that are not escalated out of the assistant. When an assistant handles a conversation from beginning to end, that conversation is contained within the assistant.)

Some of the word errors are trivial ("the" versus "a"), and some of the word errors seem important ("bookstore" versus "Bucks do I"). Fictitious Inc. should tie all analysis back to success metrics. How does the WER affect containment?

Fictitious Inc. cannot draw a straight line from WER to containment, but they can infer one by inspecting the word errors. Rather than counting errors generically, they can count errors by word. From this, they can infer if the speech-to-text model is making mistakes on words likely to affect the use case. This new view on word errors is shown in table 12.8.

Table 12.8   WER by word

Word	Errors	Total occurrences	Error rate
Bucks	1	1	100%
do	1	1	100%
a	1	1	100%
I	1	2	50%
(All other words)	0	12	0%

Table 12.8 has a small data set but suggests that the speech-to-text model will not work well when Fictitious Inc. callers ask about their Fiction Bucks balance. The error rates on "do," "a," and "I" are less likely to affect the AI. The classifier in the assistant should be resilient to minor errors with these common words.

Fictitious Inc. does not need to guess about the impact of word errors on their assistant's classifier. They can measure the impact directly by evaluating the IER.

12.2.2 Intent error rate

Fictitious Inc.'s success metric is to contain calls and complete them successfully. An important part of successfully containing a conversation is identifying the correct user intent. Speech transcription errors are not a problem if the assistant identifies the correct intent for the user. Fictitious Inc. can compute an IER through the process diagrammed in figure 12.7.

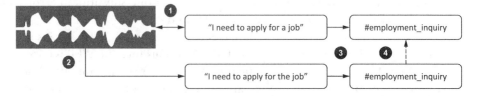

1. The audio file and correct transcription are collected.
2. The speech model transcribes the audio file.
3. **Both transcriptions are classified by the assistant into intents.**
4. **The intents are compared.**

Figure 12.7   Computing a speech-to-text model's intent error rate for a single piece of speech data

Fictitious Inc.'s IER is computed in table 12.9. Each word error is boldfaced. The expected and actual transcriptions are each classified; then the expected and predicted intents are compared.

Table 12.9 Intent errors in Fictitious Inc.'s test data

Expected (correct) transcription	Actual model transcription	Expected intent	Predicted intent	IER
"reset my password"	"reset my password"	`#reset_password`	`#reset_password`	0%
"I need to apply for **a** job"	"I need to apply for **the** job"	`#employment_inquiry`	`#employment_inquiry`	0%
"how many Fiction **Bucks do I** have?"	"how many fiction **bookstores** have?	`#loyalty_points`	Unknown	100%
				Total: 33.3%

The IER puts the performance of the speech-to-text model into context. Fictitious Inc. had to infer what a 23.5% WER meant for their users. The IER does not need any inference. A 33.3% IER means that the AI assistant will fail to predict the user's intent correctly 33.3% of the time.

> **Representative data alert**
>
> The IER is directly usable as shown in this section if the speech data is representative of production usage. If production data has a different distribution of intents or user demographics, the IER will be skewed.

IER is a great way to evaluate how a speech-to-text model impacts the assistant's intent identification. When the wrong intent is predicted, several success metrics go down, including user satisfaction and call containment. A low IER is important.

Not every message in a conversation includes an intent. The IER alone is not sufficient to evaluate the impact of a speech-to-text model on an assistant. Let's look at one more metric: SER.

12.2.3 Sentence error rate

For audio segments that are not expected to contain intents, Fictitious Inc. can evaluate a speech-to-text model using SER. SER is the ratio of sentences with an error compared to the total number of sentences. SER is a good metric to use when an entire string must be transcribed correctly for the system to succeed. We have seen that intent statements do not need to be transcribed 100% accurately for the system to succeed; the AI assistant can still find the right intent if some words are inaccurately transcribed.

We can stretch the definition of a sentence to include any stand-alone statement a user will make. In Fictitious Inc.'s password reset flow, they ask for the user's date of birth. The date of birth can be treated as a full sentence. If the speech-to-text model makes a single mistake in transcribing the date of birth, the entire date will be transcribed incorrectly. Table 12.10 shows a computation of SER for Fictitious Inc. audio files containing dates. Each word error is boldfaced. Each transcription contains a single sentence.

Table 12.10 Sentence errors in Fictitious Inc.'s test data for dates

Expected (correct) transcription	Actual model transcription	SER
"January first two thousand five"	"January first two thousand five"	0% (No error)
"**One** eight nineteen **sixty-three**"	"June eight nineteen sixteen"	100% (Error)
"**seven** four twenty oh one"	"eleven four twenty oh one"	100% (Error)
		Total: 66.7%

SER is a good metric for evaluating any conversational input that must be transcribed exactly correctly. Fictitious Inc.'s password reset flow collected and validated a User ID, date of birth, and an answer to a security question. They should not execute a password reset process if they are not perfectly sure they are resetting the right user's password, so transcribing these responses accurately is important.

In Fictitious Inc.'s appointments process flow, they collect a date and time for the appointment. Again, these data points must be captured exactly correctly, or the user may be given a completely different appointment than they expected. AI assistants commonly collect data that must be captured correctly. The assistant can always ask the user to confirm any data point before proceeding, but any sentence errors will prolong the conversation since the user will be prompted to repeat themselves.

SER computation

For some data inputs, you may run a postprocessing step on the speech-to-text model transcription before comparing it to the correct transcription. In numeric inputs, "for" and "four" should both be treated equivalently as the numeral "4." Similarly, "to" and "too" are equivalent to "two."

Your speech-to-text model may enable this automatically. This functionality is sometimes called *smart formatting* or *recognition hints*.

Once Fictitious Inc. has evaluated the performance of their speech model, they can decide if the performance is sufficient, or if they need to train a custom model to get even better results. They now have a baseline to compare their custom model against. Let's explore how they can train their own custom speech-to-text model.

12.3 *Training a speech-to-text model*

Most AI platforms integrate with speech engines, and most of these speech engines support customized training. The major speech engine providers offer differing levels of customization. Fictitious Inc. should target the minimum level of customization that meets their needs. Speech training has diminishing returns, and some levels of customization take hours or days to train.

Before Fictitious Inc. does any training, they should select an appropriate base model for their use case. Base models are available for use without any custom training and come in multiple flavors. Fictitious Inc. is starting with English, but they will likely have a choice between US English, UK English, or Australian English. Within a language and dialect, Fictitious Inc. may have choices between models optimized for audio coming from telephone, mobile, or video. The choices are summarized in figure 12.8.

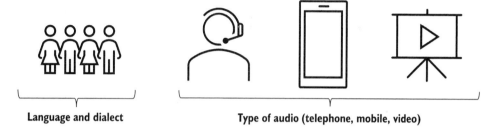

Language and dialect   **Type of audio (telephone, mobile, video)**

Figure 12.8 Speech platforms offer several types of base models, optimized for different languages/dialects as well as different audio channels. Choose the base model most suitable for your application.

Why so many choices in base models?

Audio data is encoded differently in different technology applications. Narrowband technologies (like a telephone network) compress the audio signal to a narrow range of frequencies. Broadband technology uses a wider range of frequencies, producing a higher quality audio. Like any model, speech-to-text models need to be trained on representative data. Be sure to match your use case to the right base model.

The base models are trained by the speech platform provider with data that they own. Each base model is generally trained with language and audio data from a variety of different users, both native and non-native speakers. Speech platform providers are making strides toward producing models with less bias, but Fictitious Inc. should definitely test their model against a representative user set to verify this.

After Fictitious Inc. has selected a base model, they can begin training a custom model. The custom model is an adaptation or an extension of a base model. The overview of a custom model training process is shown in figure 12.9.

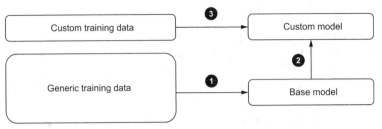

1. Select a base model trained by the speech platform.
2. Create a custom model that extends a base model.
3. Train the custom model with custom data.

Figure 12.9   Summary of the custom speech-to-text model training process

> **Terminology alert**
>
> Speech-to-text providers use differing terminology. Technically, custom speech models are adaptations of base models. In this view, base models are trained, and custom models are adapted or customized rather than trained.
>
> *Speech adaptation* is the process of building a new custom model that extends a base model with custom data.
>
> For the sake of simplifying our mental model of AI assistants, this chapter will use the simpler term training, which is close enough for our purposes.

Fictitious Inc. will generally not have access to the generic training data; this data is usually owned by the speech platform. The platform will expose a base model that Fictitious Inc. can extend into a custom model. Fictitious Inc. will train that custom model with their specific data.

> **NOTE**   In this section, we will use small training data sets to illustrate the key concepts.

In practice, Fictitious Inc. would use several hours' worth of data to train their custom models.

Depending on their speech platform provider, Fictitious Inc. will have three customization options available to them:

- A *language model* is a collection of text utterances that the speech engine is likely to hear.
- An *acoustic model* is a speech-to-text model that is trained with both audio and text.
- A *grammar* is a set of rules or patterns that a speech-to-text model uses to transcribe an audio signal into text.

Fictitious Inc. can use different training options for different parts of their AI assistant. Let's start with the simplest option: language models.

12.3.1 Custom training with a language model

Training a custom language model is the simplest form of speech training that Fictitious Inc. can do for their assistant. A *language model* is a collection of text utterances that the speech engine is likely to hear. Fictitious Inc. can build a text file from one or more of these sources: transcriptions of call recordings, or intent and entity training examples in their assistant. This text file is the training data for the language model. Fictitious Inc.'s language model training data file is depicted in table 12.11.

Table 12.11   Fictitious Inc.'s language model training data

language_model_training_data.txt
reset my password
I need to apply for a job
how many Fiction Bucks do I have?

This table is the only table in this book that shows a one-column training data table. This is not a mistake. Language models use unsupervised learning. This means they are only given inputs—no outputs are specified anywhere in the training data. A language model is trained by teaching it how to read the specific language in the domain it is trained on.

Children are often taught how to read by learning letters and the phonetic sounds they make. For instance, the English language contains 42 distinct phonemes. Once you master the 42 phonemes, you can sound out almost any English word (even if it takes a while). Mastery of the phonemes lets you pronounce words you have never encountered before.

A language model reads a training data file in a similar way. An example is shown in figure 12.10. The base model in the speech platform is trained on how to phonetically read. In the figure, we see how the language model breaks the phrase "How many Fiction Bucks do I have" into phonemes.

1.	How	many	Fiction	Bucks	do	I	have
2.	.haʊ	.ˈmɛ.ni	.ˈfɪk.ʃin	.ˈbʌks	.ˈdu	.ˈaɪ	.ˈhæv

1. The model is given textual input.
2. The model converts the text to a sequence of phonemes.

Figure 12.10   A language model learns phonetic sequences from textual input.

A speech-to-text model transcribes an audio signal into a sequence of phonemes. Most speech engines generate several transcription hypotheses: a primary hypothesis and one or more alternate hypothesis. The base model from a speech platform may transcribe the audio signal in "How many Fiction Bucks do I have" as shown in figure 12.11.

"Books" and "bucks" are phonetically similar. A base model is likely trained on data that includes the word "books" (ˈbʊks) more than the word "bucks" (ˈbʌks). This is

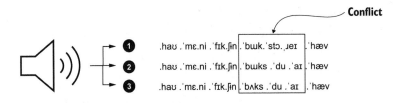

1. Hypothesis: How many Fiction bookstore have?
2. Hypothesis: How many Fiction books do I have?
3. Hypothesis: How many Fiction Bucks do I have?

Figure 12.11   A speech-to-text model generates several alternative hypotheses for the audio rendition of "How many Fiction Bucks do I have?" This base model does not immediately recognize the Fictitious Inc. term "Fiction Bucks."

especially true when we consider the sound in context. There are much fewer instances of the phrase "Fiction Bucks" than the phrase "fiction books." The former is used only at Fictitious Inc., but the latter is used all over the world. Given a difficult choice between two phonetically similar phrases, the speech-to-text model chose the phrase it had seen the most before.

When Fictitious Inc. adds language model training to their speech-to-text model, the speech-to-text model gives higher precedence to Fictitious Inc.'s specific language. Fictitious Inc.'s language model training data includes their domain-specific term "Fiction Bucks." This encourages the model to transcribe "bucks" (ˈbʌks) instead of "books" (ˈbʊks), especially when adjacent to the word "Fiction." Figure 12.12 shows how the custom speech-to-text model works after Fictitious Inc. trains it with a language model.

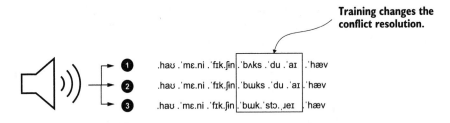

1. Hypothesis: How many Fiction Bucks do I have?
2. Hypothesis: How many Fiction books do I have?
3. Hypothesis: How many Fiction bookstore have?

Figure 12.12   A speech-to-text model generates several alternative hypotheses for the audio rendition of "How many Fiction Bucks do I have?" Language model training helps the speech-to-text model select the best alternative from similar-sounding phrases.

Language model training is perhaps the quickest way to improve speech transcription. The training is fast because it only uses textual data. Even better, this text data should already be available from the utterances used for intent and entity training. Audio data is still required to test the model after it is trained. Still, language models are not a panacea.

> ### Check your speech platform to see if it offers language models
> Several of the speech-to-text providers surveyed for this book included language model functionality, but some do not. The most common terminology is language model, but some providers refer to it as related text. Check your platform's documentation.
>
> Some speech-to-text platforms offer a light version of language models called hints or keywords." Rather than training a full custom language model, a speech transcription request can be accompanied by a list of words that may be expected in the audio being transcribed.

Some speech platforms do not offer language model training at all. These platforms can only be trained with pairs of audio files and their transcripts. Language models also rely on the speech platform's built-in phonetic reading of words. In a language model, you cannot show the speech platform exactly how a word sounds with an audio example; you can only train the model on what words are likely to occur in relation to other words. Because the model is not trained with audio, it may fail to understand words pronounced with various accents, especially for domain-specific and uncommon words.

The benefits and disadvantages of language models are summarized in table 12.12.

Table 12.12   Benefits and disadvantages of language models

Benefits	Disadvantages
<ul><li>Training is relatively fast.</li><li>Does not require any audio to train a model (audio is still required to test).</li><li>Can reuse intent and entity training utterances as language model training data.</li></ul>	<ul><li>Not all speech platforms offer language models.</li><li>Relies on the platform's built-in phonetic reading of words; does not explicitly train the model how these words sound.</li><li>May be insufficient if the user base has a wide variety of accents.</li></ul>

Language models are a great option if your platform provides them, but not every platform does. Let's look at the most common speech-to-text model training option: the acoustic model.

12.3.2   Custom training with an acoustic model

Fictitious Inc. has collected audio files and their associated text transcripts. This is exactly the fuel required to train an acoustic model. An *acoustic model* is a speech-to-text model that is trained with both audio and text. An acoustic model generally uses supervised learning with the audio as an input and the text as the answer. When this model is trained, it learns to associate the acoustic sounds in the audio with the words and phrases in the text transcripts.

Terminology alert
Many speech platforms do not give a special name to acoustic models. They may just call them custom models. An acoustic model is trained with both audio and text. This is the default training mode in many speech platforms and the only training possibility in some speech platforms.

An acoustic model is an especially good option for training a speech-to-text model to recognize unusual words across a variety of accents. By pairing an audio and a text transcript together, the speech-to-text model directly learns what phonetic sequences sound like and how they should be transcribed.

The phrase "Fiction Bucks" is specific to Fictitious Inc.'s jargon and a base speech-to-text model probably won't ever have encountered that phrase. Fictitious Inc. likely needs to train the speech-to-text model to recognize it. Figure 12.13 shows a variety of ways that the phrase "How many Fiction Bucks do I have" may sound across a variety of accents.

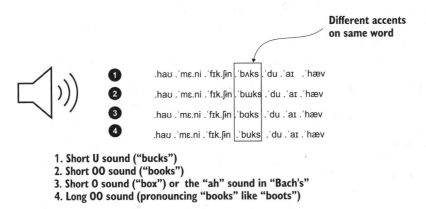

1. Short U sound ("bucks")
2. Short OO sound ("books")
3. Short O sound ("box") or the "ah" sound in "Bach's"
4. Long OO sound (pronouncing "books" like "boots")

Figure 12.13   Phonetic sequences for "How many Fiction Bucks do I have" in several different accents. An acoustic model can be trained to transcribe each of these the same way.

When Fictitious Inc. samples audio from a variety of user demographics, they may get some or all of those pronunciations of "Fiction Bucks." They can train an acoustic model with each of these pronunciations and the model will learn to transcribe each of them to the same phrase, even though they sound different phonetically.

Acoustic models generally use a supervised learning approach. This means the speech-to-text model is directly trained to associate audio signals to text transcripts. The model learns to identify variations of phonetic sequences that should get identical transcriptions. Acoustic model training is also useful for training a model to recognize uncommon words or words with unusual spelling. Acoustic training is also useful for loan words—words borrowed from another language. If a speech engine does not know how to pronounce a word, it is likely to need acoustic training to transcribe that word.

Save some data for testing the model

Acoustic models need to be trained with a lot of data, five hours minimum, preferably 10 to 20 hours. But don't use all of your data for training the model. Optimally, use 80% of the data for training and save 20% for testing. You want to be able to test your speech-to-text model against data it was not explicitly trained on. That 20% of the data becomes the blind test set for your speech-to-text model.

Acoustic models are widely available on speech platforms and are sometimes the only option provided in a platform. The primary benefit of acoustic models is that they are given a direct translation guide from audio to phonemes to text via their audio and text transcript training data. Acoustic models are the best option for training a speech-to-text model to recognize different accents.

Acoustic models have some downsides too. Acoustic models often require a large amount of training data to be effective. A minimum of five hours is generally required, with 10 or 20 hours being preferable. This volume of data is computationally expensive to process. Acoustic model training generally takes hours to complete, and sometimes takes days.

The benefits and disadvantages of acoustic models are summarized in table 12.13.

Table 12.13 Benefits and disadvantages of acoustic models

Benefits	Disadvantages
▪ Default training option for most platforms. ▪ Good when the user base has demographic diversity and varying accents. ▪ Trains the model on the exact sounds made by words and phrases.	▪ Training time can be lengthy, up to a day or two in some cases. ▪ Can require a large volume of data (five hours minimum, 10 to 20 preferred).

Language models and acoustic models are both good options for training a speech-to-text model to recognize open-ended language. "How can I help you" is an open-ended question and will have a wide variety of responses. This is why we usually train a language or acoustic model on intent-related utterances.

Sometimes an assistant asks a constrained question, where the structure of the expected input is known. When the assistant asks, "What's your date of birth," the response is very likely to be a date. Some speech platforms offer a training option that constrains the transcription options. Let's explore this option.

12.3.3 Custom training with grammars

A *grammar* is a set of rules or patterns that a speech-to-text model uses to transcribe an audio signal into text. Fictitious Inc. can use a grammar anywhere in their assistant where the expected user utterances fit a finite set of patterns. Fictitious Inc.'s first possibility for grammars is in collecting user IDs. A Fictitious Inc. user ID is a series of 4–12 letters followed by 1–3 numbers. This can be coded in the regular expression [A-Za-z]{4,12}[0-9]{1,3} as shown in figure 12.14.

> **Terminology alert**
> Every speech platform I investigate that offered this functionality called it grammar. Hooray for standardization!

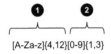

[A-Za-z]{4,12}[0-9]{1,3}

1. Four to 12 letters
2. One to three numbers

Figure 12.14 Regular expression for Fictitious Inc.'s user ID pattern. Their user IDs are always 4–12 letters followed by 1–3 numbers.

The expected range of Fictitious Inc. user IDs is small enough that it fits in a 24-character regular expression. Fictitious Inc. can use a grammar to recognize user IDs. The speech-to-text model learns several rules from the grammar including the following:

- The phoneme ˈtu means "two", not "to" or "too."
- The phoneme ˈfɔɹ means "four," not "for" or "fore."
- "M" is possible as ˈɛm. Never use the similar-sounding phonemes for "him" ˈhɪm or "hem" ˈhɛm. The model will avoid other words starting with soft "h" sounds ("A" versus "hay" and "O" versus "ho," to name a few).
- The phoneme for "deal" ˈdil is better interpreted as "D L" ˈdi ˈɛl.

The grammar for Fictitious Inc.'s user ID pattern packs a lot of training into a small space. Fictitious Inc. also collects dates a couple of times in their conversational assistant: date of birth (in the password reset flow) and date of appointment (in the create appointment flow). There are a large number of possible dates, but ultimately dates can be captured in a finite set of rules. Figure 12.15 shows 36 possible month formats and 62 possible day formats. (There are actually a few more: callers can use "oh," "zero," and "aught" interchangeably.)

EXERCISE 1 Can you build a list of possible year formats?

Month is one of these.

Day is one of these.

January	One	Oh One		One	Thirteen	Twenty-five	Oh One	One One	Two One
February	Two	Oh Two		Two	Fourteen	Twenty-six	Oh Two	One Two	Two Two
March	Three	Oh Three		Three	Fifteen	Twenty-seven	Oh Three	One Three	Two Three
April	Four	Oh Four		Four	Sixteen	Twenty-eight	Oh Four	One Four	Two Four
May	Five	Oh Five		Five	Seventeen	Twenty-nine	Oh Five	One Five	Two Five
June	Six	Oh Six		Six	Eighteen	Thirty	Oh Six	One Six	Two Six
July	Seven	Oh Seven		Seven	Nineteen	Thirty-one	Oh Seven	One Seven	Two Seven
August	Eight	Oh Eight		Eight	Twenty		Oh Eight	One Eight	Two Eight
September	Nine	Oh Nine		Nine	Twenty-one		Oh Nine	One Nine	Two Nine
October	Ten	One Oh		Ten	Twenty-two			One Oh	Two Oh
November	Eleven	One One		Eleven	Twenty-three		Three Oh		
December	Twelve	One Two		Twelve	Twenty-four		Three One		

Figure 12.15 There are a finite number of ways to give a date in month-day format. (There are a finite number of ways to give a year too.) Some users prefer to say "zero" or "aught" instead of "oh" in their dates.

Date formats

There are multiple date formats, including month-day-year, day-month-year, and year-month-day. It's impossible to write a grammar which covers all three at once (how would you unambiguously transcribe "oh one oh two twenty oh one"?) Pick one.

Month-day-year is the primary pattern in the United States but not in most of the world. If your user base is broad enough that they might use multiple formats, be sure to give the user a hint. Fictitious Inc. could ask "What is your month, day, and year of birth?" instead of "What is your date of birth?"

The number of ways to express a date within a given date format is large but finite. Still, it is a frightening proposition to write a single regular expression to handle all of the possibilities within a date format. Most speech platforms that have grammars offer some sort of rules engine which can break the work into a manageable number of pieces. The next listing shows how to code a set of rules to match date phrases.

Listing 12.1 Pseudocode for month-day rules engine

Complex rules can be broken down into simpler rules. A date is a month and a year

There are two major patterns to months, either the name of the month or the number.

```
$date_phrase = $month and $day
$month = $month_name or $month_number
$month_name = January or February or March or April or May or June or July or
⇒ August or September or October or November or December
$month_number = $one or $two or $three or $four or $five or $six or $seven or
⇒ $eight or $nine or $ten or $eleven or $twelve
$zero = zero or oh or aught
$one = one or $zero one
$two = two or $zero two
$three = three or $zero three
```

We first capture the twelve numeric variations.

The "zero" logic is captured once and reused.

```
$four = four or $zero four
$five = one or $zero five
$six = one or $zero six
$seven = one or $zero seven
$eight = one or $zero eight
$nine = one or $zero nine
$ten = ten or one $zero
$eleven = eleven or one one
$twelve = twelve or one two

# $day is left as an exercise for the reader
```

EXERCISE 2 Can you build a grammar for $day?

Most speech platforms with grammars use strict interpretation when applying a grammar. This means they try very hard to force-fit an audio signal into the specified pattern, and if the audio doesn't fit the pattern, they may not return a transcription at all. This is in stark contrast with language models and acoustic models, which will happily attempt to transcribe any input. Fictitious Inc.'s user ID regular expression `[A-Za-z]{4,12}[0-9]{1,3}` is strict. If the user says, "I don't know" or "agent," the speech engine can't force-fit that into the grammar and may not return a transcription at all. The following listing shows one way to make the user ID grammar more forgiving and lenient so that it can transcribe more phrases than valid user IDs.

Listing 12.2 Pseudocode for a more forgiving and lenient user ID grammar

```
$user_id = $valid_user_id or $do_not_know or $opt_out
$valid_user_id = regular_expression("[A-Za-z]{4,12}[0-9]{1,3}")
$do_not_know = "I don't know" or "I don't have it" or "No idea"
$opt_out = "agent" or "representative" or "customer service" or "get me out
➥ of here"
```

Grammars come with significant trade-offs. The strict nature of a grammar allows the speech-to-text model to more accurately transcribe inputs that match an expected pattern. The strictness has a cost when its inputs do not match the expected pattern. This strictness can be alleviated by encoding additional patterns into the grammar, but this makes the grammar more complex and difficult to manage.

Grammars are relatively quick to train. No audio input is required for training; only an encoding of the grammar rules is needed. Most speech platforms with grammars allow you to build complex rule patterns into the grammar itself. Some platforms let you combine grammars with language and/or acoustic models.

Grammars are not suitable when the range of expected inputs does is unconstrained. Fictitious Inc. cannot use a grammar to collect responses to their open-ended question "How may I help you?"

The benefits and disadvantages of grammars are summarized in table 12.14.

Table 12.14   Benefits and disadvantages of grammars

Benefits	Disadvantages
■ Most accurate method for capturing constrained inputs ■ Useful when the input follows a set of rules ■ No audio required for training, only rules	■ Only suitable when the expected input is constrained ■ May fail to transcribe unexpected responses or digressions

Create your own grammar, if your speech platform does not provide one

If you can write code that is executed between speech-to-text transcription and before the assistant acts, you can write your own grammar in code. Your grammar will actually be a postprocessor. For instance, when the speech-to-text model returns "January to for twenty ten" your post-processor can replace the "to"/"for" with numbers, giving "January two four twenty ten."

A general comparison of language models, acoustic models, and grammars is found in table 12.15.

Table 12.15   Comparison of language model, acoustic model, and grammar

Feature	Language model	Acoustic model	Grammar
Availability in speech platforms	Sometimes	Always	Sometimes
Trained with	Text only	Audio and text pairs	Rules only
Tested with	Audio and text	Audio and text	Audio and text
Training time	Minutes	Hours	Seconds
Open-ended questions	Works well	Works well	Does not work
Constrained questions	Works well	Works well	Works best
Training method	Unsupervised learning	Supervised learning	Rules
If the user says something unexpected	Works	Works	Does not work well
Ability to handle varying accents	Good	Best	Mostly good

Fictitious Inc. can train multiple speech-to-text models for different parts of their assistant. The model can default to using a language model and/or an acoustic model and use a grammar in specific parts of the conversation (asking for user IDs and dates). Just as Fictitious Inc. plans to iteratively train and improve their intent classifier, they should expect to iteratively train and improve their speech-to-text model(s).

Summary

- Speech-to-text models transcribe from audio to text.
- AI assistants can be resilient to some transcription mistakes. Don't evaluate a speech-to-text model based on pure accuracy; evaluate it based on how transcription mistakes affect the assistant. IER always affects the assistant; WER does not.
- Testing a speech-to-text model always requires audio with matching transcripts. Language models are trained only with text. Acoustic models are trained with audio and text. Grammar models are programmed with rules.
- Language models and acoustic models are best for transcribing open-ended inputs and can also transcribe constrained inputs. Grammars are best at transcribing constrained inputs and are completely unsuitable for open-ended inputs.

appendix
Glossary of terms
and abbreviations

Abbreviation/term	Definition/meaning
Accuracy	A measure of how correct an algorithm is. Accuracy is calculated as the number of correct predictions divided by the total number of predictions. Sometimes referred to as *overall accuracy*.
Acoustic model	A speech model that is trained on pairs of audio and text. Each audio file is accompanied by its textual transcript. The acoustic model learns the exact sounds associated with each of the transcripts.
Agent-assist AI assistant	An AI assistant pattern where the user interacts with a human agent, but the human agent is using an AI assistant.
AI assistant	An automated assistant that uses artificial intelligence (AI). It receives natural language input and performs a task for a user. The task may include answering a question, turning on the lights, or resetting a password.
All-in-one classifier	A classifier that is trained to distinguish between many intents. This classifier will predict one of N different intents, each with an associated confidence value, and the confidence values will sum to 1.
Ambiguous utterance	A textual phrase that by itself does not represent a single clear intent. If a user says "account," we don't know if they need to open an account, close an account, or check their account status.
Application programming interface (API)	A software interface that is meant to be used by other software. This is in contrast to a user interface (UI) or graphical user interface (GUI) that is meant to be used by humans.

Abbreviation/term	Definition/meaning
Bag of words	A classification algorithm that counts the number of times each distinct word occurs per intent in the training data and uses these counts to learn intent patterns. The algorithm does not apply any intelligence in processing the words beyond counting them. Due to this naivete, bag of words is one of the simplest algorithms to implement.
Baseline	A measurement of the as-is or default state. When evaluating a custom machine learning model, it is useful to compare its performance against a completely untrained model.
Bias	Unequal treatment or preference given to one group when compared to another. Machine learning algorithms infer from the data they are trained on; if the training data is biased, the algorithm will amplify that bias. Great care should be taken to build a data set representative of the user population.
Binary classifier	A classifier that is trained to recognize only one intent. A reset password classifier classifies phrases into positive (is reset password) or negative (is not reset password) classes. An AI assistant can use N different binary classifiers to classify N total intents. When multiple binary classifiers are used, their confidence values will not sum up to 1.
Blind test	A test of a machine learning model where the model is tested with data it has not seen before. Blind testing ensures that the model will work well with previously unseen instances when the model is deployed.
Classifier	Classification is a method of organizing objects into one or more categories. Classifiers are algorithms that perform classification. For instance, books may be classified as fiction or nonfiction.
Command	A verb-centered action an AI assistant should take, often clarified by additional parameters. "Turn on" is a command, clarified by the parameter "all the lights."
Command interpreter	An AI assistant pattern where the user interacts with the assistant to accomplish a single task, and then the interaction is over.
Command parameter	A noun-centered phrase clarifying a command or action. In the phrase "turn on all the lights," "all the lights" is a command parameter, clarifying the command "turn on."
Commit	A discrete change to one or more files in a source control management system.
Commit log	A history of changes made to one or more source code files.
Compound utterance	A statement containing two or more distinct user intents or goals. "I want to reset my password and also find out when the store opens" includes intents for "reset password" and "find store hours."
Confidence	A probability estimate given by a classifier. This estimate is correlated with, but not equal to, the likelihood that the classifier's prediction is correct.
Confirmation prompt	A question asked by an AI assistant that confirms the assistant understood. If the user says, "What time are you open" and the assistant says, "To confirm, was that store hours?", the assistant used a confirmation prompt.

Abbreviation/term	Definition/meaning
Confusion matrix	A grid that compares a classifier's actual predictions against the expected (correct) values. One axis of the grid is the correct intents, the other is the classifier's predicted intents. Each square in the grid corresponds to the number of times the correct and predicted intent combination occurred.
Constrained question	A question that has a finite number of expected responses. "What's your five-digit zip code?" and "Which store, Elm or Maple?" are both constrained questions.
Containment	The percentage of conversations handled entirely by the AI assistant. (A conversation that is not escalated to a human is contained.)
Context variables	These variables are used by AI assistants to maintain user-specific or conversation-specific state. For instance, an assistant may store the user's first name in a context variable so that it can later personalize responses to that user.
Conversational AI; conversational assistant	An AI assistant that interacts with an user in a fully conversational manner. These are also commonly called chatbots or voice bots.
Coverage	The ratio of how many requests an AI assistant attempts to answer divided by the total number of questions it receives.
Customer relationship management (CRM) systems	A software system that stores all interactions a corporation has with their customers. Conversation transcripts from AI assistants are often stored in CRM systems.
Development environment	An internal place where developers write and test code before sharing it with others. Development environments are where the latest code is tweaked and improved until it stabilizes.
Dialogue engine	AI assistant component that manages dialogue state and coordinates building the assistant's response to the user.
Dictionary	A static list of terms with the same or similar meaning.
Digression	When a user changes topic in the middle of a conversational flow.
Disambiguation	When a conversational AI asks a clarifying question. If the user says, "I need help with account," the assistant can ask a disambiguating question: "Do you need to open an account, close an account, or check your account status?"
Drop-off	The point at which a conversational flow fails. If the user is asked for their user ID, and the system does not get a valid user ID, the conversational flow has a drop-off on this user ID question.
Entities	Segments of a user utterance that modify or augment the intent. In "Set an alarm for 9 p.m.," the intent "set an alarm" is modified by the entity "9 p.m." Entities are usually nouns or noun phrases.
Escalation	When a conversational AI redirects a user to another channel for resolution, usually to a human. See also *hand-off*.

Abbreviation/term	Definition/meaning
Event classifier	An AI assistant that classifies an incoming message and routes it for further processing. There is no conversational element to this AI assistant. This pattern is also referred to as classification and routing.
Fallback condition	Often used in conversational AIs to handle the case where the assistant did not expect or understand the user's input. This is also called a default condition. An assistant might respond to the fallback condition with "I'm sorry, I don't understand."
False negative	A prediction that was made when it should not have been. If the user asks for a password reset and the assistant responds with store hours, there is a false negative for the password reset intent.
False positive	A prediction that was made when it should not have been. If the user asks for a password reset and the assistant responds with store hours, there is a false positive for the store hours intent.
Feature (in machine learning)	A characteristic of an input that a machine learning algorithm can use to infer how to get to an output. Machine learning algorithms generally use many different features. The bag of words text classifier creates a feature for every word in its training data.
F-score	An accuracy metric for evaluating machine learning models that considers two different types of errors. The most common F-score is F1, which is the harmonic mean of precision and recall.
Functional testing	Software testing that verifies the behavior of a system. Does the system do what it is supposed to do? A functional test may include making sure that the reset password dialogue flow resets a user's password.
Fuzzy matching	A method of string matching that does not require exact matching. Fuzzy matching helps AI assistants be adaptive to spelling mistakes and typos. Fuzzy matching dictates that "Mapel" is equivalent to "Maple."
Grammar	A strict set of rules or patterns for evaluating input. Speech models can use grammars when the number of possible inputs is finite.
Ground truth	A curated set of data that has been verified as true. Ground truth data can be used for both training and/or testing machine learning models.
Hand-off	When a conversational AI redirects a user to another channel for resolution, usually to a human. See also *escalation*.
Hot-fix	A fix to a software defect that is so important it bypasses or accelerates the usual release planning.
Intent	The meaning or goal in a user utterance—what the user wants, or is trying to do. #reset_password and #set_alarm are example intents. Intents are generally centered on verbs. By convention, intent names are often prefixed with a # sign.
Intent error rate	Method for evaluating speech-to-text transcription accuracy. Intent error rate is a ratio of the number of utterances that are misclassified due to speech transcription errors versus the total number of utterances.

Abbreviation/term	Definition/meaning
Jargon	Terms used by only a small percentage of people who know a language. Jargon is usually domain-specific.
k-folds cross-validation test	A test of a machine learning model where the training data is split into *k* distinct sets (*k* is an integer, often 3, 5, or 10). *k* different models are trained, and each model omits a different $1/k$ of the training data for a test set. The results from the *k* different tests are aggregated into the *k*-folds cross-validation test results.
Labeled data	A set of data with (input) features and (output) labels, used for training a machine learning algorithm. Also called *ground truth*.
Language model	A speech model that is trained only with text. The text includes utterances that the model is likely to hear. The language model learns what words and phonetic sequences it should expect to transcribe.
Load testing	Software testing that verifies a system can be used by many users at once without degradation in response time or functionality.
Logisitic regression	A regression algorithm where the target output is a discrete value. Classifiers commonly use logistic regression to predict 0 or 1.
Machine learning	A software algorithm that learns by example. A machine learning algorithm is given data and asked to infer rules associated with that data. Machine learning stands in contrast to traditional programming where a programmer explicitly codes a set of rules into a software program, and then runs that program against some data.
Misclassification	A classification error. If for a given utterance, the system should predict X but instead predicts Y, the prediction of Y is a misclassification.
Model (machine learning model)	The output of a machine learning algorithm. The model encapsulates the patterns and rules learned by the machine learning algorithm. A model is used to make a prediction against some input data.
Natural language understanding (NLU)	A process where computers extract structure and meaning from natural language.
Net promoter score (NPS)	A 0-10 scoring system based on responses to "How likely is it that you would recommend our company/product/service to a friend or colleague?" The highest scores (9 and 10) are referred to as promoters, and the lowest scores are referred to as detractors.
Notebook	An artifact in Python development that combines code and presentation. Code in a notebook can be manually executed step-by-step or automatically in batch mode, and the output from that code can be stored in the notebook itself.
Ontology	A method of organizing concepts and categories within a given domain.
Open-ended question	A question where the response can have nearly infinite variety. "How can I help you?" is an open-ended question.
Opt out	When a user asks to leave the AI assistant and interact with a human instead. Common opt-out phrases include "agent," "representative," "speak to a human," and "get me out of here."

Abbreviation/term	Definition/meaning
Orchestrator	Optional AI assistant component that coordinates calls to APIs to drive business processes and provide dynamic response data.
Parameters	Arguments, usually noun-based, which modify a command. The command "set an alarm" requires a parameter of "alarm time."
Parts of speech tagging	A natural language understanding technique that identifies the grammatical part of speech (noun, verb, adjective, and so on) for each word in the input. Parts of speech can be used as features in a machine learning algorithm.
Phoneme	Distinct units of sound that can be combined into words. A spoken word is a phonetic sequence.
Precision	An accuracy measurement that punishes an algorithm for false positives, such as when the algorithm predicts an event it should not. Equation: (true positives) / (true positives + false positives) An assistant that predicts a "reset password" intent for any utterance will never miss a "reset password" intent but will not be precise.
Production environment	The place where real users interact with deployed code.
Production logs	Application logs or other low-level data from production systems.
Question-and-answer bot	A conversational AI without multi-step process flows. The user asks a question, the assistant responds, and then the user may ask another new question.
Representative data	A sample of data that has the same distribution of characteristics as the entire population.
Recall	An accuracy measurement that punishes an algorithm for false negatives, such as when the algorithm misses an event it should have predicted. Equation: (true positives) / (true positives + false negatives) An assistant that never predicts a "reset password" intent for any utterance will never have a false positive "reset password" detection but will have terrible recall.
Repository (source code repository)	A place where source code files are stored and versioned. GitHub is a popular source code repository.
Reprompting	When a conversational AI admits it does not understand the user's request and asks them to restate it.
Response	Whatever the assistant returns back to the user, after a user sends an utterance to the assistant.
Rule-based	A traditional programming approach where explicit rules are coded into a software system. Rule-based programming is rigid and predictable, but gets increasingly complex and brittle as more rules are added.
Self-service AI assistant	An AI assistant pattern where the user interacts directly with the AI assistant.

Abbreviation/term	Definition/meaning
Sentence error rate	Method for evaluating speech-to-text transcription accuracy. Sentence error rate is the ratio of sentences with an error compared to the total number of sentences.
Skill	A conversational AI component containing the dialogue configuration.
Slots	A method for dynamically capturing information required to complete a task. The information can be collected at any time and in any order. When information is missing, the user will be prompted for it. Creating an appointment is a good use case for slots. An appointment requires a date, time, and location. The user can say "I need an appointment for Elm on Tuesday at 3 p.m." (filling all slots at once) or "I need an appointment" (filling no slots, so the assistant will ask additional questions until all the slots are filled).
SMART goal setting	A methodology for setting goals that increases the chance of a goal being met. Definitions vary, but a popular expansion of the SMART acronym is Specific, Measurable, Achievable, Relevant, and Time-bound.
Source control management (SCM)	Tracking and managing changes to a series of files, particularly source code files. Git is a popular source control management system.
Speech adaptation/ speech customization	The process of building a new custom speech-to-text model that extends a base model with custom data.
Speech-to-text	An algorithm for converting audio input into text input. Internally, the speech-to-text service identifies partial word sounds (phonemes) and combines them into logical word groupings. Also called speech recognition.
Success metric	A discrete metric for measuring if an AI assistant is meeting the needs of its creators. Success metrics align the entire team around a common vision for success.
Successful containment	The percentage of conversations handled entirely by the AI assistant where the assistant successfully completes the user's goal. A conversation starting with "reset my password" is only contained if it ends with the user successfully resetting their password.
Supervised learning	A family of machine learning algorithms where the algorithm is given inputs and their associated outputs (labels), and the algorithm is trained to infer the relationships and rules that transform the inputs into the outputs. Supervised learning algorithms require ground truth in the form of labeled data.
Synonyms	In the context of AI assistant entities, synonyms are words or phrases that can be treated equivalently. "User ID," "UserID," and "User Identifier" can be treated as synonyms.
Synthetic data	Data that did not come from real users. Synthetic data is often created by subject-matter experts based on their memory or insight into how users are likely to interact with a system.
Test data	Data that a model was not explicitly trained on. Because the model has not seen this data, it can be considered blind to it. A test set is often called a blind test set. The true test of a model is how accurately it can make predictions on data it hasn't seen before (this is what will happen in production). A test set is a convenient way to approximate this.

Abbreviation/term	Definition/meaning
Test environment	An internal place where a team can test code before releasing it to production.
Two-strikes/ three-strikes rule	A metaphor borrowed from baseball. When a baseball batter swings and misses it's called a strike. After three strikes, the batter is out. Similarly, if an AI assistant misunderstands the user, we can call that a strike. If the assistant misunderstands the user three times (or twice, in the two-strikes rule), the assistant should hand the user off to get their resolution elsewhere.
Time to resolution	The time between a user requesting assistance and the user getting resolution for that request.
Training data	A set of data used to train a custom machine learning model. Each row of training data generally contains an input and a labeled output. (The labeled output is the answer for the input.)
Transcription	The process of extracting text from an audio stream.
True negative	A correct prediction corresponding to the default case. If the user's utterance does not contain an intent and the assistant reacts with the fallback condition, this is a true negative. The user may make a typo when entering "I can't log in," accidentally submitting "I can" as their utterance; this statement does not contain an intent.
True positive	A correct prediction that is not the default case. If the user asks to reset their password, and the assistant detects the reset password intent, this is a true positive.
Unsupervised learning	A family of machine learning algorithms where the algorithm is given only inputs and is asked to identify relationships in that data. The algorithm will discover its own inferences; these are unlikely to align perfectly with the expected inferences.
User persona	A fictional character meant to encompass the role and characteristics of a user of an application. An example user persona is a technically savvy user who prefers to shop online using an application on their smartphone.
Utterance	Anything a user types or says to an AI assistant.
Wake word	A word or phrase that activates an AI assistant, telling it to start listening for a command. Famous wake words include Amazon's "Alexa," Google's "OK Google," and Apple's "Hey Siri."
Word error rate	Metric for evaluating speech-to-text transcription accuracy. Word error rate is a ratio of the number of incorrect words in the model's transcript divided by the number of words in the correct transcript.

index

RELATED MANNING TITLES

Machine Learning Bookcamp
by Alexey Grigorev

ISBN 9781617296819
475 pages (estimated), $49.99
Fall 2021 (estimated)

Deep Learning with Python, Second Edition
by François Chollet

ISBN 9781617296864
400 pages (estimated), $59.99
Fall 2021 (estimated)

Deep Learning with PyTorch
by Eli Stevens, Luca Antiga, and Thomas Viehmann
Foreword by Soumith Chintala

ISBN 9781617295263
520 pages, $49.99
July 2020

For ordering information go to www.manning.com